CRITICAL LIVES

The Life and Work of

Thomas Edison

Rudolph Valier Alvarado, Ph.D.

Manos.
It was really hard finding a selection
on Edison, so I grabbed this one
as soon as I saw it.
Happy Birthday.
(a little late)
Vasiliki 4/28/02

ALPHA

A Pearson Education Company

International Standard Book Number: 0-02-864229-5
Library of Congress Catalog Card Number: 2001095864

04   03   02   8   7   6   5   4   3   2   1

Interpretation of the printing code: The rightmost number of the first series of numbers is the year of the book's printing; the rightmost number of the second series of numbers is the number of the book's printing. For example, a printing code of 02-1 shows that the first printing occurred in 2002.

Printed in the United States of America

Publisher:
   Marie Butler-Knight
Product Manager:
   Phil Kitchel
Managing Editor:
   Jennifer Chisholm
Acquisitions Editor:
   Mike Sanders
Senior Production Editor:
   Christy Wagner
Cover Designer:
   Anne Jones
Book Designer:
   Sandra Schroeder
Production:
   Mary Hunt
   Ayanna Lacey

CRITICAL LIVES

Thomas Edison

Introduction

The life story of Thomas Alva Edison begins with a driven, determined boy, and ends with the greatest inventor the world has ever known. Born in a modest home in Milan, Ohio, and raised in Port Huron, Michigan, his father and mother instilled in Edison a number of personality traits that served him well throughout his life. His insatiable desire to be his own man came from his father. Self-confidence in his abilities and in himself came from his mother. These character attributes and a great many others prepared Edison to shape a world, and more specifically an America, during a time of dramatic change.

During Edison's early life, America achieved its manifest destiny, extending from sea to shining sea; the southwestern United States was acquired from Mexico; the 1849 Gold Rush led thousands of speculators to journey West; the expansion of railroads brought economic prosperity; the Civil War pitted brother against brother, followed by a time of reconstruction in which Americans struggled to unite once again.

What was it about this time in history that impacted Edison? Nothing affected Edison more than the communications technology of the day, specifically the telegraph. The telegraph, like the computer today, was the leading technological field during Edison's adolescence and young adulthood, and most people were intrigued by the possibilities the invention offered and wanted to learn more. Some became experts at a young age, much like the children of today who know more about the family computer than the parents who bought it. Thomas Alva Edison spent a good part of his time as a child acquiring telegraph parts and the batteries that made them work, learning all he could, passionate about telegraphy with an intensity that never left him. In an era when children were expected to get out on their own at an early age, telegraphy became Edison's first career.

Telegraphy offered Edison an unusual situation that fostered his independent spirit and economic needs. He worked the late shift, often with little or no supervision, which gave him an opportunity to spend his hours on the clock learning about the field of telegraphy, while doing just enough to keep his job. The profession provided Edison with the necessary funding to support himself and to pay for materials needed to conduct experiments and to further his self-education. The job was also ideal for Edison, stricken with wanderlust, to travel the Midwest, where the Civil War telegrapher positions were plentiful due to America's Civil War. Edison was able to stay informed as to the latest developments in telegraphy and, most importantly, meet and form friendships with people who would later play major roles in his career and personal life. Finally, the experience and time it afforded him gave him the necessary tools to move beyond telegraphy and into the role of inventor once he moved to the Northeast.

Decisions made at critical crossroads in Thomas Alva Edison's life radically altered his future, decisions so dramatic that another choice would have meant that discoveries might not have happened; thus significantly altering history. Of course, Edison could not foresee the consequences of these decisions, but, once committed, he never strayed or lost hope when others would have given up. Even when experts denounced his intentions, he had faith in his vision and an ability to persevere to the end. This did not always benefit Edison. Even so, when decisions proved not to be in his best interests, in business, experimenting, or inventing, the ever-optimistic Edison took what he learned and applied it to projects or experiments that followed whenever possible. Edison found use in all that he did—and often succeeded when failure seemed certain.

Ultimately, the story of Thomas Alva Edison is not only one of a man who created an incredible number of inventions that benefited mankind, but of a person who took full advantage of the opportunities life sent his way, unafraid of hard work or failure. Few people will ever match Edison's inventive output, but all of us could make a greater contribution to the world by emulating the spirit that propelled him. Examination of his life, the critical thoughts, and crucial moments allows us to understand and foster that spirit within us.

Chapter 1

The Merchant Prince

Good things come to those who hustle while they wait.
—An adage Thomas Alva
Edison had well established by
the age of twelve

The first Edisons in America were three-year-old John—Thomas Alva Edison's great-grandfather—and his widowed mother, who emigrated from their ancestral home near Zyuder Zee in the Netherlands to Elizabethport, New Jersey, in 1730. Of their early life in the British colonies little is known. Mother Edison never remarried, and when she passed away, she left a valuable estate to her son. At forty-two, John married Sarah Ogden on October 10, 1765, in the First Presbyterian Church of Hanover, New Jersey. Over the course of their marriage Sarah gave birth to five boys and five girls. Originally from Hampshire, England, the Ogdens were a prominent, wealthy family, whose early ancestors in America founded Elizabethport. Sometime after their marriage John sold his mother's estate. He and his wife, Sarah, lived on a seventy-five-acre farm in the township of Caldwell, Essex County, New Jersey, coincidentally less than fifteen miles from where Thomas Alva Edison would, one hundred and eleven years later, erect his Menlo Park laboratory. Aside from his land, British records indicate that John owned his home, one slave, a mare, fifteen sheep, three beehives, and a variety of goods valued at 288 pounds sterling.

The American Revolution cut John's prosperous existence short: He sided with the British. In 1776 he moved his family to Staten Island to protect them and returned to New Jersey as a soldier. He fought against revolutionary forces but was taken prisoner and served thirteen months before being sentenced to death for treason. Thanks to the intervention of the Ogden family, his life was spared, and, after his release, John and his family, including Thomas Alva Edison's grandfather, Samuel, fled to Canada. They settled in the province of Digby, on the western coast of Nova Scotia, where a number of Loyalists were granted refuge for their undying support of the British Crown.

John's oldest son, Samuel Ogden Edison, met and married Nancy Stimson in 1792. They in turn had eight children. The sixth, Samuel Jr., Thomas Alva Edison's father, was born on August 16, 1804. The Edisons were farmers, and remained in Nova Scotia for twenty-eight years until they moved to the township of Bayham, Ontario, where they homesteaded six hundred acres of virgin pineland along the Otter River, two miles from Lake Erie. Migrating from Nova Scotia to New York City by ship, the Edison family spent the summer traveling over eight hundred miles by ox team and wagons to their new home.

On this land, the Edisons grew numerous and prominent, so much so that the township became known as the Edison Settlement. The township grew to include a main street, a schoolhouse, a Baptist church, a tavern, and a cemetery on land donated by the Edisons, and in time came to be known officially as Vienna. Samuel Sr. became a community leader and served as a captain in the First Middlesex regiment under Colonel Thomas Talbot during the War of 1812. In August of the same year, he took part in the British-Canadian victory at Detroit.

Not much is known of Samuel Ogden Edison Jr.'s childhood in Vienna. As an adult, he was a commanding figure, standing over six feet three inches tall with an athletic build. He worked as a carpenter and a tailor before settling into life as a tavern proprietor. On September 12, 1828, he married the local schoolteacher, Nancy Elliott, a quiet and patient woman, "of medium height, stout, with large brown eyes, and brown hair." Her family had moved into the area when her father accepted the post of minister at the Baptist Church. After their wedding, the couple moved into a home Samuel built, where they raised four children.

Edison's father, Samuel Ogden Edison Jr.

(© *Courtesy of Edison National Historic Site*)

Involved in politics as his forefathers, Samuel hosted rebel meetings in his establishment in the months preceding the Canadian Rebellion of 1837. He joined the cause led by William Lyon Mackenzie, serving as a captain in rebel forces seeking, as Americans had, no taxation without representation. Their goal was nothing short of the overthrow of the Canadian government in Toronto. An attack on government buildings was led by Mackenzie in December 1837. Crushed by regular soldiers, Mackenzie and his men were sent running. When word of the defeat reached Samuel and his column of men from Vienna and Port Burwell, they had no choice but to flee for their lives. Like Mackenzie, Samuel escaped to America, but not before managing to stop by his home in Vienna to bid his wife and children good-bye and hiding for the night in a barn near his father's house. The next morning Samuel raced to the American border, eighty miles away. In pursuit were regular soldiers, tracking dogs and Native-Canadian guides. His journey lasted two and half days, until he reached the frozen St. Clair River, where he crossed into Port Huron, Michigan.

From Port Huron, Samuel made his way to Milan, Ohio, a small, thriving community a few miles from the southern shore of Lake Erie. There he established himself as a lumber and grain-feed dealer, shingle maker, and land speculator. In the spring of 1839, his family arrived from Vienna, smuggled across Lake Erie in a boat belonging to Captain Alva Bradley.

The same year, a three-mile canal was completed from Milan to the navigable portion of the Huron River, which in turn provided Lake Erie boats access to Milan. The canal swelled the town's population from roughly six hundred people to well over fifteen hundred. During the 1840s, Milan became one of the leading grain-shipping ports in the world, as well as a regional shipbuilding and manufacturing center.

The Edisons became one of the town's leading families. In August 1841, Samuel built the family a seven-room, Greek Revival-style brick house overlooking the canal. It was here in the early morning hours of February 11, 1847, following a night of heavy snowfall, that Thomas Alva Edison was born, the last child of Samuel and Nancy Edison, named in honor of the man who had smuggled the family across Lake Erie. Thomas joined Marion, eighteen; William Pitt, sixteen; and Harriet Ann, fourteen. A fourth child, Charles, had passed away at age six, and two other children, Samuel II and Eliza, had passed away as infants.

Edison's mother, Nancy Elliott Edison.

Thomas—or Al, as he was called as a boy—was born into a world on the brink of monumental change: There was talk of a continental railroad, families in "prairie schooners" were making their way west to California, telegraphy was making communication possible over long distances, and the steam engine was eliminating hard labor and long distances.

As a child, Edison had an innate curiosity about the world around him—curiosity that often landed him in trouble. He was publicly whipped in the town's square for burning down the family's barn just to see what would happen. He nearly suffocated when he fell into a grain-storage bin trying to figure out how it worked. He talked a friend into drinking a glass of Seidlitz powder to see if the bubbles would make him fly, and when that failed he convinced another friend to drink a glass of chopped-up worms to see if that would do any better. He also witnessed the drowning of a friend in the canal—an event that haunted him throughout his life, even though he was not responsible.

The Edisons lived in Milan until 1854, when the town economy took turn for the worse after the Lake Shore Railroad by-passed the town, taking with it the profits and the potential for sustaining economic growth generated by the canal.

> The Milan canal reached its highest level as a grain port in 1847—the year of Edison's birth. That year approximately nine hundred thousand bushels of wheat and one hundred thirty-eight thousand bushels of corn were shipped. Once the Lake Shore Railroad was completed in 1848, wheat shipments declined by over half and dropped to two hundred eighty-two thousand bushels in 1849.

The Edisons moved to the vicinity of Port Huron, Michigan, located on the southern tip of Lake Huron. They rented a comfortable home next to Fort Gratiot, located just outside of the town. Samuel carried on his lumber and grain trade business, but he never again reached the level of prosperity he had known in Milan.

Shortly after the move, young Thomas Edison came down with a case of Scarlet fever. Being her youngest child, and the only one born in America to survive, Edison's mother devoted herself to caring for him and eventually nursed him back to health. The illness kept Edison from beginning his formal education until 1855, when, at age eight, he was enrolled in a private school belonging to Reverend George Engle. The tuition to attend the school was thirty dollars a year, which included board, fuel, and English instruction. The Edisons also paid an additional forty dollars for piano lessons. One day after three months, Edison came running home in tears because a teacher had called him "addled." Nancy Edison immediately returned to the school with her boy in tow. Edison watched as his mother furiously dressed down the teacher. In gratitude for her defending him, Edison "determined right then" that he "would be worthy of her, and show her that her confidence had not been misplaced."

> Years after Edison became a successful inventor, he received a bill from Reverend Engle for twenty-five dollars. With the bill was a letter. In the letter, Reverend Engle claimed that the amount was never paid while Edison was attending his school. Edison paid the outstanding debt in full.

A gifted teacher, Nancy took responsibility for her son's education. Under Nancy's tutelage, young Edison became a first-rate student, and she set him on a path traveled by few of his peers. She read to him from such books as Gibbon's *Decline and Fall of the Roman Empire*, Hume's *History of England*, and Sear's *History of the World*, as well as literary classics from Shakespeare to Dickens. By the age of nine, he had read Richard Green Parker's *Natural and Experimental Philosophy* and undertaken the writings of Thomas Paine, which were readily available on his father's bookshelves. As for mathematics, Edison struggled to make sense of Newton's *Principia*. When he couldn't understand the concepts contained in the book, a friend of the family tried to explain it to him, but to no avail. The experience left Edison with a dislike of mathematics that lasted a lifetime.

Edison's favorite subject was science. In a makeshift laboratory in the basement of the family home, he systematically carried out every experiment found in R. G. Parker's *School of Natural Philosophy*, and later, the *Dictionary of Science*. He also made telegraphs, and with the assistance of a friend ran a mile long wire to his friend's house so he could test his models and practice sending and receiving messages. So dedicated was Edison to his studies and his experiments that one friend commented that he "was always studying out something, and usually had a book dealing with some scientific subject in his pocket."

> The trouble with our way of educating as generally followed is that it does not give elasticity to the mind. It casts the brain into a mould. It insists that the child must accept. It does not encourage original thought or reasoning, and it lays more stress on memory than on observation. The result of accepting unrelated facts fosters conservatism. It breeds fear, and from fear comes ignorance.
>
> —*Thomas Alva Edison*

By the age of twelve, Edison's day started with a walk to the Grand Trunk Railroad's depot. The company's railroad line had been recently extended from Toronto to Detroit, with stops at points in between. Edison had secured a job as a "candy butcher." His duties consisted of selling newspapers, apples, sandwiches, molasses, and peanuts to passengers. The position, as Edison discovered, was whatever he made of it. Being employed at such a young age was nothing unusual at the time; children often started working early, and were living on their own shortly thereafter. Work was nothing new to Edison; he was already on his second job. His first was growing vegetables, which he sold at a healthy profit. Edison abandoned the enterprise once he realized that "hoeing corn in a hot sun" did not suit him.

The trip to Detroit took three hours, and the train didn't return until late in the evening, arriving back in Port Huron around 9:30. The eight-hour layover in Detroit and the ride back and forth once his selling was done suited Edison fine—it was actually one of the unexpected "perks" of the job. The layover gave him time to read and get acquainted with the bustling city of Detroit, and, most important, the job provided him with the funds to support a popular habit among the youth of the day: experimenting with telegraphic equipment, as well as his own fascination with chemical experiments. It was a costly habit to which the Edison family had no money to contribute, but the job Edison found to support it would have a greater impact on his life than he could have ever imagined.

To relieve the boredom of the ride to and from Detroit, Edison transported his laboratory to an unused section of a baggage car, which, surprisingly enough, no one questioned. Always the opportunist, he also opened two stands in Port Huron, selling fruits and vegetables in one and periodicals in the other. Some of his fruit and vegetable inventory was transported from Detroit on the Grand Trunk Railroad at no charge after the savvy Edison sold his produce at half-price to the wives of the engineers and trainmen. In addition to these endeavors, Edison hired a boy to be the candy butcher on a railroad line transporting newly immigrated Norwegians to Iowa and Minnesota.

Edison's free-market enterprises meant that he had to hire and supervise employees, as well as keep financial records to watch profits and cash flow. Edison was up to the first task, but he never excelled at the second. As in later life, when creditors came knocking on the doors of his Newark factory or Menlo Park laboratory, Edison detested financial bookkeeping. He had no time for it. When his employees handed over the money earned from the day's sales, he'd shove the money in his pocket and forget about it until he reached home and divided it up with his mother, or stopped somewhere to purchase something for his laboratory.

Further proof that Edison did not hold a high regard for money can also be seen in his decision to shut down his two shops after he discovered that one of his employees was cheating him out of his profits. When a business venture did not pan out, or he felt that he was being used for someone else's financial gain, Edison the boy— just like Edison the man—simply moved on to another venture, or kept an eye out for a new opportunity, which for Edison never seemed too far away.

In the four years Edison rode back and forth to Detroit, America underwent some of the most dramatic events in its history: John Brown's raid on Harper's Ferry led to his hanging; Abraham Lincoln was elected president, and the capture of Fort Sumter triggered America's Civil War.

Thomas Alva Edison at age fourteen.

(© *Courtesy of Edison National Historic Site*)

As a businessman, Edison certainly took note of the latter, for on those days when casualty and death reports were published, he sold out of newspapers quickly. This lesson in supply and demand had little impact on him until one Wednesday afternoon on April 9, 1862, when the train pulled into the Detroit station, and Edison noticed crowds gathered around bulletin boards normally reserved for railroad schedules. People were reading *Detroit Free Press* headlines on the Battle of Shiloh, which had occurred the preceding Sunday. Edison realized that, "here was a chance for enormous sales, if only the people along the line could know what had happened."

Inspired, Edison suddenly remembered the telegraph and its ability to communicate instantly over great distances. He ran to the Detroit telegraph station and implored the operator to send news of the bloody battle to each stop leading back to Port Huron. He further suggested to the telegraph operator that the stationmasters along the way should chalk up the news on the boards listing the train's schedule. In exchange for his trouble, Edison offered the operator a free subscription to *Harper's Weekly, Harper's Monthly,* and an evening paper for six months! The deal struck, Edison headed to the *Detroit Free Press* office and requested fifteen hundred copies on credit. They refused at first, but he found his way into the office of the editor, Wilbur F. Storey. Edison told him his idea of telegraphing the news of the battle to stations along the route back to Port Huron. After listening intently to the boy's proposal, Storey sat silent for a few seconds, then wrote a few words on a piece of paper. He handed the slip to Edison saying, "Take that downstairs and you will get what you want."

Edison took the note to the distribution manager, who gave him the newspapers after Edison signed a promissory note to pay for them. He then quickly hired three boys to help him fold and place the newspapers on the train. At the first stop, a crowd was gathered at the platform. It looked like a riot had broken out, but as the train pulled into the station, people clamored to buy a copy of the *Free Press.* Before the train left the station where Edison normally sold two newspapers, he had sold over a hundred at five cents apiece. At the next stop he sold three hundred copies at *ten* cents apiece. At each stop, frantic crowds met the train, and at each stop, the price of the paper rose. In Port Huron, Edison transferred the remaining stock to a wagon and hired a small boy to sit on the newspapers, "so as to discount any pilfering." It wasn't long before every remaining newspaper was sold—at a dollar twenty-five each.

> In the United States in 1830, sixty-five daily newspapers sold approximately one hundred thousand newspapers a day combined. By 1870, there were three hundred eighty-seven, with a circulation of around three and a half million. This phenomenal growth was the result of an increased urban population and the establishment of the railroad and the telegraph, which enabled editors to obtain stories from all over the world. They also found, as on the train on which young Edison worked, that newspapers could be sold at stops along the line, especially during the Civil War, when publishers reaped huge profits thanks to news-hungry citizens.

Impressed by the young entrepreneur's initiative, two days later the *Detroit Free Press* featured a story about Edison on the front page under the heading NEWSBOY ENTERPRISE. In the piece, the "bright-eyed lad" was praised for his innovative use of the telegraph in marketing newspapers and mention was made as to the astounding amount of money he had earned. The article closed, "No fears but what that boy will get along in the world."

Edison's Shiloh bonanza taught him lessons he remembered throughout his life. The first was the art of selling an idea, a vision, to the person with the financial means to carry it out. He learned that investors would take a chance on an idea if the potential for profit was convincing enough. He learned that the market will pay almost any price if what is being offered has perceived or real value to it. He discovered that timing is everything; that knowing what to say and when to say it plays a huge role in capturing the public's imagination. He learned that when a story breaks, it must be dramatic, in order to create a news event where the atmosphere is charged with excitement and the public is left wanting more. Finally, Edison learned the value of the telegraph and its ability to communicate quickly and efficiently. Years later, Edison said that he decided the day after this experience that he would learn even more about telegraphy and take up printing.

The next day—as would be the case when Edison sold one of his inventions for forty thousand dollars and used the money to finance his Newark factory—he took part of his Shiloh bonanza and bought a used printing press from J. A. Roys, the most prominent bookseller in Detroit. After purchasing the printing press, Edison received permission to place it aboard the Grand Trunk Railroad in the same baggage car as his laboratory. Trainmen laughingly renamed the car "Edison's Laboratory and Printing Shop." Edison even enlisted the train's conductor, Alexander Stevenson, a feisty Scotsman, as his editorial assistant. With his printing press on wheels, Edison started his publishing career in the spring of 1862.

Described as no larger than a man's handkerchief, Edison's newspaper was named the *Weekly Herald*. It contained gossip, news, personal and business advertisements (such as the price of produce and agricultural products), mail information, birth and death notices, and a list of men entering the military. Articles often concerned employees of the Grand Trunk Railway, such as the success of a company detective who stopped an agent for the Hayitan government from swindling the company out of sixty-seven dollars after claiming to have lost personal baggage. In an editorial featured in one edition, the suggestion was made that the Grand Trunk Railway should "give premiums every six months to their Engineers, who use the least Wood and Oil," and challenged Port Huron officials to enforce its "law requiring Saloons & Grog shops to close on Sunday ... as they are a complete nuisance." These examples show a certain bravado, the self-confidence of a writer on his way to mastering the tone and phrasing of a journalist. With an estimated three to five hundred subscribers a month at eight cents apiece, the enterprise proved to be a success.

In the estimation of many of his acquaintances, Edison was well on his way to becoming a publisher or an editor—that is, until one fateful day when a bottle of phosphorous in Edison's laboratory accidentally fell to the floor and the baggage car erupted in flames. Edison was trying desperately to put out the fire when Stevenson rushed in and fought it with him until it was extinguished as the train pulled into the Mt. Clemens Station, where Stevenson boxed

Edison's ears and tossed him, his printing press, and his laboratory onto the platform.

Edison not only found himself stranded miles from Port Huron, he also found that he was partially deaf, a condition that would worsen throughout his life. Even though the exact reason he lost a great deal of his hearing is not entirely known, it changed his life forever, and not necessarily for the worse. Being deaf allowed him to hear only those things that *he* wanted to hear, not those things that others *wanted* him to hear. That Edison was able to turn this physical handicap into an advantage speaks highly of his character and his determination. In years to come, he would credit his deafness for his discovery of the phonograph and the carbon transmitter—the device that amplified the human voice and was used to make Alexander Graham Bell's telephone a practical instrument.

The next few months found Edison continuing his experiments in the basement of his parents' house. Not abandoning his interest in publishing, he founded a second newspaper under the name, *Paul Pry*, which could be aptly described as a precursor to today's *National Enquirer* because of its scandalous and probing stories regarding local citizens, which caused Edison to run "the gauntlet of the well-deserved kicks and cuffings naturally incident to the circulation of such a sheet." He also kept his job as the "candy butcher" on the Grand Trunk Railroad, a fortuitous occurrence, because one day while the train was stopped in Mt. Clemens Station—ironically, where Edison and his valuables were tossed off by Stevenson—Edison saved the stationmaster's three-year-old son by pulling him out of the way of a railroad car that somehow started rolling. In a show of his gratitude, the boy's father, J. U. MacKenzie, offered to give Edison formal lessons in the art of telegraphy. Edison accepted, and on the first day of his lessons, he arrived carrying his own set of telegraph instruments.

In the summer of 1862, Edison spent an average of eighteen hours a day learning the telegrapher's trade. Before long he had built on his ability to send and receive information, and become familiar with the ins and outs of the technology itself. He advanced so rapidly that MacKenzie admitted five months later that he could teach him nothing else.

With his new skills, Edison opened his own telegraph company, a line extending between Fort Gratiot to the train station. The venture was short-lived when he discovered that there wasn't enough business to support him and the established telegraph office in Walker's jewelry and stationery store. Undaunted, the young Edison went to his competitor, showed him what he could do, secured a job, then took the opportunity to gain the knowledge and experience to move to the next level, which to rural telegraphers of the time meant receiving what were called "press reports." With his employer's permission, Edison set up a cot in the back of the store, complete with a rudimentary laboratory. This enabled him to practice taking press reports whenever they came over the wire, and afforded him the opportunity to read the assorted books and journals in the store. He also become familiar with the tools used in repairing clocks and watches.

By the following year, Edison was ready for the next step. He applied, and with MacKenzie's recommendation, was hired to be the night operator at Stratford Junction, Ontario. Thomas Alva Edison was all of seventeen years old. Soon he was traveling to Canada to start a job that would leave a lasting imprint on both his personal and professional life and prepare him for life on the road as a singing line operator.

Chapter 2

A Tramp Telegrapher Comes of Age

To stop is to rust .... A harvest must be reaped occasion-
ally, not once in a lifetime.
                                    —*Thomas Alva Edison*

U se of the telegraph expanded rapidly after Samuel F. B. Morse
sent his famous message, "What hath God wrought," over
wire strung from Baltimore, Maryland, to Washington, D.C., on
May 24, 1844. By 1846, New York City was connected to
Washington, D.C. By 1851, over fifty telegraph companies were
operating in the United States, and on April 4, 1856, twelve of
these companies combined to form the Western Union Telegraph
Company.

In 1861, Western Union extended its telegraph lines from
Omaha, Nebraska, to California. Members of the eastern and western labor crews met in Salt Lake City, Utah, on October 24. From
this site, Stephen J. Field, chief justice of California, transmitted
the first transcontinental message to President Abraham Lincoln.
In his message, Field declared California's loyalty to the Union.
The completion of the transcontinental line brought an end to the
Pony Express, which had been in service for only about nineteen
months.

The fraternity of professional telegraphers did not enjoy the
best reputation. Many were single men with no interest in raising
a family or settling down. The turnover rate was high. Losing a job

was of little consequence, because demand for a telegrapher's skills was high due to the Civil War and general growth in the industry. Among those free-spirited individuals, however, were also men who would take advantage of the technology to make their fortunes, or start them on their way. This would include individuals like Andrew Carnegie, George Kennan, and Sir William Van Horne, wealthy men who early in their careers were simple telegraph operators.

Given the discipline he showed as a boy, one would expect Edison to be a reliable and dedicated telegraph employee. The truth is, Edison often fell into the category of unreliable journeyman, but for considerably different reasons than most of his counterparts. This lack of discipline was the direct result of Edison's years of self-guided employment aboard the Grand Trunk Railroad, where he had time away from the job during layovers in Detroit to do what he wanted: experimenting and reading about science and technology. Even before Edison left Thomas Walker's employ in Port Huron, Walker noted that on occasion Edison neglected customers because he was "engrossed in his experiments and scientific reading. " To escape the watchful eye of a supervisor, Edison preferred working the late shift, which not only gave him the freedom to do as he pleased, it also brought him job security, because most people didn't want the hours.

In his position as a railroad dispatcher in Stratford Junction, Ontario, Edison found the perfect job. His shift started at seven at night and ended at seven in the morning. The job was simple and straightforward: All the dispatcher had to do was listen for messages about the trains' schedules and pass the information along as necessary. To make sure telegraphers were awake and on the job, the company required them to send a message to the office every half hour.

After Edison did this, he used the spare time experimenting and reading, or taking a few catnaps, a custom that became a lifelong habit. As for the nagging problem of having to check in every half hour, what was called "sixing," Edison had a solution: a device that automatically sent the required signal to the main office at the prescribed time. This machine was a rudimentary instrument that used a notched wheel to automatically transmit the sixing signal.

The device worked perfectly—perhaps too perfectly. Before long, management started to notice the prompt and suspiciously consistent signals that the Stratford Junction dispatcher was sending. They also noticed that he didn't respond to messages sent to him shortly after his signal was sent. In short time, a railroad agent was sent to investigate; what he found did not please the company. Edison's contraption was exposed. Edison was severely reprimanded, but allowed to keep his job.

In the weeks that followed, Edison sent his signal manually, and he continued his practice of experimenting and taking catnaps. To ensure that he didn't miss sending a signal, the railroad yardman kept an eye on him, making sure to wake him if he overslept, or send the signal for him if he was away from his desk. The arrangement worked for a while, but everything changed one night when Edison received an order to hold a freight train so an oncoming train could have the right of way. Edison replied that he would take care of it, but before he could find the signalman and get the signal set, the freight train passed by. Edison ran to the telegraph office, where he sent word that he was unable to stop the freight train. In reply he received the word, "Hell." It was too late; the dispatcher, thinking that Edison was stopping the freight train, had permitted the second train to leave the station. Hoping to avoid a disaster, Edison ran to the lower station near Junction where the day operator slept. The night was dark and as he bounded down a culvert, he fell and was knocked unconscious.

Fortunately for Edison, an accident was averted when the train engineers spotted each other and were able to stop in time. The next day, Edison and his superior, Mr. Jeremiah Carter, stood before the general superintendent of the Grand Trunk Railroad, W. I. Spicer, in his Toronto office. Carter was raked over the coals "for permitting such a young boy to hold such a responsible position." Spicer then turned to Edison and told him that he could be sent to Kingston Prison for negligence of duty. Just at this moment, three executives from England stepped into the office. Spicer stood to shake hands and offer a warm greeting, while Edison quietly slipped out of the office. Once outside, Edison crawled into a caboose and kept low until the train reached Port Huron. The experience left the sixteen-year-old Edison badly shaken and worried that a Grand Trunk Railroad investigator would show up at his home to take him back to Canada.

Edison's fears were never realized, and in early 1864, he was hired as a night operator for the Lake Shore and Michigan Southern Railroad in Adrian, Michigan, then a small community sixty miles southwest of Detroit. Before leaving, he gained notice for coming to the aid of the citizens of his hometown and the Canadian city of Sarnia across the river. Ice clogging the river from the brutal winter severed the telegraph wire between the cities, with no way to repair the wire or string another one across the river's mile-and-a-half expanse. While city fathers pondered the situation, Edison convinced a railroad engineer to maneuver his train close to the riverbank. Then, Edison pulled on the train's whistle cord, producing a series of Morse code "dots and dashes": "Hello, Sarnia ... Sarnia, do you get what I say?" No response came, so Edison sent the message again. This time a Canadian engine answered. The problem was solved. The towns communicated by "train whistle Morse code" in the evenings for about a week, until the lines could be restored.

Arriving in Adrian to begin his job as night operator, Edison promised himself he would do a first-rate job. He did, and for his hard work, his supervisor granted him a small room in which to live. Edison set up a cot and soon converted the space into a little shop in which to continue his self-education by reading the latest literature on science and technology and conducting experiments.

Edison was a model employee, until one day when he was ordered by his superior to interrupt a busy telegraph line to send out an important message. Edison succeeded in stopping all but one operator transmitting over the line. When he demanded that operator stop sending, a message came back advising him that it was the superintendent of the entire railroad, and that he had no intention of stopping his message. Later in the day, the superintendent showed up and fired Edison on the spot. Edison told him that he was ordered by his supervisor to cut into the line. The superintendent asked the supervisor if this was true. The supervisor denied everything. Though innocent, Edison had no choice but to leave Adrian.

From Adrian, Edison traveled to Fort Wayne, Indiana, where he went to work as a day-shift operator for the Pittsburgh, Fort Wayne and Chicago Railroad. Preferring the night shift, in the fall of 1864, Edison moved to Indianapolis, which by the 1860s was an established railroad-shipping hub and home to over one hundred manufacturing and industrial enterprises. On his arrival, Edison found employment in the Western Union's office as a day operator taking messages from surrounding towns. The job provided him with enough income to afford a room in a boarding house nearby. This gave Edison an opportunity to visit the telegraphers' office in the evenings to practice taking "press," a habit the regular evening operator appreciated.

Edison soon discovered that the press reports came in too fast for him to write down, so he invented an instrument to aid him in his work: a Morse repeater. Consisting of two Morse registers with the ability to record incoming dots and dashes onto a strip of paper at regular speed, the messages could later be played back at a much slower rate. This gave the receiver the advantage of practicing taking a message by longhand as it came in and also provided a system of checking for accuracy.

Like his "sixing" device, Edison's Morse repeater worked perfectly. Edison and his fellow operator Ed Parmalee were able to take, and write out perfectly, lengthy press reports. They continued to use the device for a few weeks, and might never have stopped if not for one night when a presidential vote kept the news pouring in without a break, and the young operators found themselves falling an hour, then an hour and a half, finally two hours behind. When the office manager found them still writing out messages the next morning, Edison revealed his apparatus. He explained how it worked and what had caused the back up. Unimpressed, the manager banned the use of the instrument and he forbade Edison and his friend from ever practicing telegraphy at night. Edison didn't lose his position, but he was warned not to repeat his actions.

Whether Edison's Morse repeater was his first invention is arguable. The automatic "sixing" device he originated in Stratford Junction would certainly take precedence, even though it was not designed to aid the efforts of others. Regardless of which item is considered his first true invention, they certainly reveal that Edison was no ordinary telegrapher. They're also evidence that Edison had learned and understood the basic mechanical and electrical operation of telegraph technology, an understanding that would grow toward a serious consideration of how to improve the speed, accuracy, and use of the telegraph beyond a communication tool.

Opportunities were certainly there for ambitious individuals to leave their mark on the industry. Telegraph companies were interested in new advances because holding a patent on an invention gave them the exclusive right to use the instrument. If their competitors wanted a device that performed the same function, they turned to creative inventors who could alter the design of the original to get around patent rights. Even by the outbreak of the Civil War, telegraph technology was plagued by a variety of problems. Weather conditions often hampered transmissions. Messages were not received because wires were not insulated or strung properly. Messages were also limited to a radius of two hundred miles; messages that had to travel farther had to be written down and retransmitted, which required additional operators. There was also the cost of stringing mile after mile of wire so more than one message could be sent to the same location at the same time.

After inventing the Morse repeater, Edison remained in Indianapolis until the winter of 1865, when he left for Cincinnati after learning of a job opening from Ezra Gilliland, a fellow-telegrapher he had worked with on the late shift at Adrian. Cincinnati's reputation as a center for the research and development of telegraph technology had grown, and there were opportunities for telegraphers to enter management in the various telegraph offices in town. City leaders had taken advantage of the telegraph to market Cincinnati and in time it became the commercial center of the Ohio River valley, with burgeoning industries centering on pork, soups, and the production of leather.

In Cincinnati, Edison worked Western Union's day wire from Portsmouth, Ohio. The job afforded no challenge, but he continued to hone his skills by coming in at night to take press reports as well as picking up extra shifts where he could, all in an "effort to become proficient in the very shortest time." His practice paid off in September 1865, when the night operators failed to show up for work after apparently having too much to drink at a meeting to organize a chapter of the National Telegraphic Union. Having left the gathering early, Edison found himself in the telegraph office with no one to take the incoming press report. Reasoning that he couldn't be fired for trying, Edison sat down at the press table and wrote down what he could.

The next day, having taken press until three in the morning, Edison was at his regular station when the chief operator, J. F. Stevens, told him that he had been reassigned to work the Louisville wire nights with a salary of one hundred twenty-five dollars a month. It was a huge jump in pay for Edison, who up to this point had never made more than eighty dollars a month, but it wasn't the salary that gave Edison the greatest satisfaction, it was being promoted to first-class operator, a title that ranked him among the very best telegraphers in the industry.

Edison's time in Cincinnati was also significant because it marked the first time since Edison had taken to the road that he allowed himself to have a social life. Among those that Edison befriended were Ezra Gilliland, who had only been an acquaintance in Adrian; Nat Hyams, a comedian and eventual manager at Wood's Theatre, which featured burlesques; and Milt F. Adams, a flamboyant telegrapher who would eventually invite Edison to Boston. They spent evenings at the Loewen Garden, drinking beer, eating pretzels, listening to an excellent German band, and at the theatre, where Edison was drawn to the dramas of Shakespeare, especially *Othello*. So taken was Edison by the Bard that he once exclaimed, "Ah Shakespeare! That's where you get the ideas! My, but that man did have ideas! He would have been an inventor, a wonderful inventor, if he had turned his mind to it."

But friendships and becoming a first-class operator were not enough to keep Edison in Cincinnati. Before long he relocated to

Nashville, then, in 1866, to Memphis. There he found a city trying to come to grips with the aftermath of the Civil War. Rampant
in the city were lawlessness, violence, vice, and racial tension
between newly arrived Irish immigrants, newly freed slaves, and
the Colored infantry units stationed at Fort Pickering. The telegraph industry fared no better as tension mounted between the
military and private enterprise as control of established telegraph
offices went from the military to private enterprise. Amid this
unrest, Edison managed to secure a position with Western Union.
In his spare time he took up two new interests: teaching himself to
read and write Spanish, and developing a duplex system of telegraphy, whereby two messages could be sent over the same wire at the
same time.

> *Experiments with duplex telegraph systems started in Europe in the
> 1850s. Few Americans thought them feasible until the 1860s, when
> American inventor Moses Farmer demonstrated a duplex system on a
> line from Boston to Portland, Maine, and on a line from Cincinnati to
> Indianapolis. Press coverage of Farmer's demonstrations drew the inter-
> est of inventors, including the president of the Franklin Telegraph, Joseph
> B. Stearns, who three years later introduced his duplex system in Boston.*

After a few days on the job in Memphis, Edison learned that
management had been trying to figure out a way to form a direct
line from New Orleans to New York City since the end of the Civil
War. Most thought the distance made the problem impossible to
solve, but Edison took up the challenge and soon arrived at an
answer by modifying the repeater device he had developed in
Indianapolis. His success, however, was not received warmly, perhaps due to jealousy that he had done something the top men in
the office had not been able to do. When he arrived at work the
next day, he was terminated with no explanation. If professional
jealousy was the reason for Edison's dismissal, the fact that the
Memphis Advertiser published a story describing his triumph
couldn't have helped.

Edison had changed dramatically in his years as a tramp telegrapher. In a telegram sent home around this time, Edison wrote

that he no longer looked much like a boy. A second telegram informed his family that he was extremely proficient in speaking, reading, and writing Spanish. He also boasted about his ability to read French, yet was quick to point out that he could not speak the language. Unemployed, he decided to move on to Louisville in the fall of 1866.

Louisville was the antithesis of Memphis, having prospered in its role as a supply depot for Union forces and the industrial growth its location on the Ohio River brought. By the time Edison arrived, Louisville had established theaters, beer halls, and occasional lectures on physics and chemistry at Myer's Commercial College. Edison went to work for the Louisville Western Union office where, he developed a style of writing that an editorial in the industry journal, *The Telegrapher,* later described as the *"finest* they had ever seen."* Edison later explained that he had to write letters clearly and economically because he often had to use his imagination to fill in gaps in press reports that he missed or were not clearly sent over distressed wires. In one such incident, Edison reported that a candidate for the United States Senate had been elected by the state's legislature, when in truth the legislature had only adjourned for the night without electing anyone. Once again, Edison's cleverness caused him to resign his position.

Edison's reason for taking an interest in Spanish soon became evident when he journeyed to New Orleans to catch a steamship to Brazil. In New Orleans, Edison and his traveling companions found that the steamship they were to take to Brazil had been commandeered under martial law after a race riot in the city on July 30. While waiting a few days to resume their journey, Edison had a change of heart and decided to return to Louisville. Edison later confessed that he changed his mind based on advice from an old man sitting in the steamship's office who, on hearing the trio's plan, told them that "any man that left this country to better his condition was an ignorant fool."

It was fortunate for Edison that he had a change of heart, for his companions only made it as far as Vera Cruz, Mexico, where they contracted yellow fever and died within the month.

Thomas Alva Edison during his "collegiate" years as a "tramp" telegrapher.

Edison returned to Louisville, regained his position in the Western Union office, and over the following weeks settled into a routine of experimenting and reading during the day, catching a few hours' sleep, and then reporting to work as night operator.

Even after all he had been through, Edison still couldn't leave his interest in experimenting and inventing at home. When his interest in duplex telegraphy was re-ignited, he took apart all the instruments in the office and reconfigured them to fit his specifications. The move might have proven beneficial—except his experiment proved inconclusive, and left the office with no working instruments. Warned by management to leave company property alone, Edison had no choice but to continue his experiments in secret. His scheme went undetected until one night when he accidentally tipped over a bottle of sulfuric acid and it damaged the manager's desk and carpet in the room below. The next morning, Edison was told that "the company wanted operators, not experimenters," and he was fired.

Edison found himself unemployed once again. Rather than rush off to another town in search of a job, he tried to convince an acquaintance to invest one hundred dollars to help him complete his duplex telegraph. His friend refused, so Edison had no choice but to move on. He returned to Cincinnati in 1867 and rejoined Western Union, taking press copy. For a young man making the transition from tramp telegrapher to inventor, the city provided him with the technological information and mechanical services he needed to succeed. Encouraged by Charles Summers, the superintendent of telegraphs for the Indianapolis, Cincinnati, and Lafayette Railroad, who provided Edison with space in which to carry out his work, Edison experimented on a variety of items, such as a self-adjusting relay and his system of duplex. Working with another acquaintance, George Ellsworth, he developed a secret signaling system they planned to sell to the government for a large sum of money. However, Ellsworth left Cincinnati before the project was completed, and Edison soon lost interest in the venture. He also installed a private telegraph line between the downtown offices of Proctor and Gamble and their factory on the city's outskirts.

That Edison had reached a marked level of sophistication concerning telegraphy can be seen in a notebook he kept during his time, containing two lists of books that Edison was either reading or thinking of purchasing, such as Michael Faraday's *Researches in*

Electricity, Richard Culley's *Handbook of Practical Telegraphy*, and Charles Walker's *Electric Telegraph Manipulation*—works whose influence would be evident in Edison's inventions in coming years. The notebook also contained drawings of modifications to existing instruments, not surprising since Edison was always improving on the inventions of others, including diagrams for variety of repeaters, as well as designs for duplex telegraphy. That Edison's designs in the area of repeaters were of significant value even at this early stage can be attested to by the fact that models were eventually perfected from these early sketches and featured in two of the industry's premiere publications, *The Telegrapher* and *Modern Practice of the Electric Telegraph*.

> *Following the Civil War, private telegraph lines were but one of the expanded uses of the telegraph. The telegraph was also used as a fire alarm, a burglar alarm, a facsimile machine, and a version of the instrument could be installed to deliver gold and stock quotes throughout the day.*

The real insight to be gained from these early notes and drawings is an understanding of Edison's commitment to his intellectual and technical growth during his years as an itinerant telegrapher. It is apparent that Edison chose the profession with every intention of taking advantage of the freedom and opportunity it afforded. As his employment record indicates, Edison wasn't a model employee, but in his mind, experimenting and inventing came first. If he lost a job, it simply meant it was time to move on, and the telegrapher's profession again fit his needs perfectly. Edison's years on the road laid the foundation for his future success.

If Edison had remained in Michigan, he would have eventually exhausted his sources for expanding his intellectual and practical knowledge of telegraphy. Only by leaving Michigan did Edison's knowledge of telegraphy become sound not only in theory but in practice. He also wouldn't have made the professional connections with individuals who would eventually play a significant role in launching his career as an inventor.

Chapter 3

East to Boston

*Restlessness is discontent—and discontent is the first
necessity of progress. Show me a thoroughly satisfied
man—and I will show you a failure.*
                                        —*Thomas Alva Edison*

Even though Thomas Alva Edison had become a first-class operator, he had a long way to go to live up to the expectations of
those who sang his praises when he was a boy. He had spent a better part of his life as a drifter, working as a telegrapher throughout
the Midwest. He would have died with his companions in Vera
Cruz, Mexico, if he had not decided to stay in America instead of
seeking adventure and riches as a telegrapher in Brazil. He was now
twenty years old with nothing but the clothes on his back. It was
far from obvious that he would become a world-famous, accomplished man.

In Port Huron, life for Samuel and Nancy Edison hadn't been
much better. The Edison's home of thirteen years had been confis-
cated by the military and made part of Ft. Gratiot. After serving a
term as justice of the peace in 1866, Samuel found work hard to
come by. He speculated in land and might have worked as a con-
tractor. He often walked over fifty miles to Detroit, staying for days
to earn some money and return home. Nancy suffered from what
today would probably be diagnosed as severe depression.
According to friends and family, she remained secluded in the

temporary housing provided by the military. The Edisons received some financial assistance from William Pitt Edison, their oldest son, who had prospered in business as the operator of the largest livery stable in the region. With time he also became the manager and part owner of the Port Huron and Gratiot Street Railway Company.

Such was the state of the Edison's family when Thomas Alva returned from Cincinnati in 1867. Whether his days as an itinerant telegrapher had come to an end because of his mother's poor health or because he needed a quiet place to think through his next move is uncertain. Shortly after his arrival, Edison secured a position working at odd jobs at the Port Huron train depot to provide for himself and his parents. At home, he continued developing a duplex telegraph, which he tested on the Grand Trunk Railroad's telegraph wire, which ran underwater from Ft. Gratiot to Port Edward, Canada.

Life settled into a routine, but as always, when life became somewhat predictable, it was a sign that Edison's life was about to take a dramatic turn. He received a letter from his old friend and ex-roommate from Cincinnati, Milt F. Adams, informing him of employment opportunities in Boston. Adams's letter could not have come at a better time; Edison was growing restless, and was even thinking of heading east. He wrote back asking if a position could be easily found. Adams wrote back advising him of a job opening in the Western Union telegraph office, and Edison hit the road yet again. Leaving his mother in her condition must have been difficult, but the ever-practical Edison knew that he could do more for his parents financially by taking to the road than he could staying home. He was right, and once Edison made his first real money, he immediately provided financial assistance to his parents—just as he had as a child.

The city of Boston had in the postwar era become second only to New York City as the leading telegraph community in the country. The telegraph had evolved from a simple communication tool that investors turned down to an instrument that business organizations sought to control. In their effort to become leaders in the industry and the marketplace, these organizations quickly purchased the patent rights to improvements made in any facet of telegraphy, and inventors strived to expand the telegraph's capabilities. Boston was full of men who had succeeded as inventors in the field of telegraphy. There was J. B. Stearns, the forerunner in the race to develop a functional duplex system; Thomas Hill, who, though not first, had successfully developed, manufactured, and demonstrated a miniature electric-motored train; and Charles William Jr., a shop owner who provided space, machinery, and guidance to aspiring inventors and electricians. Here Alexander Graham Bell had conducted early experiments on the telephone, and Moses G. Farmer, the leading American inventor of his time, had developed and tested some of his inventions.

Above all, there were venture capitalists in Boston willing to take a well-calculated risk on a new invention and an unproven inventor. Some of these investors were also known to acquire the rights to inventions by any means necessary, which often meant an inventor would receive no royalties on their inventions. To succeed in such a competitive environment, an inventor needed more than a good imagination and undying determination, he also needed to be generally schooled and have had experience in financing, marketing, and manufacturing. It was an environment in which Edison would thrive.

The day Edison arrived in Boston, he walked straight to the Western Union telegraph office and introduced himself to the manager, George Milliken. Dressed in baggy clothes, a wide-brimmed hat, and badly in need of a haircut, Edison caught the attention of the telegraphers seated around the office hard at work. After a five-minute interview and a demonstration of his skills, Edison was offered a post and asked when he could get started. Right now, he answered. The other telegraphers took note of the Michigan boy's enthusiasm and smiled at each other as Milliken told him to come back at 5:30 that evening.

Upon his return, Edison took a seat and got to work taking a message. The sender on the other end started out slowly, but was soon going at a good pace. Edison kept up, writing down everything as it came across. Not believing that this hayseed was really writing down what was being sent, the telegraphers in the office came over and checked his progress. Unbeknownst to Edison, the boys had pitted him against the fastest sender in the company, a man in the New York City office. Sensing that his new compatriots were up to something, Edison continued writing, occasionally stopping to sharpen his pencil or get a drink of water, then returned to taking the message without missing a single word. This went on for quite awhile until Edison opened up the key and asked the man on the other end to "change off and send with the other foot." His fellow telegraphers exploded with laughter, and the comment threw off the New York telegrapher's concentration; he finally turned his instrument over to a co-worker. The freshman telegrapher had won the respect of his new co-workers.

As with this cartoon found in the January 1, 1879, issue of The Operator, *Edison, too, was "hazed" by telegraph veterans during his first day on the job in Boston.*

Rooming with Adams, Edison soon settled in as night operator on the "Number 1 press wire," from New York City. During his time off he was consumed with developing a number of inventions, and with his self-education. Nothing impacted his development more than Michael Faraday's two-volume set, *Experimental Researches in Electricity*, which he found in Cornhill's bookstore, his favorite haunt for used books. Edison was long an admirer of Faraday, because his explanations were simple and he used mathematics sparingly. Edison read both books in one sitting. Encouraged by what he read, he exclaimed to Adams, "I am now twenty-one. I may live to be fifty. Can I get as much done as he did? I have so much to do and life is so short that I am going to hustle."

> *Michael Faraday was born near London on September 21, 1791. He was the first scientist to liquefy a number of gases and to distill benzene from fish oil. His work in electrochemistry uncovered a relationship between electricity and the valence (combining power) of a chemical element, which provided scientists with the first clue to the existence of electrons. He is best known for discovering electromagnetic induction in 1831, the principle behind the electric generator. He found that moving a magnet through a coil of copper wire caused an electric current to flow in the wire. This meant that men no longer had to rely on a limited, chemically produced electrical current.*
>
> *Faraday distinguished himself by communicating the most difficult subjects so simply and effectively that even children understood. A popular lecturer, Faraday gave a series of lectures every Christmas for children, the most popular of which was titled, "The Chemical History of a Candle."*

In the weeks to come, Edison became familiar with Boston's technical community. He sought out J. B. Stearns and Charles Williams Jr., with whom he developed a friendship and in whose shop he got space to carry out his work. Inspired by the variety of applications for the use of the telegraph, Edison expanded his field of experimentation to include printing telegraphs, fire-alarms, burglar alarms, and facsimile telegraphs. He also continued work on his duplex system. In an early effort to market his work, he placed an announcement in the personal column of the April 4, 1868, *Telegrapher* announcing that "T. A. EDISON, formerly of the W. U.

Co.'s office, has accepted a position, and is now with the same Company's office, Boston, Mass." A week later, *The Telegrapher*, one of the industry's journals, published Edison's first technical article under the headline, EDISON'S DOUBLE TRANSMITTER.

In the article, Edison referred to his version of the double transmitter as an "ingenious arrangement" that allowed for the transmission of two messages "in opposite directions at the same time on a single wire." Overall, the instrument was no better than that invented and introduced by Stearns, coincidentally enough, on the same day Edison had arrived in Boston. But the article does show Edison's growth in his understanding of the technology—and in his ability to communicate his ideas on paper. In hindsight, the article was a master's thesis, proof that Edison's years on the road could be considered his "collegiate" years.

Edison had submitted the article to *The Telegrapher* in late December 1867 or early January 1868, while he was still in Port Huron. The article and the invention described were well received by the journal's editor, Franklin Pope, who published a note to the inventor in the January 11, 1868, issue, "Good! Come some more." The article would have been published earlier if it hadn't been mislaid when Pope passed the editorial reigns to James Ashley. When published, the article made some waves. *The Telegrapher*'s competitor, *The Journal of the Telegraph*, funded in part by Western Union, printed a reaction to Edison's instrument four days later referring to the apparatus as "interesting, simple and ingenious," but the piece pointed out that Edison's invention showed no original thought—an observation they might not have made if Western Union had had a stake in the device's success. Regardless of the criticism, for Edison the most important outcome of the piece was that people in Boston's technical community were becoming aware of his presence.

In the months that followed, Edison made sure to build on his name recognition by publishing an additional job announcement and articles. On April 25, he published a second job notice making clear that prior to his employ in Boston, he had been with the Western Union's Cincinnati office. The issue also contained a piece written by Edison describing his work with induction relays.

This was followed by a lengthy article titled "Edison's Combination Repeater" published on May 9. In the article, Edison was careful to point out that the device was based on original thought.

By June 1, 1868, a third instrument Edison was developing was featured in *The Journal of the Telegraph* under the title "Automatic Telegraphing." The article, written by Milt F. Adams as though he had no relationship with Edison, unveiled a variation of the repeating telegraph Edison had invented in Indianapolis. Described as "a very practical automatic apparatus which is both ingenious and curious," the instrument allowed for the rapid transmission of messages from one office to another. What made the instrument revolutionary, however, was that it did not depend on a telegrapher to write down an incoming message. Instead, an incoming message was automatically encoded onto a strip of chemically treated paper running through the receiver. The paper was then sent through a second machine for the purpose of writing out the message in readable form. Innovations of this sort were important to the industry because of the growing number of consumers sending messages across the wire.

These articles certainly attest to Edison's efforts to further establish his name and reputation, but they also represent a growing sophistication in his work, as well as his interest in a variety of instruments used in telegraphy.

> *In order to establish himself not only as an inventor but also as an industry spokesman, Edison published a number of articles during his time in Boston focusing on the telegraph industry. For instance, one article reported on improvements made to wire used for telegraphic lines, while another centered on advancements made to self-adjusting relays. In yet another piece, he wrote about a fire at a telegraphic manufacturing company. In one article he even boasted that Boston had a reputation among telegraphers and electricians "for the superior quality and finish of the work turned out by some of its leading manufacturers."*

From the outset of Edison's efforts to establish his name in Boston, he attracted the interest of investors. In April, Dewitt C.

Roberts, a telegrapher, entered into an agreement with Edison to develop a stock-printer—a device used in printing stock-ticker quotations. Roberts promised to furnish Edison with the money to patent and manufacture the instrument if he succeeded, and to provide the funds to patent and manufacture a second invention, the telegraphic vote-recorder. Before Edison could make progress on the stock-printer, Roberts left Boston in November, selling his interests in the stock-printer to Samuel Ropes Jr., a stockbroker. Knowing that Edison was close to completing his telegraphic vote-recorder, Roberts maintained control of his interests in that invention.

> *Those applying for a United States patent in those days were required to submit a fifteen dollar fee, a model, and a measured drawing. After a patent was granted, the inventor then paid an additional twenty dollars. If questions arose as to the granting of a patent, additional expenses were incurred. For this reason, inventors often hired patent lawyers. For example, when patenting his telegraphic vote-recorder Edison secured the services of Carroll D. Wright, a prominent patent lawyer.*

Edison was inspired by articles in *The Telegrapher* announcing that the New York legislature and the Washington, D.C., city council were considering the purchase of machines allowing the quick tabulation of votes. With Roberts's investment, Edison made a working model in William's shop. The instrument was simple enough: On top of each legislator's desk was a "yes" and a "no" button. By the side of the speaker's desk was a square frame containing two dials corresponding to either a "yes" or "no" vote. Below the dials appeared the number of votes cast. To place a vote, the person simply pushed the "yes" or "no" button. An electrical impulse was sent via a copper wire to the appropriate dial. All the speaker had to do was announce the results. The patent for this invention was granted on June 1, 1869: United States patent number 90,646 became Thomas Alva Edison's patent number 1.

The prototype was demonstrated to Massachusetts officials, who showed a slight interest, but did not place an order. The device was then demonstrated before a congressional committee in

Washington, where it functioned perfectly. Standing before a row of seated congressmen, Edison expected to hear that they wanted to place an order; after all, with his invention, congressmen would no longer have to sit in a crowded hall waiting for a vote to be taken manually! The committee, however, didn't like the future Edison's machine offered. One legislator was so upset by the device that he declared to Edison ...

> *Young man, that won't do at all! That is just what we do*
> *not want. Your invention would destroy the only hope the*
> *minority have of influencing legislation. It would deliver*
> *them over, bound hand and foot, to the majority. If there*
> *is any invention on earth that we don't want down here, it*
> *is this. One of the greatest weapons in the hands of a*
> *minority to prevent bad legislation is filibustering on votes,*
> *and this instrument would prevent it.*

Edison vowed that he "would never invent anything which was not wanted, or which was not necessary," but this failure did nothing to curtail the interest of investors in his work. In June 1868, John Lane, a former president of the Franklin Telegraph Company, agreed to finance Edison's development of an automatic printing telegraph, which allowed for the printing of messages on a strip of paper without an operator. For unknown reasons, the association was short-lived. In July 1868, E. Baker Welch, also a former Franklin Telegraph Company executive, backed Edison's experiments on double transmitters and fire-alarm telegraphs. He was also willing to fund Edison's patent application and finance a company to install the device in Cambridge if Edison succeeded in landing a contract to do so. When Edison didn't win the contract, Welch then paid to have Edison's double transmitter advertised in the pages of *The Telegrapher*, but his investment was apparently a loss, since there's no evidence that a single unit was ever sold. A month later, he invested in Edison's magnetograph, a telegraph that had a keyboard attached to it so a lay-person could easily send a message.

While working to develop these inventions, Edison also turned his attention to further developing the stock-printer. The leading stock-printer in use at the time was invented by E. A. Callahan, whose stock-printer allowed for the printing of gold and stock quotes on a long strip of paper. Edison examined the machine and found it impractical. The inner workings were so complicated that a specially trained attendant had to be on hand at all times. In addition, the device required a great deal of wiring, which ran up costs even further. Edison did away with the costly and unnecessary wiring, and made his machine so practical that anyone could repair it if a problem arose. He further expanded the stock-printer's capabilities by inventing a way for it to print letters as well as numbers.

By January 1869, Edison's stock-printer was finished. After securing two additional investors, Ropes started a gold and stock quote-reporting service featuring Edison's invention. Within a short time the company had thirty subscribers, and when a market was discovered for leasing telegraph instruments in private homes, Edison's magnetograph joined the product line, so the customer could type out a message without having to learn Morse code. Edison was to receive a portion of the profits and serve as manager. Based on the growing success of the business, Edison announced in *The Telegrapher* on January 30, 1869, that he "would hereafter devote his full time to bringing out his inventions."

Edison's decision to become a full-time inventor must have been made before this public declaration—it *must* have been, because at his full-time job as a telegrapher, he regressed back to behavior reminiscent of his younger days. For instance, he started noting lengthy stock market reports in writing so small that he could fit two thousand words on a single sheet. When their illegibility was brought to his attention, Edison wrote out the reports *one letter per page*: By the end of his shift, he had a stack of pages several feet thick. Demoted from his position at the press table to that of "sender," Edison resigned. His career as a telegrapher was over.

After Edison's business venture had been in operation for a short while, he discovered that his partners had managed to gain control of the patent rights to his inventions, which gave them control of the company. Feeling cheated, and rightfully so, Edison resigned.

He now focused his energies on further developing his duplex system after learning that Western Union was not satisfied with the system invented by J. B. Stearns. With yet another investment from Welch and with money from his personal savings, Edison completed an improved model of his duplex telegraph. He offered to demonstrate the machine to Western Union officials but was turned down, so he took the device to a competing firm, the Atlantic & Pacific Telegraph Company. At the present time, the company was small. It had lines running from New York to Cleveland, by way of Albany, Rochester, and Buffalo. Sufficiently impressed by the instrument and the qualities of its visionary salesman, the company agreed to a demonstration over company wires. The test would take place on a line from Rochester to New York City.

Borrowing an additional eight hundred dollars from Welch, Edison made last-minute modifications and headed to Rochester. Before departing, he fully briefed the New York City operator on what to expect once messages started flowing. He arrived in Rochester on Saturday, April 10, 1869. The test of the system started early the next morning. From the beginning things didn't go well. The operator in New York City was not responding, either because he hadn't fully understood instructions, or because the telegraph line was affected by thunderstorms. The test was repeated over several days, but faired no better; the system was a failure. However, the results of the demonstration as reported in *The Telegrapher*'s April 17 issue declared that the Edison's duplex system had "proved to be a complete success ...."

As would be the case in future newspaper stories on some of Edison's inventions, this was simply not the truth. Disgusted, Edison returned to Boston, greatly in debt and with no prospects for the future. He gave up working on his double transmitter completely.

After two years in Boston, by the end of April, the time had come to move on. The obvious choice would have been to play it safe, perhaps return to a life as a "tramp" telegrapher. But this was not an option for Thomas Alva Edison, who that night boarded a boat to New York City. As the boat made its way up New York

Harbor in the darkness, it is hard to believe that in less than thir-teen years Edison would be lighting the streets of New York City.

Chapter 4

Escaping Obscurity in the Big Apple

*I'll never give up for I may have a streak of luck before
I die.*

— *Thomas Alva Edison*

Edison spent his first night in New York City wandering the
streets. The only person he knew in town, a telegrapher from
his days on the road, was not home. Walking into a telegraph
office, he managed to borrow a dollar from a fellow telegrapher. He
bought apple dumplings and a cup of coffee.

For an inventor down on his luck, New York City was the best
place to be. It was the largest city in the United States, with a population of over one million, the nation's industrial and financial
capital, and the center for printing, publishing, fashion, tobacco
production, as well as a cultural mecca. The Erie Canal and the
expansion of railroads across the state spurred economic development, producing thousands of jobs. New York was also the home of
the United States's telegraph industry. Most telegraph companies
had their headquarters in New York City, including Western
Union. As in Boston, there were businessmen willing to provide
inventors with the capital to bring their discoveries to fruition;
and, like Boston, some businessmen were ruthless, caring for nothing else except creating or maintaining their fortunes.

The morning after his arrival, Edison paid a visit to S. S. Laws's Gold Indicator Company in the financial district. Once the president and presiding officer of the New York Gold Exchange, Laws had come up with the idea of posting the change of gold quotations on a mechanical device fixed on a wall of the Gold Room. It replaced the antiquated practice of noting prices on a blackboard. In the postwar era of active gold trading, even Laws's system didn't provide brokers and bankers with an efficient way to receive gold prices in their own offices, much less at the moment a price was changing. They had to rely on messenger boys—runners—to get this information to them. Often the price being delivered was no longer current once a runner reached their offices.

To solve this dilemma, Laws invented what he called a gold and stock indicator, a device that used the basic principles of telegraphy to deliver gold and eventually stock prices to subscribers. For a fee, an indicator was placed in a subscriber's office, receiving up-to-the-minute price quotes throughout the day. Started in 1867, by the time Edison arrived in New York City, Laws's company was making well over three hundred thousand dollars a year. It was one of two such companies dominating the field—the other being the Gold and Stock Telegraph Company.

At Laws's company headquarters, Edison met and talked to the superintendent, Franklin Pope. The author of *Modern Practice of the Electric Telegraph* and the eventual founder of the American Institute of Electrical Engineers, Pope was the former editor of *The Telegrapher,* which had accepted Edison's first article for publication. Pope knew of Edison not only from his articles but also from his work in Boston, especially his stock-printer. Naturally, Edison asked Pope if there was a job opening in the company. Pope advised him that at the moment there was none, but Edison impressed him enough that he offered him the company's machine shop for his experiments and a cot in the cellar to sleep on until he got back on his feet. Edison accepted.

Over the next few days, Edison spent his nights becoming familiar with Laws's indicator, which lay around the shop in various stages of disrepair. He spent his days searching for work, but he found nothing. He even walked by telegraph offices with "Help Wanted" signs posted in their front windows.

It was June 1869, trading on Wall Street had been fast and furious since the beginning of the month. Of heightened interest to speculators was the buying and selling of gold. Jay Gould, Jim Fisk, and a few other businessmen were laying the foundation that, they hoped, would enable them to corner the gold market. This overly active trading kept Laws's indicators humming for hours on end—until one day when the company's central indicator responsible for transmitting gold quotations to subscribers stopped working. Panic erupted all over New York City. Brokers served by Laws sent runners to his office to find out what was going on, while brokers with Laws's competitors went about business as usual. Soon the gold indicator's office was so packed with people that they spilled out onto the street. Chaos ruled. People demanded to know why service was halted; some speculated aloud that the price of gold had skyrocketed, and the government had ordered that trading be stopped. Inside, Laws yelled for Pope to "Fix it! Fix it! Be quick, for God's sake!"

The flustered Pope circled the machine but saw nothing out of place. Laws then took up the cause, but even he couldn't spot what had caused the machine to crash. All seemed lost, but, as luck would have it, Edison happened to be in the building and came running to see what the commotion was about. He watched Pope and Laws turn their frustrations over the machine on each other, and as the fierce shouting match built in volume and intensity, Edison walked over and studied the machine. After a minute he found what caused the instrument's failure: a contact spring had broken off and dropped between two gear wheels. Seeing a stranger huddled over his instrument, Laws quickly demanded to know what Edison was doing. Edison responded innocently enough that he had found the problem with the machine. Laws turned to Pope, who assured him that he should take the young man seriously.

Laws immediately demanded that Edison repair the machine, which he did in minutes. He reset the indicator's dial to zero, and trained repairmen were then sent to every subscriber's office to reset those machines to zero, thus bringing them into alignment.

Once this was done, the indicators were started. Within two hours, gold quotations were once again flowing. Edison had saved Laws's business. In gratitude, Laws hired Edison on the spot as Pope's assistant. As had been the case when Edison had saved J. U. Mackenzie's three-year-old son from a runaway train, fate once again rescued Edison from obscurity.

In July, Pope resigned to become an electrical engineering consultant. His job as the supervisor of Laws's Gold Indicator Company went to Edison, at a monthly salary of three hundred dollars. Throughout the summer, Edison modified Laws's indicator, his most valuable contribution being the removal of most of the intricate parts that were apt to break off. Edison also worked on redesigning a stock-printer Laws invented to compete with Calahan's stock-printer—the one used by Laws's rival, the Gold and Stock Telegraph Company. Edison's modifications proved invaluable. The size and number of parts in the printer were reduced and the ink ribbon was replaced with a printing wheel. An electromagnet was added to operate the unison stop—a device that kept the printer and the transmitter synchronized. Western Union, which had recently acquired the Gold and Stock Telegraph Company, took special note of Edison's refinements.

Edison kept Laws's indicator from breaking down the entire summer, and by the fall he had nearly finished his work on Laws's stock-printer. All was set aside, however, when on September 24, 1869, "Black Friday," Gould and Fisk made their final move to corner the gold market. The day started routinely enough, until Gould and Fisk starting buying up gold. Their well-timed purchases sent gold prices soaring. Edison made adjustments to Laws's indicator as it struggled to keep up with the fluctuating prices. Finally, it fell silent. Describing the excitement around him, Edison said that Mr. Speyer, the banker, lost his head and had to be restrained by five men. Everyone else in the room and the people rushing into the building were frantic. Amid the chaos, a Western Union operator commented, "Shake, Edison, we are O.K. We haven't a cent."

The panic of "Black Friday" did not subside until late in the day, when the United States Treasury flooded the open market with gold reserves. The experience of having been an eyewitness to one of history's most notable days on Wall Street left its mark on Edison. In the years after he became a wealthy man, not once did he ever gamble on the stock market, unless it was stock related to one of his enterprises.

> The gold standard system is largely fiction. Banks have a good reserve of, say, fifty percent of their note issue. This is fifty percent alleged real reserve and fifty percent real gamble, the banks taking the gambling chance that the note holders will not call on them all at one time. Finally, if things go wrong, and the note holders begin to demand the fifty percent gold, the banks fall back upon the credit of the Government and the merchants' notes through the Federal Reserve.
>
> It seems absurd to me that all our values should be based on boxes of metal in a treasury. It is an absurdity, but everyone has been educated to believe that absurdity is common sense.
>
> —*Thomas Alva Edison*

Six days later, Edison was out of a job. Laws, having had enough excitement to last him a lifetime, sold his company to Western Union, who merged it with the Gold and Stock Telegraph Company to form a subsidiary. Included in the transaction were the patent rights to Edison's inventions while working for the company, including inventions to which patents were pending. Edison resigned after Laws sold out, even though General Marshall Lefferts, the Western Union executive in charge of the new enterprise, asked him to stay.

> *While in the midst of negotiating for the purchase of the Gold and Stock Telegraph Company, Western Union's president, William Orton reported to the company's central division superintendent that, in his opinion, Edison's printing telegraph inventions were so unique that they ranked second only to those invented by George Phelps, Western Union's manufacturing superintendent, whose printing telegraph the company used. Orton further stated to the division leader that Edison was "probably the best electro-mechanician in the country."*
>
> *Edison had reached this level of notoriety less than two years after his arrival in New York City.*

After leaving Laws's company, Edison joined Franklin Pope, his former boss, and J. L. Ashley, the current publisher of *The Telegrapher*, in October 1869, to form the first electrical engineering firm in America. As advertised in *The Telegrapher*, the goal of the enterprise would be "the application of electricity to the Arts and Sciences."

To save money, Edison lived in Pope's home in Elizabeth, New Jersey, the very region where three-year-old John Edison and his widowed mother first settled in the United States, approximately one hundred and fifty years earlier. The company's shop was located in Jersey City near the Pennsylvania Railroad yards. Edison worked in relative freedom, much as he had as a boy on the Grand Trunk Railroad. His days started at six in the morning, when he rose to catch the train to New York. There he spent most of the day rooting out business opportunities before making his way to the shop where he and Pope worked late into the night.

From the outset the firm concentrated on upgrading instruments widely used in the telegraphic industry, such as fire-alarms, burglar alarms, facsimile telegraphs, and stock-printers. Before long the company introduced Edison's Universal Stock Printer, a new and improved stock-ticker that was so practical anyone could operate and repair it without any training. Revolutionary features of the device included the use of relay magnets and an improvement perhaps inspired from Edison's nights in Walker's jewelry and stationery store, an electrically driven escapement, comparable to those used in clocks, that drove the printing wheel.

In conjunction with the unveiling of Edison's improved Universal Stock Printer, the company announced that it was expanding its services to include stock market quotations at twenty-five dollars a month. Aware of the potential challenge posed by Edison's invention, Western Union offered fifteen thousand dollars for the exclusive rights to the instrument. The company accepted the offer. The money was divided equally among the three partners, even though Edison was responsible for the lion's share of thought and work that had gone into the device.

After the sale of Edison's instrument to Western Union, the company's strategy continued much the same as before: A device was conceived and developed or improvements were made to existing products. Edison spearheaded and was responsible for the success of most of the company's projects, yet he received only a third of the profits. Even so, there were benefits for Edison: His personal finances stabilized to the point that he was saving a fair amount, which enabled him to send a percentage home to his parents. This gave him great pride, evident in a letter probably written in May 1870 in which he asked his mother and father not to "do any hard work," and for his mother to buy "anything she desires." He concluded by informing his parents that they could count on him for financial assistance. "Write me," Edison wrote, "say how much you will need till June and I will send the amount on the first of that month."

Edison's patents for refinements to existing products and for original inventions began to mount. It became clear to industry observers that Pope, Edison and Company's success was due to him. Edison thought so, too, and in the summer of 1870, he left the company after growing tired "of doing all the work" for one third of the profits. Always ready to add an inventor of Edison's caliber to their roster, General Marshall Lefferts once again offered Edison a position with Western Union's newly formed subsidiary. Finding himself with no clear prospects, this time Edison accepted. Under the terms of his employment, Western Union paid the expenses of his work. In exchange, the company retained the right of first purchase of subsequent inventions. Characteristically, he never negotiated a steady salary for himself, or a price for the rights to future inventions.

Among the projects Edison worked on was the tendency of Callahan's stock-printer to involuntarily print out quotations at random, which not only caused chaos but required an attendant to then visit each subscriber to reset the indicators to zero before the central indicator could be restarted. Within three weeks Edison solved the problem by incorporating a "unison stop" into Callahan's printer, so an errant stock ticker automatically realigned itself to the rest of the system whenever it ran wild. He could not stop the machine from arbitrarily printing because, as with most equipment in use at the time, there was little understanding of electrical surges that wreaked havoc on equipment with no reasonable explanation. Even so, Edison's solution so impressed Lefferts and the board of directors that they decided to make Edison an offer for the patent rights. Summoned to Leffert's office, Edison was asked how much he would take for the improved stock-printer.

Edison thought of asking for five thousand dollars, then changed his mind to three thousand, thinking he did not want to press his luck. Even then, he didn't have the nerve to say the figure aloud. Instead, he threw the question back on Lefferts saying, "General, suppose you make me an offer."

Lefferts thought for a few seconds, then said, "How would forty thousand dollars strike you?"

Edison sat quietly. Years later he laughingly recalled that the Lefferts's offer "caused me to come near fainting as ever I got. I was afraid he would hear my heart beat. I managed to say that I thought it was fair."

On top of this astonishing sum, Edison also agreed to produce twelve hundred units of his self-aligning stock-printer, an order worth over five hundred thousand dollars. A contract was drawn, and three days later Lefferts handed Edison a check. Somewhat skeptical that the check was good, Edison immediately walked to the company's bank to cash it. The teller took the check and asked to see some proof of identity. Edison, failing to understand because of his deafness, took the check and stormed out of the bank. He marched to Lefferts's office demanding to know what was going on. Lefferts and his secretary had a good laugh after realizing that this was the first check Edison had ever tried to cash. Reassuring him that the company could cover the check, Lefferts sent his secretary to the bank with him just in case something else went wrong. Stepping up to the teller's window a second time, Edison was asked how he wanted the transaction handled. In cash, he responded. When the teller finished counting out forty thousand dollars, Edison had a stack of ten- and twenty-dollar bills over a foot high. With patrons staring, Edison stuffed the money into his pockets as best he could. He boarded the ferry to New Jersey and hurried to his room in a Newark boarding house, where he hid the money under his mattress. He did not leave his room for the rest of the day. That night he lay awake, worried that a thief would rob him of his fortune. By morning, Edison could no longer stand the thought of so much money under his mattress; he shoved the bills into his pockets and went directly to Lefferts. He confessed his anxiety about having so much money in his possession. Smiling, Lefferts suggested he deposit the money in the bank.

Edison suddenly found himself with money in the bank and facing the challenge of manufacturing twelve hundred of his realigning stock tickers. His first order of business was to secure a site in which to set up the manufacturing of the instruments. The factory would be located in Newark, where the cost of doing business was low and the availability of skilled labor high. Over the next few weeks, Edison and his partner, William Unger, a Newark mechanic whom Edison respected, searched the city until they found a suitable space on the third floor of a building on Ward Street. They called their enterprise the Newark Telegraph Works. Unger would remain a partner until 1872, when he left for New York City.

Horse-drawn wagons delivered the necessary machinery, and advertisements for machinists were placed in newspapers throughout the area. Applicants were surprised to find that the proprietor was twenty-four years old. Chief among those hired who would remain associated with Edison in the years that followed was Charles Batchelor, "Batch," as colleagues called him. Born in Britain and raised around machines, Batchelor was familiar with their workings and blueprints. This enabled him to work on projects with nothing more than rough sketches or ideas that called for an ability to improvise. Sent to America by the J. P. Coates Company, a thread manufacturer, to manage the installation of machinery at the Clark Thread Mills in Passaic, New Jersey, Batchelor wandered into the shop one day and met Edison. When he returned the next day and asked for a job, he was hired; he would work and remain a friend to Edison until his dying day.

John Kruesi, a master machinist and clockmaker from Switzerland, was placed in charge of manufacturing heavy machines and invention prototypes. He would one day build Edison's phonograph from a freehand drawing. John and Fred P.

Ott, brother mechanics, would spend their lives working for Edison. Fred eventually starred in the world's first copyrighted film, *The Record of a Sneeze*, filmed using Edison's movie camera. The final member of Edison's early team was Sigmund Bergmann, a German whose work ethic rivaled even Edison's. In years to come, Bergmann would open his own shop in New York City, where he would manufacture a number of Edison inventions, beginning with his phonograph.

Before the end of the month, Edison's shop was fully staffed and equipped. In his only letter home during the winter of 1871, Edison wrote, "I have a shop which employs 18 men and am fitting up another which will employ over 150 men. I am now what 'you' Democrats call a 'Bloated Eastern Manufacturer.'"

It's doubtful that his mother understood the good fortune that had befallen her son; her chronic nervous condition had grown worse. Edison longed to see her but couldn't trust anyone to look after his interests, so for the moment he did not return home. The decision choice proved devastating: On April 11, 1871, a telegram arrived from Port Huron informing him that his mother had passed away. Edison rushed home. He attended her funeral, returning quickly to Newark after the burial.

In time, Edison's staff grew to over two hundred and fifty, and a night-shift was added. Several offshoot enterprises were started at various locations. The American Telegraph Works was established to manufacture additional orders and to develop or perfect existing products. At their peak, Edison and his men were working on forty-five inventions at the same time. Much like he would do at his Menlo Park laboratory, Edison supervised all efforts. Men were expected to follow his instructions to the letter. As for the enterprise's finances, Edison managed them in much the same way as he had his childhood endeavors: financial bookkeeping consisted of two hooks screwed into a wall: one for incoming bills and the other for past due bills. At "the first intimation that a note was due" Edison "hustled around and raised the money."

Employees' work schedules were demanding, and expectations were extremely high. Edison's philosophy was to work as long as it takes to get the job done—work came first, everything else second.

Even so, Edison often surprised his men by giving them the day off, or taking them on a fishing excursion. Away from the shop and on special occasions, the men came to know Edison's personal side. They came to respect him not only for his work ethic, which surpassed that of almost every man, but for his sense of humor, which was also a step or two ahead of most men.

Among Edison's achievements in this period, he discovered what he referred to as "etheric force," after noticing a flash in the core of a vibrator magnet being used as part of an experiment. With this phenomenon in mind, he examined vibrator magnets used in stock-printers and the electric pen while the instruments were in operation. As before, sparks were emitted from the interior of the vibrator magnet. Edison had discovered radio waves, which years later would be the basis for the vacuum tube, which in turn would serve as the foundation for the electronics industry. Not fully understanding the importance of what he had discovered, after a series of experiments, a few notations in a laboratory notebook, and a brief splash in newspapers, the discovery was set aside.

As he had always done, Edison kept a book of notes and drawings of all the work taking place. The first notebook for the Newark factory was dated July 28, 1871. Inside, it read: "This will be a daily record containing ideas previously formed, some of which have been tried, some that have been sketched and described, and some that have never been sketched, tried or described." He would continue keeping these notebooks for the next thirty-five years.

His business matters under control, in the spring of 1871, Edison accepted an offer from the Automatic Telegraph Company to make improvements to an automatic telegraph for which it owned the patent rights. The automatic telegraph was growing in importance because it allowed for the rapid transmission of messages across a telegraph wire. The first such device had been invented by Alexander Bain over twenty years earlier; however, the instrument was neither reliable nor practical. Bain's device called for the perforations of dots and dashes on a long strip of paper. The perforations were done by hand using a hole-punching machine on a long strip of paper, then the paper was pulled through a metal cylinder and a metal stylus. When the stylus passed over the perforations and came into contact with the metal drum, an electrical impulse was sent along the wire. This allowed for the transmission of an estimated four hundred words a minute, a substantial increase over the fifty words an operator was capable of sending. When the system was introduced in the United States in the 1870s, the stylus's inability to transmit the distinct sound of a dot and a dash caused messages to become slurred over long distances.

George D. Little designed the model to which the Automatic Telegraph Company owned the patent rights. With a few modifications, the instrument worked off the same principle as Bain's, and suffered from the same slurring of signals. At the time that the Automatic Telegraph Company had purchased the rights, they were not aware of the instrument's shortfalls. Edison attacked the challenge in his customary way: He read everything he could find on the topic. At the same time he conducted experiments using a working model of Little's machine.

During this same period, Edison met sixteen-year-old Mary Stilwell, after she and her sister sought refuge from a driving rainstorm in the doorway of his Newark factory. He invited them inside, where introductions were exchanged. Edison was taken by Mary and offered her a job.

> To save money, manufacturing companies hired women and boys to do menial labor. In Edison's Newark Telegraph Works, as in most of his shops, women and boys were hired to assemble a variety of Edison's instruments, a testament to the simplicity of Edison's inventive mind.

After a brief courtship, Edison married Mary on December 25, 1871. Family tradition also holds that on their wedding night, Edison took his bride to the house he had purchased for them— and left her to return to the factory. He did not return home until after midnight, and then only because an associate inadvertently interrupted his work. By the time Edison returned home, he found his bride in tears, afraid she had done something to upset him. The experience left Mary so shaken that she asked permission for her sister, Alice, to come along with them on their honeymoon to Niagara Falls, to which Edison agreed.

Mary Stilwell, the first Mrs. Thomas Alva Edison.

(© *Courtesy of Edison National Site*)

Returning to work on Little's automatic telegraph, Edison set about solving the machine's tendency to slur transmissions. The improvements would take Edison two years to complete. For his efforts he would receive forty thousand dollars. When tested over a wire running from Washington, D.C., to New York City, over twelve thousand words were transmitted in twenty-two and a half minutes, an average of five hundred words a minute. After this successful test, officials with the Automatic Telegraph Company paid Edison to go to England in April 1873—his first trip overseas—to demonstrate the device to British Post Office executives. The demonstration went well, but no orders were placed for the invention.

Upon Edison's return, Jay Gould, the entrepreneur who had tried unsuccessfully to corner the gold market, stepped forward and openly acknowledged that he was the owner of the Automatic Telegraph Company. Gould, who by this point in his career had added to his wealth by gaining control of a number of railroad lines, the Atlantic and Pacific Telegraph Company, as well as a number of key telegraph patents, planned to use the patent to Edison's automatic telegraph as a way to gain control of Western Union.

Before leaving for England, Edison had entered into a verbal contract with Western Union president William Orton to solve lingering problems with Joseph Stearns's duplex telegraph. Edison promised to develop a system by which two messages could be sent in the same direction at the same time, what would come to be known as a "diplex" telegraph. As with all duplex telegraphs at the time, two messages could be sent on one wire at the same time, but only in separate directions. By the spring of 1873, Edison had not yet solved the problems associated with a diplex system; however, he was successful in creating his version of a duplex system. While different enough from Stearns's model to gain Edison a patent, it was only a slight improvement. However, Edison had an idea for developing a quadruplex system—a method by which two messages could be sent at the same time, but in opposite directions. Edison approached Orton for funding to research and develop the idea. Once again, Orton agreed to sponsor Edison's efforts, and once again, a verbal contract was made.

Working with George B. Prescott, a chief engineer for Western Union, Edison completed his work by July 1874. The system was then tested for Western Union officials on a wire running from New York to Albany and back. Rainstorms near Albany promised to wreak havoc on the demonstration, but once the proceedings began, Edison's invention worked perfectly.

> Inasmuch as every mile of wire actually built does the work of four miles of wire, the quadruplex system represents 216,000 miles of phantom wire, worth $10,800,000.
>
> On these $10 million worth of wires there is no repairing to be done. The value of those phantom wires is, therefore, represented by a saving of $860,000 in repairs at $4 a mile annually, besides the interest on the $10,800,000 which it would have taken to build them.
>
> —*Thomas Alva Edison, from the* Scientific American, *1892*

Of this major achievement that turned the telegraph world on end, and received coverage in the nation's newspapers, Edison stated that …

> *This problem was of the most difficult and complicated*
> *kind and I bent all my energies to its solution. It required*
> *a peculiar effort of the mind, such as the imagining of*
> *eight different things moving simultaneously on a mental*
> *plane, without anything to demonstrate their efficiency.*

Orton promised to pay Edison five thousand dollars for the exclusive rights to the invention, as well as two hundred and thirty-three dollars annually for each circuit placed in use. However, for unknown reasons, Orton did not follow through on the agreement. Having lost his home following the Panic of 1873 and desperately in need of cash to support his various enterprises, Edison struck a deal with Jay Gould for the rights to his quadruplex patent: The price was thirty thousand dollars. By the time Orton managed to send a letter to Edison in January 1875 advising him that Western Union was ready to finalize their deal, Edison informed him that rights for the quadruplex telegraph were under Gould's control. Furious and feeling betrayed, Orton brought a lawsuit against Edison and Jay Gould on behalf of Western Union. Throughout the trial, Western Union attorneys painted Edison as a traitor, while Gould's legal representatives argued that it was Western Union's intent to swindle Edison on the basis of nothing more than a verbal agreement.

In his defense, Edison stated that at the time he made the agreement with Orton, he'd forgotten that the rights to the invention actually belonged to George Harrington, a telegraph investor, based on an agreement reached in 1871. The deal was recorded at the patent office, where Gould had purchased Harrington's interest. On researching Edison's claim, Western Union attorneys found that someone had altered the patent office records of the transaction in an effort to have the agreement read in Edison and Gould's favor.

For his part, Edison further stated that Western Union's general superintendent, General Eckert, advised him that the company was no longer interested in the quadruplex and introduced him to Gould, who was more than willing to make an offer. Of course, Eckert had not revealed to Edison that he was in negotiations with Gould to leave Western Union to join Atlantic and Pacific. In the end, the courts sided with Western Union; however, in 1881, Gould had the last laugh when he acquired control of Western Union. He was to rule over the company until his death in 1892.

Of the takeover, Edison stated that, "When Gould got the Western Union, I knew no further progress in telegraphy was possible, and I went into other lines."

Since his arrival in New York City in 1869, Edison had risen from obscurity to national renown. He had managed to survive cutthroat business practices and earn a great deal of money, which he funneled into his various ventures. With the assistance of his men, by the start of 1876, he had been awarded over two hundred patents. Even with all of the success he was enjoying, by 1875, the twenty-eight-year-old Edison was becoming discontented with his life in Newark. He longed to simply invent full time, as he had done while he was with Pope, Edison and Company, but the constant need to manage staff and oversee what was by now a large industrial organization kept him from it. In addition, by 1876 the Edison family had grown to include a daughter and son, whom Edison playfully nicknamed Dot and Dash—and the industrial town of Newark was no place to raise children.

After more than seven years—the longest time Edison had spent anywhere since leaving his home in Port Huron—it was time to move on yet again.

Chapter 5

The Invention Factory

*My one ambition is to be able to work without regard to
the expense .... I want none of the rich man's usual toys.
I want no horses or yachts—I have no time for them.
What I want is a perfect workshop.*

—*Thomas Alva Edison*

By the fall of 1875, Edison had decided to move his base of operations and rededicate himself exclusively to the business of
inventing. The only question was where to move to. Edison left it
to his father, Samuel. A widower for four years, Samuel and
Charley, William Pitt Edison's son, came to Newark in 1875 to
maintain the Ward Street factory, a position that paid Samuel
twenty dollars a week. Edison now asked his father to find the site
of his own laboratory.

Edison set parameters before Samuel began the search in early
December 1875: The location had to be near New York City; a
railroad had to be in close proximity, and the price had to be right.
Discovering Menlo Park, New Jersey, by the end of the month,
Samuel succeeded on all three counts. A failed real-estate development, Menlo Park was the ideal location: It was twenty-five
miles south of New York City and only twelve from Newark; a railroad line stretching from New York City to Philadelphia served the

area, and land was cheap, which enabled Edison to acquire two tracts of land and a house that had served as the office for the Menlo Park Land Company for a grand total of five thousand two hundred dollars. Land was also for sale around the tract on which Edison's laboratory was to be built leaving room for expansion. The sleepy hamlet's population was small; there were additional houses available for Edison employees, and, aside from a small saloon near the railway depot, there were no social activities to distract Edison's assistants.

To finally have arrived financially and professionally at a point where he could establish a permanent laboratory for the sole purpose of inventing must have seemed like a dream come true for Edison, yet he kept these feelings to himself. In one interview after another for the rest of his life, he maintained that his primary reason for leaving his Newark factory was due to a suit brought against him by a landlord for rent owed on a space he had leased. Whether or not this was the case, once Edison made up his mind to leave Newark, it was as good as done. It was a bold move. No one had ever before established an "invention factory" whose purpose was only to invent commercially viable products, and critics declared that Edison's lack of formal scientific training would prevent his success.

Work on the laboratory started in the spring of 1876 with Samuel supervising construction. Building plans called for the laboratory to be one hundred feet long and thirty feet wide, consisting of two floors with tall windows lining either side. A covered porch would run the width of the front and serve as a balcony for the second floor. White-painted clapboards would cover the building's frame as well as the carpenter's shed directly behind the laboratory; detailed trim work would complete the exterior. Surrounding the structures would be a white picket fence to keep out cows, chickens, pigs, and the occasional bill collector. This phase of construction amounted to two thousand seven hundred dollars.

On the first floor there was an office and a small library. Beyond this, a small chemical laboratory and a testing room ran along one wall while on the other side of the long hall were a galvanometer table, a hydrolytic press, stacks of condensers, materials used for the production of batteries, and a glass case containing selected Edison inventions from which parts were freely borrowed. At the far end was the machine shop, with an assay bench, two small rooms, carbonizing furnaces, an upright steam engine, a sink, and a fume chamber. Under the staircase leading up to the second floor was a cubbyhole in which, legend holds, Edison was known to catch a few winks of sleep every now and then. Within two years, additional structures were constructed, including a carbon shed, a glasshouse, and an expanded machine shop. Another two-story structure was built later, into which the office and the library were moved.

The heart and soul of the laboratory, however, was on the second floor, where Edison's factory for inventions was finally realized. On this floor were work-stations that allowed a number of inventions to be developed at the same time. There were cabinets containing equipment and, in one corner, Edison's desk, where a telegraph sender and sounder sat waiting. Surrounding these items were shelves holding thousands of bottles of chemicals. Gas jets provided light for the structure. No expense was spared in obtaining the best scientific equipment and chemicals available—everything Edison needed to test his ideas efficiently.

The oddest piece of machinery in the laboratory was a pipe organ, which sat against the second floor's back wall. Given to Edison in early 1878 by Hilborne Roosevelt, a designer and manufacturer of pipe organs and cousin of Theodore Roosevelt, the pipe organ gave visitors a clue that this was not a run-of-the-mill workshop, but a dynamic workplace where the unconventional ruled.

The placement of workstations and equipment (with the exception of the organ and the amount of chemicals kept on hand) was common in most workshops of the day, but the greatest influence on how each work table functioned probably came from Charles Williams's shop in Boston, which also had work going on a number of projects at the same time. However, at Williams's shop, men worked for themselves, which often meant that ideas were not freely shared. In Edison's shop, men worked for him, on his ideas.

A distinctive feature of the laboratory was the notebooks laying about, in which Edison and his assistants kept detailed notes and sketches of their work, a practice that by the end of Edison's career would produce over thirty-five hundred bound and unbound notebooks.

As the laboratory neared completion by the end of March 1876, men in horse-drawn wagons delivered machinery and crates loaded with tools and instruments from the Newark factory. (A number of men at the Newark factory remained on the payroll until work tapered off.) Edison's wife, Mary, and their two children moved into the six-room Victorian house that once housed the failed land-development company's office. Charles Batchelor and John Kruesi also acquired homes for their families. At least at the beginning, single men were left to make their own living arrangements.

Besides Batchelor and Kruesi, a fortunate few would make the move to Menlo Park. Edison gave the matter of whom he would bring with him as much consideration as he had selecting the laboratory's location. Here, too, certain parameters had to be met. Those selected had to be dedicated to their work and ready to live a monastic life. They had to be willing to take orders and follow Edison's instructions to the letter. Once given an order, they could not offer an opinion unless asked. They had to be willing to work long hours with relatively low pay—if they were paid at all. Most importantly, they had to be trustworthy and loyal—secrets had to be kept. Two qualifications were above all others: First, a man had to know his area of specialization like the back of his hand, and second, he had to be efficient with his time. "We have got to keep working up things of commercial value," Edison had said, "that is what this laboratory is for. We can't be like the old German professor who as long as he can get his black bread and beer is content to spend his whole life studying the fuzz on a bee!"

Selected to join Batchelor and Kruesi were the brother machinists John and Fred P. Ott, Sigmund Bergmann, and a dozen others. The years to come would add Francis R. Upton, an American mathematician and graduate from the College of New Jersey (later known as Princeton), whom Edison playfully nicknamed "Culture." Upton would play a vital role in researching and developing Edison's incandescent lamp. Ludwig Boehm, a German glassblower, had the honor of making the glass lamps used in Edison's incandescent lighting experiments and their first public demonstration. Arriving after Boehm was eighteen-year-old Francis Jehl, who in retirement wrote a memoir of his years at Menlo Park and assisted Henry Ford in reconstructing the laboratory at Ford's Greenfield Village in Dearborn, Michigan. On the business side, Edison hired William Carmen, who would be the Menlo Park bookkeeper until 1883. Ernest J. Berggren was Carmen's assistant. Samuel Mott was Edison's patent draftsman. S. L. Griffin, an Edison friend from his days as a telegrapher, served as Edison's personal secretary, and Samuel Insull as Edison's business secretary. With these men taking care of his business, Edison could focus his attention on inventing.

With his team and laboratory in place, Edison was so sure of success that he boldly proclaimed to his friend Dr. George Beard that from Menlo Park would come "a minor invention every ten days and a big thing every six months or so." As Edison had made clear to his staff prior to being selected to join him at Menlo Park, they would work around the clock to complete an experiment, or to manufacture a prototype of an invention. Work was fast and furious. Results were expected. Edison demanded it. Through it all, however, he was, as Jehl said, "Respected with a respect that only great men can attain."

No one worked harder than Edison, who one day received a letter from J. U. MacKenzie, the Mt. Clemens stationmaster who had mentored him as a teenager, advising him to "quit for meals regularly … carry on enjoyable conversation with members of your family … and devote your evenings to domestic pleasure and enjoyment—never work on Sunday!" Edison couldn't bring himself to do as MacKenzie advised. As in Newark, he hardly spent time at home, leaving Mary to raise their children. A reporter for the *New York Herald* observed, "Edison himself flits about, first to one bench, then to another, examining here, instructing there; at one place drawing out new fancied designs, at another earnestly watching the progress of some experiment."

Edison's Menlo Park complex in its completed form as painted during the winter of 1880–81. The office/library is at the front, the laboratory is at center, and the machine shop is at the rear.

All, however, was not work at Menlo Park. On occasion, Edison would take the men fishing as he had done in the early days of his Newark factory, or he gave them the day off without warning. The men also enjoyed sitting around the pipe organ listening to music while enjoying a break or a meal. Edison himself played the organ once in a while, pecking away with one finger, and nothing brought a bigger smile to his face than surprising someone dozing off to sleep with his "corpse reviver": a wooden box with a crank and a wooden gear inside that made a horrible sound when the crank was turned. Edison liked to spin a good yarn or two, and enjoyed listening to stories by others as much as he liked to tell them. His men held impromptu singing programs in which they parodied the popular songs of the day.

Edison was not naïve enough to think that good times interspersed between long hours of hard work were enough to ensure the loyalty and respect of his staff. Edison knew that one thing motivated men more than anything else: money. "In those days," as John Ott later recalled, "we all hoped to get rich with him."

Edison (center) sits surrounded by his staff on the second floor of his Menlo Park laboratory. The reconstructed laboratory is today located at Henry Ford Museum and Greenfield Village in Dearborn, Michigan.

(© *Courtesy of Edison National Historic Site*)

Edison didn't open the till and start handing out cash. If any-thing, Edison locked the cashbox and threw away the key! A man had to prove he was worthy of a paycheck, and not just to Edison, but to those working around him. Men who succeeded in securing a paycheck or who were hired on a salary were seen as having proved their worth to the organization, and, even more important, to the "Old Man"—the nickname respectfully given to Edison by his employees, even though most of them were considerably older than he was. Aside from a steady paycheck, Edison also rewarded those worthy with bonuses in the form of stocks in the various companies that sprang from Menlo Park. This additional benefit would make wealthy men of more than one Edison employee. Of course, once Edison's reputation grew to immortal proportions, men willing to work for free came knocking at his door. For instance, in his letter of application, Dr. Otto Moses, a researcher and analytical chemist wrote, "As it is of more importance to secure work, than for me to be paid for it, I will not now propose that question ... for the present, my philosophy is to know, and to conquer Nature rather than Fortune."

Over the course of the first few months, Edison and his men focused on the continued technical improvement of various instruments used in telegraphy and the refinement of Edison inventions originated in Newark. The first significant project undertaken, however, was the development of a "speaking telegraph," an investigation Edison was hired to undertake by Western Union president William Orton. By now Orton and Edison had set aside their differences over Edison's quadruplex. With a formal agreement in hand, Orton hired Edison to research and develop the instrument for a monthly fee of five hundred dollars. It was Orton's hope that Edison could invent a "speaking telegraph," or telephone, as the device came to be known, which would rival that invented by Alexander Graham Bell and Elisha Gray.

On February 14, 1876, Alexander Graham Bell filed a patent application for his telephone. Two hours later, Elisha Gray filed a caveat for his telephone. The inventions described in the documents were almost exactly the same. In the months that followed, there was speculation that a crooked patent office employee had reversed the order in which the materials were turned in. In the court case that resulted, Bell was awarded the patent outright. Thus Gray missed being credited with one of the greatest inventions in history.

In early 1876, Orton had missed an opportunity to purchase the rights to Bell's telephone after Bell, in desperate need of money, offered them to Orton for a reported hundred thousand dollars. Calling the telephone "nothing more than a toy," Orton had turned down the offer, knowing if the instrument ever did pose a threat to Western Union, he could hire someone to develop a similar product for close to nothing at all. Only after Bell's public announcement of the discovery of the telephone in March 1876 and the subsequent success that Bell and his investors had in luring customers from Western Union, did Orton fully realize the value of the telephone. Taking steps to correct his unfortunate decision, Orton purchased the rights to Gray's telephone, and hired Edison to discover a telephone superior to Bell's.

Edison undertook the challenge by examining Bell's telephone, which by now included a receiver and a transmitter. He found that Bell's *receiver* worked well enough, but his *transmitter* didn't. The problem lay in the design of the device, which used a soft, thin piece of metal as a diaphragm. When a person spoke into the transmitter the sound waves caused the piece of metal to vibrate. The metal would then make contact with a bar magnet that had a long piece of thin copper wire wrapped around one end. When the metal diaphragm came into contact with the magnet, it started a fluctuating current in the magnetic coils corresponding to the sound waves. The impulses ran through the line to the receiver, which used a design similar to the first. Variations in the magnetism vibrated the diaphragm, thus replicating the human voice. The only problem was that the impulses were not very strong; once the signal reached the receiver, a person's voice was barely loud enough to hear.

Meanwhile, at the Centennial Exposition of 1876 in Philadelphia, Bell was receiving accolades for his telephone. The exposition celebrating America's first one hundred years of freedom featured exhibits highlighting ten decades of progress and expansion. Items exhibited before the over ten million people who attended the event included Bell's telephone, George H. Corliss' fourteen-hundred horsepower steam engine, and George Westinghouses' air brake for railroad cars. Also displayed were fifty-ton locomotives, the continuous-web printing press, the self-binding reaper, the typewriter, the refrigerator car, gas stoves, arc lamps, machines used to make products ranging from button holes to shoes, and dynamos—today known as electric generators.

Also represented alongside these innovations were most of Thomas Alva Edison's inventions, minus his automatic telegraph, which was being used at the exposition by the Atlantic and Pacific Telegraph Company, the "official" telegraph service provider for the event. At thirty, Edison already held more patents than most of the people represented. One of the prizes awarded Edison was for his automatic telegraph, considered "a very important step in land telegraphy."

One of the ten million individuals attending the Centennial Exposition in 1876 was William Ford, father to the automobile magnate Henry Ford. On his return home, William presented his children with gifts from the event and told them stories of the innovative items he had seen. Henry Ford was only four years old at the time. Twenty-nine years later, he would meet Edison, forming a friendship that would last the rest of Edison's life.

Edison attended the event with his wife and children, but soon returned to Menlo Park, where for the rest of the year he and his staff conducted thousands of experiments in an effort to invent a transmitter that would emit a clear and loud voice. As indicated in notebook records on January 20, 1877, Edison finally "succeeded in conveying over wires many articulated sentences." He accomplished this by connecting a small spring in the center of a metal diaphragm to three platinum points submerged in a bowl of carbon granules. Passing through the platinum points was a current generated by a battery. When the voice caused the spring to vibrate, it caused the carbon granules to compress and release, thus altering the battery's current. The result, even in this crude form, was a superior sound. The secret lay in the carbon granules, which had a high resistance to electrical current.

With these results, Edison was granted additional funding from Western Union to continue his research. He placed the carbon granules inside a metallic disk, which he referred to as a "carbon button." He placed one carbon button in the transmitter so that the metal diaphragm, now without a spring attached to the center, came into contact with it when sound waves caused it to vibrate. He placed a second carbon button underneath the first, held ever so slightly apart. A current generated by a battery was then made to flow through each carbon button. When sound waves caused the first button to vibrate it came into contact with carbon button underneath. When this happened, the strength of the signal moving down the line was considerably stronger, which resulted in even a louder and clearer voice coming out of the receiver. Still not satisfied, after a series of experiments Edison found that if the battery's current was made to run through the primary circuit of an induction coil, then through a second coil, the resulting impulses were strong enough to travel hundreds of miles. On April 27, 1877, Edison finally filed a patent for his "speaking telegraph transmitter."

In tests conducted for Western Union officials on a line extending from Philadelphia to New York City, Edison's transmitter was used with Gray's receiver. Together the instruments functioned perfectly. To sell the product, Western Union established the American Speaking Telephone Company. When approached by Orton to purchase the patent rights, Edison was asked how much he would take for them. As he had done in previous negotiations, Edison asked Orton to make an offer. Orton suggested one hundred thousand dollars. Edison accepted. However, Edison requested the amount be paid to him over the lifetime of the patent—seventeen years. Edison could have taken the original sum and made six thousand dollars a year in interest alone, but as he later explained, if he would have taken the cash up front, it would have been gone before he knew it. In accepting six thousand dollars a year, he would have a steady income for the next seventeen years.

While Edison was conducting transmitter experiments, he was conducting a number of other investigations at the same time on commercially viable products such as submarine cable devices, carbon microphones, condenser microphones, dynamic microphones, typewriters, sound measuring apparatuses, mimeograph machines, and even on incandescent lamps, which for the moment proved inconclusive. Of those products completed, Edison's "electric pen" showed the greatest promise. More important, when the patent application for the instrument was filed on March 13, 1876, it ended a stretch lasting more than a year in which he failed to file a single patent application. Like the early tests on incandescent lamps, which had been set aside but to which he would return, the electric pen had been conceived in 1874 in Newark. Time and again Edison had returned to the invention, trying to perfect it. The culmination of his efforts was being awarded a prize at the Centennial Exposition for his electric pen, because of its "practically and simplicity of design," already an Edison trademark.

The electric pen consisted of a small electric motor which got its current from two Bunsen batteries. The motor drove a small crank attached to a long stylus in a pen case. When turned on, the stylus's rapid up-and-down action punctured a sheet of wax paper held in place by a hinged frame that could open and close. After a letter was written, the frame was opened and a clean sheet of paper placed underneath. The frame holding the original was then lowered on top of the piece of paper. A felt-covered roller coated with printer's ink was then run back and forth over the original, producing a copy. By the time the device was ready to market, Edison had so perfected the application that over three thousand copies could be made from a single original. The patent rights, as well as to those pertaining to Edison's mimeograph machine, were sold in 1877 to A. B. Dick of Chicago, who sold the machine for between twenty-four and thirty-four dollars. At one time, an estimated sixty thousand electric pens were in use the world over.

After being on the market for a year and a half, it became apparent that Bell's receiver was superior to that of Gray's and that Edison's transmitter was superior to Bell's. To get around patent restrictions, both companies made *slight* alterations to each other's instruments. This practice, however, would be challenged, not in America, but in Europe after Edison's transmitter was demonstrated before the Royal Institution in the fall of 1878. The problem arose when Bell's receiver was used with Edison's transmitter. Bell's telephone company had recently formed a subsidiary in Britain. When Bell's British agent learned what had taken place, he demanded an end to the practice. Western Union officials once again turned to Edison, this time to invent a receiver that would challenge Bell's. Edison, by this time deeply involved in developing his incandescent lamp and electrical distribution system, accepted the challenge.

Over the months that followed and after hundreds of experiments, Edison solved the problem. In Edison's receiver, as with early experiments with his transmitter, a small spring was attached to the receiving diaphragm. A cylinder made of ordinary chalk was then placed in such a way that the spring pressed down on the side of it. The telephone wires were then connected on either side of the chalk cylinder. When the chalk cylinder was turned with a crank, the electrical impulses received through the wires were conducted through the chalk cylinder. The impulses then caused the metal diaphragm to vibrate as they passed through the spring attached to the diaphragm, thus reproducing the human voice.

In March 1879, Charley Edison traveled to Britain, where he demonstrated his uncle's receiver and transmitter before the Royal Society of London. The demonstration was immediately hailed as a success, even though time would prove that Bell's receiver was still superior. Also, while Edison had been developing his receiver, Bell had devised a carbon transmitter that proved to be just as effective as Edison's. How long would this cat-and-mouse game go on? The matter was brought to an end by the British government in 1869, after telephone companies were merged to form a monopoly under government control. When it was announced that telephone companies wanting to do business in Britain would have to acquire a license, the Bell and Edison camps announced that they would not. Consequently, the British government brought a lawsuit against Edison, but for unknown reasons did not pursue litigation against Bell.

Unsure of what the outcome of a legal case might be, Orton decided to settle the matter once and for all. He approached Bell with an offer to merge Western Union's telephone subsidiary with Bell's telephone company. Bell accepted the proposal as long as the terms were right. They were. In the final agreement, Western Union sold its subsidiary, the American Speaking Telephone Company, including Edison's transmitter patent, to Bell. In return, Bell would pay Western Union twenty percent of the income generated from telephone rentals over the life span of the patent; an amount that eventually totaled three and a half million dollars.

In Britain, the companies came together to form the United Telephone Company, which for ten percent of its profits was granted a thirty-year license by the British government.

In the late 1880s, the telephone started out in homes as a plaything for the rich, costing over one hundred fifty dollars to lease for year. However, buy the end of the century subscriptions grew and the prices dropped dramatically, so that by 1914 ten million telephone customers existed in the United States.

From the start, Edison's Menlo Park laboratory itself was proving to be his greatest invention. In the decades to come, companies the world over would emulate Edison's invention factory, where research and development reigned over all in an effort to create commercially viable products. Edison's reputation would continue to grow, especially with businessmen in need of his undying enthusiasm and abilities. Even so, for all that he had accomplished, Edison's name might not have reached legendary status outside of professional circles if not for an event in 1877 that lifted him into immortality.

Chapter 6

The Wizard of Menlo Park

I've made a good many machines, but this is my baby, and I expect it to grow up to be a big feller, and support me in my old age.

—*Thomas Alva Edison*

The birth of the phonograph was rooted in Edison's work on the telephone and the telegraph. The instrument that set Edison on the path to its discovery was called the embossing telegraph, a device he referred to years later as the "father of the phonograph," which used cardboard discs on which telegraph messages were embossed in a spiral pattern. The idea itself was as old as most telegraph technology. As a tramp telegrapher in Indianapolis, Edison had designed a Morse repeater that allowed for this very thing. In Newark, he had improved on this method by further perfecting Little's automatic telegraph, which recorded incoming messages on a strip of paper that were then transcribed and either handed to a customer, or sent down the wire until it reached its final destination. Now Edison attempted to create an instrument that recorded a message on a cardboard disk that could then be quickly sent down the line without an operator having to tap out the message again.

All of the work Edison had done in this area in the past used a sounding device—the part on a telegraph that makes the clicking sound—to record a message. Now he was using a stylus to make indentions on cardboard, similar to the dimples that allow the blind to read the Braille alphabet. The stylus was made to go up and down by the current of an incoming message. All an operator had to do was remove the disc, place it on another instrument, and send it out in a matter of seconds. He could send the message out using the device that received the message, or, by sending it out on another machine, keep the line free to receive another incoming message.

The day of the discovery was July 18, 1877. Edison and Batchelor were conducting experiments on the embossing telegraph when an expected surge of electrical current from the telegraph line caused the disc underneath the stylus to spin faster than normal. At this point in the developmental process, the disc was made of paper coated with wax. As it spun out of control, the stylus ran over the indentions from previously sent messages. When this happened Edison thought he heard a faint sound. He kneeled next to the instrument and literally bit into a side of the device. He did this because over the years he had learned, because of his deafness, to use his nasal cavity to conduct sound, and the only way to do this was to bite into the device. Once Edison was in position, Batchelor sent a strong current through the machine. This time there was no doubt: A sound was made when the stylus came into contact with the indentions. The up-and-down movement of the stylus reminded Edison of a telephone's diaphragm.

Edison had been conducting experiments with diaphragms in an attempt to clearly transmit hissing consonant sounds. A number of diaphragm models lay on a nearby table. Edison paused, then walked over to the models. He took one of them and held it in his hand. In early experiments on materials for use as a diaphragm, Edison would place his finger below and in the center of the material and judge its effectiveness by sounding notes in front of it and feeling the vibration with his finger. In subsequent experiments on Bell's transmitter, he had attached a small spring to the center of the thin metallic disc Bell used as a diaphragm. When the metallic disc was made to vibrate the spring moved up and down. "Naturally enough," Edison later recalled, "the idea occurred to me: If the indention on paper could be made to give forth again the click of an instrument, why could not the vibrations of a diaphragm be recorded and similarly produced?"

After studying the diaphragm for some time, Edison turned to Batchelor saying, "Batch, if we had a point on this, we could make a record on some material which we could afterwards pull under the point, and it would give us the speech back."

Batchelor took the device to Kruesi, who placed a metallic point in the center of the diaphragm. Edison then mounted the contrivance on a piece of wood in such a way that the point barely came into contact with a strip of wax paper Edison had laid underneath the point. This done, Edison yelled, "Hello! Hello!" into the diaphragm as he pulled the strip of paper. As Edison yelled, the vibration of his voice moved the point up and down, thus leaving indentations the length of the paper. Edison then ran the strip of paper underneath the point making sure that point ran over the indentations. "We heard a distinct sound," Edison stated of the experiment, "which a strong imagination might have translated into the original 'Halloo.'"

Edison recorded his findings with his notes on the rest of the day's experiments. "Just tried experiment," Edison wrote, "with a diaphragm having an embossing point & held against paraffin paper moving rapidly the vibrations are indented nicely & there's no doubt that I shall be able to store up & reproduce automatically at any further time the human voice perfectly."

Contrary to popular belief, Edison did not spend the next few days manufacturing his phonograph and then rush out the door to publicly demonstrate the device. Instead, he used the idea on which the phonograph was built throughout the summer and fall of 1877 in an effort to record the human voice coming over the telephone, not so that it could be heard when played back, but so it could be transcribed automatically. Thinking that telephones would be used commercially rather than privately, the idea was to develop a method similar to that of the automatic telegraph by which a message could be recorded and written out later, thus leaving lines open.

> The idea that sound waves could be recorded was nothing new. In 1837, French inventor Leon Scott had demonstrated that this was possible by duplicating patterns of sound vibrations on a piece of paper coated with lampblack. In the experiment, Scott used a diaphragm made of pigskin with a pig's bristle attached in its center. The piece of paper was wrapped around a cylinder and the diaphragm placed in such a way that the bristle underneath barely made contact with the piece of paper. The cylinder was then rotated as Scott spoke into the diaphragm. The vibrations of his voice caused the pig's bristle to move up and down, thus preserving a print of Scott's voice. When the voiceprint was compared with those made by others it was found that the voiceprint recorded on the paper was the same.

A few days after his initial discovery involving his embossing telegraph, Edison attached a diaphragm outfitted with a point to the end of a telephone receiver. When tested, a faint imprint of the caller's voice was left on the wax paper. The problem was that a voice transmitted over a receiver wasn't loud enough to leave a distinct indentation. In experiments that followed, it was discovered that if the strip of wax paper was folded in half and then opened, the "ridge" running down the middle and facing the point allowed the point to leave a distinct impression on the paper. Once this breakthrough was made, attention turned to developing an instrument that could transcribe these indentations into the written word. The work was done under strict secrecy. Edison approached Western Union president William Orton with the idea of selling them the patent rights to the invention that might result but was turned down after Orton saw "no conceivable use for it."

By October, rumors started to circulate about the latest developments at Menlo Park. On October 23, General Ben Butler, Edison's attorney in the quadruplex trial, wrote Edison a letter, asking him to send word about the machine he had invented for playing back the human voice. In closing, he warned Edison to keep his discovery a secret. On November 5, *The New York Times* made brief mention of Edison's forthcoming "phonograph."

Edison did not respond to Butler's inquiry, nor did he go public with his unique line of experimentation. He might have stayed on this course if not for the appearance of an article in the

November 3 *Scientific American* in which it was revealed that Dr. Rosapelly and Professor Marey had succeeded in graphically recording "the movements of the lips, of the vail of the palate, and the vibrations of the larynx," which could lead "to the application of electricity for the purpose of transferring these records to distant points by wire."

Reacting Rosapelly and Marey's disclosure, Edward H. Johnson, an assistant who had been with Edison since 1871, wrote a letter and sent rough sketches to the editor of the *Scientific American* detailing Edison's phonograph. In his letter, Johnson responded to Rosapelly and Marey's "prophecy" of sending a message across a wire by informing them that Edison had already fulfilled the prophecy. He went on to write that Edison was going to do this by recording the human voice on a strip of paper. The voice could then be saved until such a time that it was played back automatically "with all the vocal characteristics of the original speaker ...." The recording, Johnson claimed, could be saved for over fifty years and then played back, "long after the original speaker was dead." Contrary to most accounts, Johnson's letter was first published on November 6 in the *New York Sun*—and not in the *Scientific American* of November 17. In a response to the letter, which was published under the headline, "ECHOES FROM DEAD VOICES: Wonderful Possibilities of Mr. Edison's Latest Invention," an editorial response to the article exclaimed that, "Nothing could be more incredible than the likelihood of once more hearing the voice of the dead ...."

When the letter appeared in the *Scientific American* of November 17, under the heading, A WONDERFUL INVENTION, the *Scientific American* editor wrote in a preface:

> It has been said that Science is never sensational; that it is
> intellectual not emotional; but certainly nothing that can
> be conceived would be more likely to create the profound-
> est of sensations, to arouse the liveliest of human emo-
> tions, than once more to hear the familiar voices of the
> dead. Yet Science now announces that this is possible, and
> can be done .... The possibility is simply startling ....
> Speech has become, as it were, immortal.

The news of Edison's discovery was so unbelievable that a business associate wrote him days after reading the *New York Sun's* story warning him that in his opinion someone had published the account in a "calculated effort to injure his reputation." In truth, Edison wasn't capable of delivering on the claims in Johnson's letter. Yes, he did have a principle on which his experiments were based; however, the device that came to be known as the phonograph did not yet exist. It's not known exactly what experiments Edison conducted trying to invent what became the first phonograph; oddly enough, no records indicate exactly what the steps were in solving this problem. However, in among drawings of the instruments Edison was considering for transcribing the human voice into written words, there are a few crude drawings of instruments that resemble the phonograph. Regardless of the steps taken, by November 29, 1877, Edison had completed a rough drawing for a prototype of his phonograph, which he gave to Kruesi to manufacture.

Changes in the final design make it evident that Edison had clearly focused on the instrument during the twenty-three days since it was made public. Gone was the idea of a long strip of wax paper being pulled under a point attached to a diaphragm. In its place was now a wide piece of tin-foil wrapped around a metallic cylinder with a helical grove cut into it from one end to the other. A diaphragm device with a point at its center was on either side of the cylinder: One to make a recording, the other to play it back. The points attached to the diaphragms were designed to fit into the grove cut in the cylinder. Before recording, the point of the recording diaphragm was adjusted so that it barely touched the tin-foil. Meanwhile, the point on the diaphragm used to play back the recording was pulled away from the cylinder. The cylinder was made to go around by a hand crank attached to a metal rod that ran through the length of the cylinder. The cylinder and the metal shaft were designed so that they traveled horizontally as the hand crank was turned. In handing the job over to Kruesi, Edison later stated, "I didn't have much faith that it would work, expecting that I might possibly hear a word or so that would give hope of a future for the idea."

As Kruesi neared completion of the instrument, he asked Edison what it was for. Edison told him that he was going to use the machine to make a record of the human voice and then use the machine to play it back. Kruesi thought it absurd. Kruesi wasn't the only skeptical person in the group; as the story goes, Edison bet James Adams, a laboratory assistant, fifteen cigars, Batchelor a barrel of apples, and Kruesi two dollars that the device would work. When it was finished, the phonograph was placed on the bench in the rear of the laboratory. The tin-foil was put on; Edison then shouted the nursery rhyme, "Mary Had a Little Lamb," into the recording diaphragm. He then set the reproducer, and turned the crank.

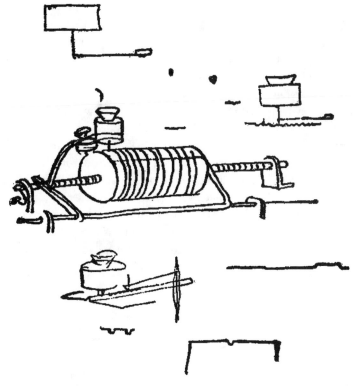

Edison's first conceptual drawing of his phonograph.

(© *Courtesy of Edison National Historic Site*)

The group waited. Suddenly Edison's voice was heard, loud and clear, reciting the story of Mary and her lamb. On hearing the machine come to life Kruesi exclaimed, "*Mein Got in Himmel!* [My God in Heaven!]"

"I was never so taken aback in my life," Edison later reminisced, "everybody was astonished."

Throughout the rest of the night, Edison and his assistants made one recording after another, making minor adjustments. Everyone present agreed that the instrument had to be introduced to the public, and soon. However, being granted a patent application could take months. Edison knew that recent articles concerning his phonograph had made the public hungry to learn more, and eager to see the device in action. For Edison, there was only one thing to do; he would have to go public, not just to prove that his phonograph worked, but to protect his claim to its invention. After all, he had already made the guiding principles behind the device publicly known. If he went public with the thing itself, no one would dare steal his idea once it was judged successful.

The next morning, December 7, Edison, Batchelor, and a model of the newly minted phonograph traveled to New York City and the offices of the *Scientific American*, where Edison set the phonograph on the desk of one of the editors, Alfred Beach. Unwrapping his package, Edison informed Beach that he had with him the instrument that was capable of recording and reproducing the human voice. A crowd quickly gathered as Edison set up his contraption. When he turned the handle on the device, to everyone's astonishment, the phonograph spoke! It inquired as to the health of those gathered, said it hoped people were impressed by it, acknowledged that *it* was doing fine, and then bid everyone good night.

In his December 22 column, Beach, still enchanted by the device, exclaimed that it was impossible for a man "to listen to the mechanical speech without experiencing the idea that his senses are deceiving him."

The Michigan hayseed was now thirty years old. He could not have more perfectly timed his decision to demonstrate his phonograph in the offices of the *Scientific American*. Newspapers soon broke the story of Edison's invention: Life for Thomas Alva Edison would never be the same. In the weeks that followed, Edison further modified the phonograph. The repeater diaphragm was removed, leaving only the one diaphragm to record and play back, and a funnel was attached to the top of the diaphragm, allowing for the concentration of sound waves on the diaphragm. One problem persisted, however; the tin-foil was only good for so many recordings before it had to be discarded and the recording lost. It was a major drawback that would be solved in time. For now, the machine's uniqueness made it quite easy to overlook this drawback.

By the first of January, Edison submitted a new and improved model to the patent office, and patent no. 200,251 was granted on December 24. To publicize and draw the interest of potential investors, he delivered a second model to the corporate offices of Western Union in New York City, where it was displayed and demonstrated, and others were demonstrated throughout the Northeast. Crowds filled the halls at each demonstration, with more attention as newspapers started to take notice of the device.

With all the publicity, by the end of January, Edison reached agreements with three different groups of investors to sell and manufacture the device. The most prominent group was headed by Gardiner Hubbard, a member of a wealthy Boston family and the father-in-law of Alexander Graham Bell. The group established the Edison Speaking Phonograph Company. For his part Edison received ten thousand dollars up front and a twenty percent royalty on all phonographs sold.

One of the investors in the Edison Speaking Phonograph Company was Hilborne Roosevelt, who in 1878 presented Edison with a pipe organ for his Menlo Park laboratory. Hilborne's organ manufacturing company was at one time the largest manufacturer of organs in the United States. Aside from this enterprise, Hilborne was also partner in a Bell Telephone franchise for Manhattan. Edison first met Hilborne after conducting experiments with his transmitter and electromyograph receiver over lines belonging to Hilborne's franchise.

A second contract was drawn up with the Ansonia Clock Company to develop talking clocks, and a third with two New York entrepreneurs for use of the device in toys. These ventures proved unsuccessful, but Hubbard's group decided to market the phonograph as a "novelty" item until Edison completed work on a practical version. The group also decided to lease five hundred models, manufactured by an old friend of Edison's, Sigmund Bergmann, who had left Menlo Park for New York City in 1877. The machine could be leased by anyone willing to be trained to operate the device, pay a hundred dollars, and turn over a share in the profits. With their lease, a person would be granted a region in the United States in which to demonstrate the instrument. The venture was so successful that Edison's royalties for a week's worth of shows in Boston alone amounted to eighteen hundred dollars— an astonishing figure considering that spectators were charged twenty-five cents apiece.

On at least one occasion in New York, Edison led one of these demonstrations. He paid Jules Levy, a renowned cornetist, to have several of the tunes he played recorded. As the host of the evening's event, Edison took center stage and played back the recordings at various speeds. He then recorded himself reciting "Bengen on the Rhine," followed by a couple of songs and a speech. All of this was on one piece of tin-foil. Just about this time, Levy stepped up and recorded yet another tune on the same piece of tin foil. When played backed, the conglomeration of sounds resulted in nothing but noise. The audience roared with laughter as Levy stood helpless.

The right to market Edison's phonograph in Britain was purchased by the London Stereoscope and Photographic Company in March 1878, even though Edison had only filed what in America would be called a caveat for his invention in Britain. In the agreement, Edison was paid seven thousand five hundred dollars and he promised to make further modifications to the phonograph. After making these improvements, he was obligated to send the company two of the models.

> *People all over the world are familiar with Nipper, the little black-and-white dog next to a phonograph horn, an ear raised and a quizzical expression on its face, listening to "his master's voice." Nipper was a terrier-bulldog mix, acquired as a pup in 1884 by Mark Barraud, a scenic designer from France living in England. After Barraud's death, Nipper lived with his brother, Francis, an artist whose work once hung in the Royal Gallery. One day, Nipper and Francis were visiting another brother, Philip, a professional photographer, at his studio in Liverpool. The ever-curious Nipper sat by a speaking machine listening to the sounds emanating from the large funnel. With his camera, Philip recorded the image that inspired his brother's painting. In the completed piece, Nipper was seated beside an Edison Commercial Phonograph, the cylinder type sold in Britain by the Edison-Bell Consolidated Phonograph Company.*

Before long, the phonograph craze had reached such proportions that newspaper reporters were sent to Menlo Park to conduct interviews with Edison. In the feature articles that followed, he proved himself willing to give his time freely, with a personality that made for "excellent copy." He was described as "sadly in need of a shave ... but the fire of genius shone in his keen gray eyes ...."

> *Men who worked with Edison during his itinerant telegrapher days lined up to bask in the glory of their former associate. Ezra Gilliland, a friend from Edison's days in Cincinnati wrote a piece for the Cincinnati Gazette titled "Thomas Alvey Edison." George "Fatty" Stewart published "The Napoleon of Science," an account of Edison's days in Boston. George Bliss, an operator and an investor in Edison's electric pen and mimeograph machine, published a biographical sketch of Edison in the* Chicago Tribune.

On April 2, 1878, the most famous of all articles was published in *The New York Daily Graphic*. In the course of the interview, the *Graphic's* reporter asked Edison, "Aren't you a good deal of a *wizard*, Mr. Edison?"

"Oh no!" replied Edison with a laugh. "I don't believe much in that sort of thing."

Eight days later, the *New York Graphic* ran a story under the headline "The Wizard of Menlo Park." The piece bestowed upon Edison the nickname that would propel him to mythic proportions.

From the first reporters' visits to Menlo Park, Edison stressed that he saw the phonograph as primarily a business not an entertainment tool. When the phonograph debuted, entertainment dollars were nothing compared to the money in the business community. To stress this to businessmen, and perhaps add stature to his views, Edison published an article in the *North American Review* titled "The Phonograph and Its Future," writing that he foresaw the phonograph as an instrument for letter writing, recording of books for the deaf, teaching elocution, telling time, preserving languages and family history, and using with the telephone to preserve conversations. He was also sure to mention that the device could be used in toys and to record music.

By spring 1878, Edison's reputation had grown to such an extent that he was invited to Washington, D.C., to present and demonstrate his phonograph for the National Academy of Sciences. He accepted and, accompanied by Charles Batchelor, arrived on the morning of April 18, 1878, dressed in a checkered three-piece suit, his hair neatly cut and combed. Uriah Painter, Edison's representative in the capital, met them at the train station and informed them that Congress and President Rutherford B. Hayes had asked for a demonstration of his phonograph, but that the president could not meet with Edison until later at night. Painter then accompanied them to the studios of Matthew Brady, the famed Civil War photographer, where a series of photographs were taken of the three men and the phonograph. A Brady sitting was considered "a rite of passage for the rich and famous, a sign of having arrived" by Washington's elite.

Later in the afternoon, Edison, Batchelor, and the phonograph arrived at the National Academy of Sciences. The hall was filled with an enthusiastic crowd overflowing onto the sidewalks outside. As he was introduced, Edison prepared the phonograph, then stepped to the side. The audience expected him to make a brief introduction. Instead, Edison started turning the phonograph's crank. As the audience stood dumbfounded, a voice suddenly spoke: "The Speaking Phonograph has the honor of presenting itself to the Academy of Sciences." Stunned, the audience did not know whether to clap or jeer—in case it was a hoax.

In the midst of his whirlwind tour of Washington, D.C., to demonstrate his phonograph, Edison's photograph was taken at the studio of famed Civil War photographer, Matthew Brady, a clear sign that Edison had "arrived."

(© *Edison National Historic Site*)

Batchelor then stepped up to the instrument. Edison turned the crank as Batchelor sang, shouted, whistled, and made the sound of barn animals into the phonograph's mouthpiece. Edison rewound the cylinder and replaced the stylus. Again, he turned the crank; the sound of Batchelor's antics filled the hall. Three ladies fainted. Finally convinced that Edison's phonograph was no trick, the audience burst into applause.

After this successful demonstration, Edison and Batchelor exhibited the phonograph in the offices of the *Philadelphia Enquirer* before a group of newspapermen from around the country. Once again, the phonograph was a hit. Edison and Batchelor then informally met with Science Academy members at the U.S. Observatory. Around eleven o'clock that evening, Edison and Batchelor arrived at the White House, where they were greeted by President Hayes. He was alone, but once he heard his voice coming from the phonograph, he was so taken by the experience that he woke his wife and guests, and the demonstration did not end until three in the morning. Early the next day, the phonograph was displayed at the Capitol for congressmen who were amazed by the machine in action.

The British patent for Edison's phonograph was filed a few days after his demonstration at the White House with an application titled "Recording and Reproducing Sounds" and a detailed report containing sixty-seven drawings and a number of methods for recording the voice, including a sheet of paper, on a continuous strip of paper, and on a disk. The patent was granted in August 1878. William Preece, head of the British Postal Telegraph System, had the honor of demonstrating the device for the elite of British society. Not an enthusiastic supporter of Edison, Preece had visited Edison in July 1877, and wrote in his personal diary that Edison was known in the United States "as the Professor of Duplicity ...." He went on to say that "William Orton [Western Union's president] told me in England of Edison, 'that young man has a vacuum where his conscience ought to be.'"

Edison's whirlwind tour of Washington, D.C., left him exhausted. Even so, the day after his arrival he was back at work. By May, Edison and the laboratory were legendary in the nation's newspapers. One newspaper likened Edison to Faust, while another predicted the laboratory would become "the electrical mecca," where "pilgrims of science" would pay homage to Edison, the "high priest of the temple." It wasn't far from the truth. The mayor and the city council of Newark came calling, pleading with Edison to move back. Daily throngs of visitors to the laboratory continued to grow, leaving him with little time for inventing. "Hereafter," one reporter wrote of the crowds, "there can be no actual certainty of privacy in any conversation unless held in a desert."

By mid-June, Edison had become "so much annoyed by the curiosity-seekers" that he served notice that his laboratory could no longer receive visitors. He would meet with businessmen, but only if they had an appointment. Who could blame him? Fan mail had grown to an average of eighty to a hundred letters a day. Most letters asked Edison for money, or requested he invent a particular device to cure a physical handicap, like deafness. Stockton L. Griffin, a telegrapher who had worked with Edison in Cincinnati, was hired as Edison's personal secretary to handle the deluge of mail, reading each letter and forwarding only those dealing with business. Not that it mattered: Edison didn't stop long enough to read those, either.

Edison's plea for privacy did little to slow visitors. Much of this was his own doing; he continued to grant interviews suggesting that visitors were more than welcome. Two articles were titled "An Afternoon with Edison" and "An Evening with Edison." In July, his health "gave way under the strain," and the normally complacent Edison decided to break "away for a Western trip as far as California."

The trip, characteristically enough, was a working vacation, providing Edison with an opportunity to test a tasimeter, an instrument designed to measure minute changes of temperature. His gadget would be tested in Rawlings, Wyoming, where a total eclipse of the sun was to take place on or around July 29. Accompanying Edison was George F. Barker, a long-time supporter and friend who was professor of physics at the University of Pennsylvania and editor of the *Journal of the Franklin Institute*.

Edison's experiment proved inconclusive, but, during their nightly discussions, Barker spoke of the challenges of transforming electric current into light. Edison listened carefully and later confessed that, "It happened that at the time I was more or less at leisure, because I had just finished working on the carbon-button telephone, and this electric-light idea took possession of me."

On his return to Menlo Park, Edison set aside the phonograph, the invention of the century, for an incredible ten years. The possibility of incandescent light became his passion. Investors in the phonograph, like Gardiner Hubbard and Hilborne Roosevelt, were left feeling betrayed. Edison would come back to the invention—he always operated this way—but *when* was anybody's guess. For the moment, the world watched and waited for the Wizard's next creation.

Chapter 7

Edison Turns Off the Dark

Genius is one percent inspiration and ninety-nine percent perspiration.

—*Thomas Alva Edison*

In the weeks after their arrival from the West, Edison seemed to have a change of heart about undertaking the question of incandescent lighting. However, Professor Barker and Grosvenor P. Lowery, Edison's attorney and staunch supporter, kept on him to give electric light serious consideration. Lowery, who would also be Edison's liaison with Edison light investors, kept Edison informed of progress made in electrical illumination, while Barker tried to convince Edison to take time off from work to tour the brass-manufacturing shops of William Wallace in Ansonia, Connecticut. Wallace was the co-inventor of the first American electric dynamo—what today is called an electric generator—and a leader in the introduction of arc lights to American cities. Barker wanted Edison to visit Wallace's shop to view the eight brilliant, five hundred-candlepower arc lights used to light the interior of the shop. He also wanted Edison to see the eight-horsepower Wallace-Farmer dynamo that supplied the electricity that powered the lights.

Joining the two were Batchelor and his brother James, who was visiting from England; Professor Charles Chandler of Columbia University; and Charles Davis, a telegrapher and a member of the Menlo Park staff. The *New York Herald*'s star reporter, Marshall Fox, joined the group to cover the event. Entering Wallace's shop, Edison was captivated. He ran from the lights to the dynamo and then to the instruments that controlled the lights. He lay on the floor and crawled over tables to look at everything that caught his attention, seeming like a child on a playground. After a moment he took a piece of paper and a pencil from his pocket and started figuring how much power each light was using in ratio to the power generated by the dynamo, and further calculated how much coal it would take to run the dynamo for a day, a week, a month, a year. He then defiantly turned to Wallace and said, "I believe I can beat you making the electric light. I do not think you are working in the right direction."

> *In Edison's day,* candlepower *was the measure of a light's intensity. A light of one candlepower literally meant the light produced was equivalent to the light of one candle. In Edison's Menlo Park laboratory, the candlepower of a lamp was tested in the Photometer room located on the first floor.*

Later that night Edison, as a gift to Wallace, signed his name and wrote the date, September 8, 1878, on the goblet in which his drink was served: It was a challenge tailor-made for Thomas Alva Edison. In an interview with the *New York Sun* following his trip to Wallace's shop in Connecticut, Edison declared, "I saw the thing had not gone so far but that I had a chance."

Back home, Edison noted his charge simply enough in a laboratory notebook under the heading *Electricity vs. Gas as General Illuminants:* "Object, Edison to effect exact imitation of all done by gas, so as to replace lighting by gas by lighting by electricity. To improve the illumination to such an extent as to meet all requirements of natural, artificial, and commercial conditions."

Well aware of the state of electrical lighting before entering the race, Edison knew that he was pursuing a goal that had been declared impossible by many knowledgeable scientists. Even his own research in 1876 and 1877, as sparing as it was, had proven that, for the moment, arc lighting reigned supreme and was the technology on which the hopes of the industry rested.

Sir Humphrey Davy, a professor of chemistry at the Royal Institution in London, had demonstrated the arc light for his peers in 1808. In Davy's exhibition, a two thousand-cell battery was used to produce an electric current that ran through a small gap between two carbon rods laid on a horizontal line facing each other. As the current oxidized the carbon, an electric arc between the rods produced a garish white light. Even though Davy's demonstration was successful, further development was not feasible without a machine capable of producing enough current. Michael Faraday would not discover the principles behind this machine, which would be known as a dynamo, until 1831.

> Dynamos produce electric current. If a loop of wire is turned between the ends of a horseshoe-shaped magnet, an electric current flows in the wire. Dynamos change the energy of motion into electrical energy. The energy to work a generator's moving parts can come from wind, running water, or steam produced by heat from fuels such as oil or coal.

Edison knew that arc lights were a proven commodity. The first triumphant commercial use having taken place in the Dungeness Lighthouse in Kent, England, in 1862. Proven worthy of further commercial development, a European named Paul Jablochkoff and an American named Charles Brush succeeded in producing commercially viable arc systems for streets and large public areas. Before long, arc lights were illuminating the streets of Paris; New York; Cleveland; San Jose, California; and Wabash, Indiana. However, for all their success, Edison and his contemporaries working in incandescent lighting knew that arc lights were extremely limited in their commercial use. They were too bright and smelly. They flickered. They weren't economical except for very large installations, and even then they were best when used outdoors. Carbon rods had to be replaced often—a dangerous job—and the average person could not bother with them without risking electrocution. Arc lights were impractical.

Before Edison took an interest in incandescent lighting, there was no viable system for electrically lighting a residential structure. That honor was held by natural gas. This industry was born in

1821, when a gunsmith named William Hart completed the first natural-gas well in Fredonia, New York. The gas was piped from the twenty-seven-foot well to nearby buildings, where it was used for lighting. A second well was drilled near Westfield, New York, in 1826. By 1865, over three hundred natural gas companies in the United States were distributing manufactured gas. The first long-distance pipeline was completed in 1872. The twenty-five mile wood pipeline carried natural gas to hundreds of consumers in Rochester, New York. Also in 1872, the first iron natural-gas pipeline extended five miles to Titusville, where two hundred and fifty consumers used over four million cubic feet of gas daily. By the 1870s, gas companies were also well established in Europe. Gas, too, had its shortfalls. It was costly. There was a risk of explosion. It was smelly. It darkened walls, destroyed paintings, and, when accidentally extinguished, could kill someone while they slept. A customer's only alternative was to light their home with oil lamps.

All this was about to change. On September 13, 1878, Edison filed his first caveat for incandescent lighting, "Caveat of Electric Spirals." Edison believed that the answer was a long strip of platinum, shaped into a number of spirals and combined with a current regulator that would shut off an electric current when the platinum filament grew too hot. He had clearly given the matter serious consideration in the six days since his visit to Connecticut, given the description of the forty-four regulators he offered as possible solutions.

In an interview with Marshall Fox, on September 16, 1878, Edison broke the news to the world: The problem of incandescent lighting was a thing of the past. With results in hand, he exclaimed, "I have it now! With the process I have just discovered, I can produce a thousand—aye, ten thousand—[lamps] from one machine. Indeed, the number may be said to be infinite."

He added that he had arrived at this juncture by "an entirely different process than that from which scientific men have ever sought to secure it. They have all been working in the same groove, and when it is known how I have accomplished my object, everybody will wonder why they have never thought of it, it is so simple."

The "entirely different process" Edison spoke of was rooted in his past. As a telegrapher and inventor, he had become an expert at dealing with all matters relating with electrical currents.

> With the invention of the electric battery by Alessandro Volta, men found that electricity passing through a high-resistance wire offered heat and light similar to that of a piece of iron heated in a furnace. The challenge, however, was to find filament material that could stand up to the electric current. In most cases, once the electricity was turned on, the filament burned out instantly. With time, a platinum filament proved able to withstand the enormous heat and "shock" created by an electric current.
>
> In America, the inventor Moses Farmer used lights containing a platinum filament in his house in Salem, Massachusetts, as early as 1859. Powered by electric batteries, the lamps did not last long, and each one produced less light than a single candle.

Already casting an eye to the future, Edison told Fox of his plans to eradicate gas lighting in lower Manhattan, replacing it instead with his complete lighting system. The electrical lines would be powered by Wallace's dynamos and run under the streets. In most cases, the electrical lines would come into homes through piping previously used for gas. (When the future of the phonograph was raised in interviews shortly thereafter, Edison stated, "The little feller ... is taking care of itself ... comatose for the time being. It is a child and will grow up to be a man yet; but I have a bigger thing in hand and must finish it to the temporary neglect of all other phones and graphs.")

The next day, Grosvenor P. Lowrey began the legal paperwork and financial negotiations with potential investors for what became the Edison Electric Light Company. By October 16, the company secured incorporation papers in New York City. Joining Edison's venture were a number of New York financiers, eight of whom were involved in telegraphy. They had paid fifty thousand dollars for the privilege, but they stood to make millions if the venture succeeded.

In the days leading up to the announcement of the company's incorporation, Edison telegraphed Theodore Puskas, his European agent responsible for securing investors and the promotion of his inventions, and predicted that the light would be a sensation. He boasted that William H. Vanderbilt, "the largest gas stock owner in America," and his friends had invested in the company, and that he was going to receive an advance of fifty thousand dollars, on top of which he would maintain half of the capital stock in the company and earn thirty thousand dollars a year in royalties.

A nationally recognized and respected figure after the interest generated by his phonograph, Edison's remarks sent gas stocks plummeting. Critics such as William E. Sawyer and Joseph W. Swan, each working at perfecting an incandescent light, declared that Edison did not have the scientific know-how to solve the problem. William Preece, the head of the British Postal Telegraph Service and one of England's leading electricians, emphatically stated that, "for all his accomplishments, this was one that even Edison could not conqueror."

Time proved the critics right. A month and a half passed. Edison had spent little time at the laboratory. Doctors reported that he was home in bed, suffering from "a case of neuralgia." To the delight of gas company executives, rumors circulated that he was close to death and had given up on the hunt for light. Lowery rode to Edison's defense in a scathing rebuttal to one such rumor printed in a New York City newspaper, exclaiming that he had spoken to Edison's personal physicians and that they had assured him that Edison was in fine health. To underscore that all was well, he added, "For two weeks past, Mr. Edison has been daily and nightly, as usual, at work in his laboratory upon the electric light …."

Lowrey's response was true. Edison's health had suffered for a short time, but after a break, he was back in the laboratory, hard at work. He continued experiments on a variety of filaments such as platinum, titanium, rhodium, and others. He even tried tungsten, the metal used in light bulbs today, but at the time there existed no way of forming the metal into a thin wire. It was decided that platinum was the best choice. With an average resistance to electrical currents seven times greater than copper, the material could be heated up to five thousand degrees without burning out. His confidence growing, or perhaps to thoroughly squelch the rumors of his untimely demise, by October 20, 1878, Edison was once again singing the praises of his incandescent light to the *New York Sun*, announcing that he hoped to have his electric lights ready in *six weeks!*

Thomas Alva Edison as he would have appeared during his Menlo Park years.

(© *Courtesy of Edison National Historic Site*)

Meanwhile, progress was being made on the new workshop, to be outfitted with the best machine shop tools and machinery, at the rear of the laboratory. At one end, a Babcock and Wilcox boiler would power a C. H. Brown steam engine, which would eventually supply the power to the dynamos that would supply the electricity to light Edison's lamp.

At the laboratory, however, progress stalled. In one experiment after another, Edison could not lengthen the time that a platinum filament would glow once an electrical current was applied. Asked by a reporter when he thought he would be finished with the invention, Edison replied that all seemed to be going well, but, "There are the usual little details that must be attended to before it goes to the public."

Aware of investors' growing concern, Lowery convinced Edison that he should hire someone with knowledge in the "physical sciences." He had the perfect candidate. Francis R. Upton, two years older than Edison, was a graduate from the College of New Jersey (later called Princeton) and had studied at the University of Berlin under Hermann von Helmholtz on the use of mathematics in explaining the dynamics of electricity. Upton immediately became a valuable assistant to Edison. He quickly confirmed that platinum was the best material for use as a filament, and the vacuum created inside a bulb before a filament was tested would have to be even greater. Edison needed a Sprengel pump, a device used for the removal of air or gases from an enclosed space.

It just so happened Upton's alma mater was in possession of such a pump, and Upton was sent to pick it up. On the return trip, he disembarked from the train at Metuchen, two and a half miles from Menlo Park; unfortunately, the late train did not stop in Menlo Park. He lugged the Sprengel pump on his back all the way to the laboratory. Hauling the device wouldn't have been easy: The body of a Sprengel pump was a plank six feet tall and three to four feet wide with a long tube of glass roughly half-an-inch in circumference that snaked back and forth over the length of the plank board. When the exhausted Upton arrived at the laboratory, he was put to work setting up the device, and by the break of dawn a number of tests had been conducted using the device.

> *A Sprengel pump has a mercury reservoir at the top of a long, narrow, vertical tube. The mercury—a heavy substance—is allowed to dribble down the tube. These droplets move past a side pipe in the tube connected to the light bulb. Air in the bulb rushes into the gap between the drops of mercury, which push this air down the tube. As each drop of mercury passes, more air from the light bulb rushes into the space. At the bottom of the long tube the mercury and the air come out. After the pump has run for long enough, nearly all of the air has been sucked out of the light bulb and down the vertical mercury-drop tube.*

By creating a greater vacuum with the Sprengel pump, Edison was able to extend the life of the filament to an average of eight minutes. He informed Lowrey of the development, who informed him that investors were becoming concerned. A demonstration was held on April of 1879. Edison showed the men his improved lamp, turning it off in less than eight minutes. The "successful" demonstration, as well as Edison's charismatic personality, undying enthusiasm, and salesmanship, left the backers satisfied that it would only be a few more months before Edison was successful.

In the weeks that followed, even with the increased vacuum and trying everything from plantinoiridium, boron, chromium, molybdenum, and osmium, Edison's efforts to lengthen the life of a filament beyond eight minutes failed. He had no choice but to stop all experiments with metals as a filament. All those months of investigative work were for naught—or were they? As Francis Arthur Jones suggested in his authorized biography, Edison achieved victory at this moment in the eyes of those around him, because he never gave up hope. He "was a monument of encouragement to his associates—always good-humored, always cheerful, always certain that the next day would see the victory."

After deciding that a filament made of metal was not the answer, Edison turned his attention to carbon. He had used carbon in his telephone transmitter and even in early incandescent lighting experiments in 1876 and 1877, which were quickly abandoned. However, none of his previous work with carbon influenced his decision to take up the material again. In Edison's legendary account of his decision, he took up carbon again after he found himself seated at his desk on the laboratory's second floor "rolling between his fingers a piece of compressed lampblack mixed with tar for use in his telephone."

Edison knew from previous experiments that carbon would take an electric current. However, he did not know how long a carbon filament would last in a lamp from which the air had been almost completely removed. There was only one way to find out: Place a piece of the material inside a lamp and give it a charge. It sounds simple enough, but it took over six hours. First, the material had to be placed inside a horseshoe-shaped mold and slowly "cooked" in a furnace for a number of hours, allowing the material to burn while remaining in one piece. The material was then carefully removed from the mold, and two strands of copper wire were attached to each end of the horseshoe. The filament was then placed inside a glass bulb so that the two wires extended out from the bottom of the bulb. A cork coated with a glue-like substance was inserted into the end of the bulb, and the two wires were attached to the wires that would provide the electricity. The air inside the lamp was then removed with the Sprengel pump and the tip of the bulb was sealed with a glassblower's torch.

For most of the early steps in this process, Edison and Batchelor encountered no problem. However, when they tried to place the filament inside the glass lamp, it broke, so they had to repeat the process all over again because they only had one mold. Even so, Edison and Batchelor persisted until at last they had a carbon lamp ready for testing.

> Besides the various metals one might have expected Edison and his team to investigate as a filament, there were a number of items tested that might come as a surprise. For example, tests were also conducted on coconut hair and shell, horsetail hair, fish line, cork, and a strand of hair from a man's beard.

The lamp proved to be promising. However, they soon realized that the lampblack and tar combined weren't strong enough to hold their structure once an electrical current was sent through it. Something was needed to give the material substance. Edison's solution was brilliant: he coated a piece of ordinary cotton sewing thread with the lampblack and tar material. (Ironically, Batchelor had come to America as an employee of a British sewing-thread company, to oversee the replacement of outdated machinery in the company's American factories.) Over two days, Edison and Batchelor went through an entire spool of Clarke's thread. They did not manage to come up with a filament until the evening of the second day. They inserted the carbon in the lamp and removed the air. They turned on the current and, as Edison later stated, "The sight we had so long desired to see met our eyes."

The current was increased and light kept shining. The current was increased further until the filament finally broke after fourteen and a half hours. A second lamp was tested: This one lasted for over twenty hours … thirty hours … forty hours …. "The longer it burned," Edison recalled later, "the more fascinated we were. None of us could go to bed …. We sat and just watched it with anxiety growing into elation. The lamp lasted about forty-five hours, and I realized that the practical incandescent lamp had been born …. These experiments had taken place on October 21 and 22, 1879, a full thirteen months from the day Edison had promised to deliver.

Incredibly, Edison continued to test a variety of materials, hoping to find a filament that was better than the one he'd found. He succeeded. In less than two weeks he replaced the sewing-thread filament with carbonized cardboard. Lamps were manufactured as quickly as possible, each one unique, to test whether size and shape played a role in increasing the life of the filament. Meanwhile, crews from Western Union planted light poles in the ground and hung electrical wire outfitted with Edison's lamps throughout Menlo Park. Lights were also installed in homes of Edison, Batchelor, and Mrs. Sarah Jordan, who operated the boarding house.

As days and weeks passed, commuters on passing trains spied the bright lights on the darkened horizon. They reported seeing small globes of light dancing from Edison's laboratory down the road. Edison's neighbors came calling. They too spread stories of the brilliant lights burning from sundown to sunrise.

To accommodate the bachelor employees of Menlo Park Laboratory, Edison engaged the services of a distant relative, Sarah Jordan, a widow from New York City to operate a boarding house. In a sizable Victorian house, the men had six rooms on the second floor, and a parlor and dining room on one side of the first floor. Sarah, her thirteen-year-old daughter, Ida, and their helper, Kate Williams, lived on the side opposite the dinning room and the parlor on the first floor. Their quarters were strictly off limits to the men. The kitchen was located in a back room. At the height of their business, these three women fed, cooked, and cleaned for as many as sixteen boarders. With the rise in popularity of Edison's incandescent lamp, Mrs. Jordan soon opened a "lunch room" to serve hungry tourists and employees who didn't reside there.

By December, new rumors of Edison's breakthroughs sent gas stocks tumbling once again. Edison Electric Light, with its limited amount of available stock, raced to $500, $1,000, $3,500 per share. The end was nowhere in sight. At its peak, the stock reached a whopping $8,000 a share before the price settled at $5,000—an astonishing run because it was based only on speculation. Edison, an owner of 2,000 shares, became a millionaire ten times over, at least on paper. Edison paid his tidy profit no attention. Instead, he summoned Fox and gave him a tour of Menlo Park, and then let the publicity do the rest.

Edison's timing was perfect. The public pounced on the story. Anyone who was anybody was reading the *New York Herald* on December 21, 1879. The headline read, "Edison's Light, It Makes a Light, Without Gas or Flame, Cheaper Than Oil. Success in Cotton Thread." The opening paragraph to the exclusive read:

> Edison's electric light, incredible as it may appear, is pro-
> duced from a little piece of paper—a tiny strip of paper
> that a breath would blow away. Through this little strip of
> paper is passed an electric current, and the result is a
> bright beautiful light, like the mellow sunset of an Italian
> autumn ... [there are] no deleterious gases, no smoke, no
> offensive odors—a light without flame, without danger,
> requiring no matches to ignite, giving out but little heat,

vitiating no air, and free from all flickering; a light that is
a little globe of sunshine, a veritable Aladdin's lamp.

This incredible introduction read more like the prologue to a new Jules Verne science-fiction thriller. How could Edison turn off the dark in fifteen months when scientists of the highest caliber had made only rudimentary and crude progress? Suddenly, almost instantaneously, Edison claimed to have unlocked the secret. The story was too fantastic!

The *Herald's* managing editor, Thomas D. Connery, grew furious. He went to the daily editor demanding to know who had written the story. He was informed that Marshall Fox, the newspaper's star reporter, was the author. "But," Connery explained, "doesn't he know that it has been absolutely demonstrated that that kind of light is against the laws of nature? ... How could he allow himself and the paper to be so imposed upon? ... We must do something to save ourselves from ridicule!"

> *Edison not only awarded shares in his enterprises to his assistants. On at least two occasions, he also showed his gratitude to newspaper reporters by awarding stocks to them For example in January 1878, Edison presented Marshall Fox of the New York Herald and William Croffut of the Daily Graphic with shares in his newly formed Edison Electric Light Company. To Fox went eight shares, to Croffut five. Valued at one hundred dollars when presented, by the end of the year they would trade for forty-eight hundred dollars apiece.*

Connery's concern was justified. The leading scientific minds not only doubted that Edison had actually succeeded in creating a working incandescent lamp, they also questioned a number of innovations needed to make an electrical lighting system a reality. They questioned Edison's claim of having invented a dynamo with a ninety percent efficiency rating—astounding when the highest rating to date was anywhere from thirty-eight to forty-one percent. One scientist argued that if Edison was successful, it could not have happened without "destroying the doctrine of the conservation and correlation of forces."

Still, the stringing of wires along selected Menlo Park streets and homes continued. Edison accepted a proposal from Lowery to stage a public exhibition of his lighting system. The event would take place on December 31, 1879. However, before this date it became evident that invitations wouldn't be necessary because people were already rushing to Menlo Park.

Edison did not object to the growing crowds. In the end, he decided to open the laboratory a week before the official unveiling. Two days after Christmas the American correspondent of the *London Times* arrived by train. The president of the Philadelphia Local Telegraph Company and an assistant editor of the *Philadelphia Ledger* accompanied him. Arriving around noon, the trio spent hours touring the facility, the streets, and the houses. Of the experience, the *London Times*'s correspondent, Joel Cook, wrote that he spent Saturday night with Edison examining Edison's lamp, generator, meter, and regulator. What he found was that the system was a complete substitute for gas and at a cheaper rate. The light produced was "bright, clear, mellow, regular, free from flickering or pulsations ... [it was] better than gas, more regular, and emitting so small heat no danger exist[ed] from fire ...."

On December 31, incoming trains from New York were doubled. Fashionable ladies, gentlemen, and newspapermen trudged through the freshly fallen snow. Celebrities included Henry Ward Beecher, Chauncey M. Depew, General Ben Butler, and Carl Shurz. William Sawyer, Edison's American challenger in the area of incandescent lighting, appeared to be intoxicated. He yelled and objected that the display was nothing more than an elaborate hoax. Of the event, the *Herald* reported that ...

> *people came by hundreds in every train. They went pellmell through places previously kept sacredly private. Notices not to touch or handle apparatus were disregarded, the assistants were kept on the jump from early till late guarding the scores of delicate instruments with which the laboratory abounds .... The railroad company ordered extra trains to be run and carriages came streaming from near and far. Surging crowds filled the laboratory,*

machine shop and private office of the scientists, and all
work had to be practically suspended.

Dressed in his work clothes, his vest unbuttoned, and his bow
tie discarded, Edison worked the crowds, explaining how his lighting system functioned and boldly proclaiming that his lamps would
soon light up all of New York City. From there, Edison prophesized,
his lighting system would find its way to every city of the United
States, and the world!

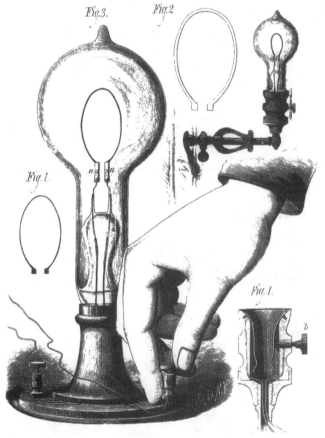

Edison's incandescent lamp, socket, filament, and wall fixture
as featured in the Scientific American three days after they were
introduced to the public on December 31, 1879.

Edison's claims were contested by a variety of doubters who in all probability were hired by competing gas companies to undermine confidence in Edison's lighting system. In describing the efforts of one such individual to short-circuit a string of lights Edison stated that he recognized the man as "a well-known electrician," a "graduate of John Hopkins University."

As the evening at Menlo Park drew to a close, Fox remained behind. His assignment was to spend a night at Menlo Park and write about what he observed in the waning hours after Edison's greatest triumph over nature. In describing what he experienced, Fox wrote that as he returned to the laboratory after a short rest, he saw the random movement of shadows in the windows. Men were still inside working, or so he thought, for as he drew nearer he heard the notes of a song from the musical *HMS Pinafore* being played on an organ inside the laboratory.

Entering the laboratory, Fox made his way upstairs. At the far end of the structure he saw eight or nine assistants seated on stools and benches. One man named MacGregor sat at the organ as the men improvised a song from the musical:

> MacGregor: *I am the Wizard of electric light,*
> *And a wide-awake Wizard, too.*
> *I see you're rather bright and appreciate the might*
> *of what I daily do*
> *Quadruplex telegraph or funny phonograph,*
> *It's all the same to me;*
> *With ideas I evolve and problems that I solve*
> *I'm never, never stumped, you see.*
>
> Chorus: *What, never?*
>
> MacGregor: *Well hardly—*

Sensing that Fox was not sure if he should go or stay, MacGregor stopped. Batchelor invited Fox to have a seat. Before long, Ludwig Boehm, the young glassblower from Germany, played the zither and another song commenced. Not long afterwards, as Fox noted, another man walked in and took a seat at the end of a bench. He sat and listened and then after the song was finished said, "That was very nice." To Fox's surprise it was Edison.

The men ate crackers and herring, and all but Edison drank a beer with their late supper. Edison drank a glass of water. As the night wore on, a few men were lost to sleep. Fox observed that the rest, including Edison, "were a merry crowd of seven there at one in the morning. The inventor's face beamed with good humor, and he joked with the boys who are on such a pleasant footing with him, intimate in expression, but it was always a pleasure to see the respectful alacrity with which they looked after him at all times ...."

In the hours that followed, Edison spoke to Fox about his early days in Boston, in New York and of his tramp days as a telegrapher traveling the country. With dawn fast approaching, Fox gathered his belongings and was about to step down the stairs to the first floor. As he was leaving the laboratory, he looked back in time to catch the inventor with his coat over his arm, looking for a soft spot on the benches upon which to sleep. Thomas Alva Edison was only thirty-two years old, but the reverence with which his men treated him, the brilliant success of the lamp's public demonstration, and Fox's respectful words made him seem much older.

Edison's New Year's Eve demonstration was a fantastic success. Investors in the Edison Electric Light company turned over an additional $57,568 for continued research and development—more money than had been spent in all of 1879. For investors in Edison's light, prospects were looking good, *very* good. In showing the promise of not only his incandescent light but his lighting system, it seemed that Edison stood ready to lead civilization into the Modern Age. Still, Edison knew that lighting a few homes and a stretch of road was nothing compared to lighting an immense area. The preliminary success of his lighting system would have been enough to sustain most inventors for years to come, but not Edison. He knew that improvements still had to be made to all aspects of his lighting system in order to make it commercially feasible. Still, in the aftermath of Edison's display, it was hardly arguable that he had succeeded in inventing a complex lighting system capable of competing with gas-company monopolies. His next challenge would be to sell this vision to those around him.

Chapter 8

The March on New York City

*Everything is so new that each step is in the dark. I have
to make the dynamos, the lamps, the conductors, and
attend to a thousand details the world never hears of.*
—Thomas Edison

On the day following the public demonstration of Edison's electric light and distribution system, Joseph W. Swan, Edison's chief rival in Europe, reminded the world that he had carbonized paper in the shape of a horseshoe fifteen years earlier. William Preece, one of England's leading electricians, declared, "The subdivision of the light is an absolute *ignis fatuus.*" On January 5, William E. Sawyer, Edison's American competitor, boldly declared that he was ready to back up his "assertion that Mr. Edison cannot run one of his lamps up to the light of a single gas jet for more than three hours." The *New York Herald* suggested that Mr. Sawyer visit Menlo Park with the hope that "perhaps Edison would keep up the illumination many hours extra for the sake of converting the doubting Thomas."

Edison knew that he would have to counter these comments immediately to maintain the positive momentum his demonstration had generated. He personally invited and led a reporter from the *Scientific American* on a tour of his laboratory on January 10, 1880. The reporter wrote favorably about the work since the demonstration, even praising Edison's lamp for enabling the group to read the *Scientific American* from a distance of 100 feet and for its simplicity in design. "It seems that the subject of general electric lighting is now reduced to a mere question of time," the reporter wrote. A week later, a follow-up article stressed Edison's simple approach to solving scientific queries, as well as his drive to develop a complete lighting system that not only served the needs of the public, but made it practical to set up and affordable. In both articles, Edison made sure to say nothing about the harsh criticisms being leveled by his competitors.

Taking criticism of Edison to a personal level, *Nature*, the leading scientific journal in Europe, alleged in mid-February that he was "thirty-five years behind the time in his new invention," referring to a patent for an incandescent lamp awarded in 1845 to Edward King, an Englishman.

To rebut criticism and curb personal attacks, Edison secretly underwrote the expense for an American journal, *Science*, which soon announced, "While others talked he has worked, and in a few short weeks all will be ready, when those who are competent can see and judge for themselves."

Taken by news of Edison's triumph was Henry Villard, an Edison investor, who owned a number of manufacturing and railroad line companies. He asked Edison if he could equip the SS Columbia, a 334-foot, 3,200-ton steel vessel belonging to a company he owned, with a lighting system. The ship was built in a Pennsylvania shipyard, but was to sail to California by way of Cape Horn in the summer of 1880. Knowing that the commission would bring publicity and a way to further test his model of a centralized power station, Edison agreed.

Four of Edison's "long-waisted Mary Anns," as his dynamos were called, were placed in the ship's engine room along with two steam engines to drive them. The dynamos would supply power to 115 Bristol board filament lamps. When work was completed, the SS Columbia made its way through the Delaware Bay, its lights bouncing off the still water, awing spectators on shore. Skeptics worried about the danger of fire aboard the ship, but the ship arrived in San Francisco two months later, all systems intact, including Edison's lamps.

Edison was indeed preoccupied with perfecting his lighting and electrical distribution system down to the last detail, experimenting on a number of innovations he would incorporate, including underground wiring, safety fuses to counter short circuits, insulating materials for wiring, light switches, fixtures, regulators, and meters to measure the amount of electricity used by a consumer. Edison knew it wasn't ready for mass marketing: The carbonized cardboard filament of his light bulb was neither sufficiently durable nor long-lasting, and the exceedingly high cost of copper meant that the wiring to light the area Edison had in mind would be a prohibitive expense at two hundred thousand dollars.

For Edison to make rapid progress, his managerial methods had to change. No longer could he afford to micromanage every project. He had to give men a certain amount of freedom to conduct experiments or manufacture components of his lighting system without first getting his approval. Based on this necessity, he assigned specific tasks to staff members or to teams of researchers and machinists. Describing this new approach to research and development Edison stated ...

> *I instructed them on the general idea of what I wanted*
> *carried out, and when I came across an assistant who was*
> *in any way ingenious, I sometimes refused to help him out*
> *in his experiments, telling him to see if he could not work*
> *it out himself, so as to encourage him.*

Edison now needed additional laboratory assistants: men willing to take risks, men of vision, men of passion, and men of daring. When word circulated, that Edison needed such workers, men hurried to Menlo Park, drawn to the Wizard's laboratory by the mystical reputation surrounding Edison. Otto Moses, an analytical chemist, draftsman, and outstanding researcher, was hired and placed in charge of the library. Charles Clark and Julius Horning were trained engineers. William Hammer, George Crosby, and Albert Herrick were young men who were paid little, if anything, as they gained experience and responsibility. Wilson Howell paid a visit to the laboratory and was so taken by the experience that he returned the next day in search of a job, willing to work without pay just to learn about electricity from Edison. Howell was soon placed in charge of devising a means for insulating underground electrical wires. As for Edison, he once again turned his attention to the question of the filament. The cardboard filament used for the public demonstration had served its purpose, but its short life span it would never do for mass marketing. Not long after taking up his work, Edison announced ...

> *Paper is no good. Under the microscope it appears like a lot of sticks thrown together. There are places where the fibres are packed and other places where there are few fibres, dense spots and great open holes. Now I believe that somewhere in God Almighty's workshop there is a vegetable growth with geometrically parallel fibres suitable to our use. Look for it. Paper is man made and not good for filaments.*

Edison and his men tested thousands of materials hoping to discover the molecular make-up Edison spoke of. The answer came in almost the same type of inspirational burst as when Edison completed his first successful filament, but instead of rolling a mixture of lampblack and tar between his fingers, on a hot day Edison noticed a fan lying on a table in his home. The rim of the fan was made of a long strip of bamboo that, when placed under the microscope, Edison determined to be worthy of testing. Batchelor had the bamboo strip carbonized and placed inside a lamp. Edison later stated, "We were gratified to see that the lamps were several times better than any we had succeeded in making before." Soon afterwards, Edison sent a man to Japan, where the bamboo originated, to have the material shipped to Menlo Park.

Finally satisfied that his incandescent lamp was ready for massproduction, Edison hired over a hundred additional men to manufacture the lamps in a factory converted from a barn across the road from the laboratory. Edison, Batchelor, Upton, and Johnson, financed the entire ten thousand dollar operation. Before long approximately one thousand lamps a day were being completed. When Edison's system went into use in 1882, production of lamps for that year was roughly one hundred thousand. Ten years later, this would increase to an astounding four million a year, and by 1903 forty-five million.

Edison's distribution system was his other major concern. The only existing solution was to run a main wire requiring an exorbitant amount of copper from a generator the length of area to be lit. Because copper was extremely expensive, this system was not economical. Even more important was the fact that by the time electricity reached lamps at the end of the line, the light produced was too dim. Edison needed the entire problem laid out before him. He had his men lay out an area of half a square mile, then had them designate areas within this space as either a building or a home. Trenches were dug to carry electrical lines to each site. A building would be equipped with a large number of lamps, a home with fewer. Wiring would also be provided to each site for domestic use.

Edison's solution was so ingenious, yet so simple, that when Sir William Thomson, the distinguished physicist, was asked why no one had ever thought of the method before, he responded, "The only answer I can think of is that no one else is Edison." First of all, Edison's main wire was roughly three-quarters of the size of those being used to supply power to arc lamps, and his main wire was not connected to the generator providing the electricity. Instead, Edison's main wire ran along the area to be lit, for example, a city block. Small-gauge copper wiring was then connected to this main wire and run to local distributing circuits. From this point an even smaller gauge wire ran into a customer's house, where it supplied power to a circuit panel. Smaller wires branched off the circuit panel and into the various rooms to be lit. An electrical current was then sent to the main wire from a number of "feeder" wires connected to their own generators, which were all located at the central plant. These feeder wires were connected to the main wire at equal distances from each other down the length of this wire. By adding generators and by feeding the current produced into the main wire at various points, electricity was maintained at a steady rate, allowing lamps inside homes to burn brightly regardless of how far down the line they were. The amount of copper required was drastically reduced, so that the cost of lighting a nine-block area went from two hundred thousand to roughly thirty thousand dollars—an astonishing savings.

Throughout the summer, critics such as Sawyer argued that Edison was making no headway and that he should come clean by declaring stock in the enterprise worthless. Gas and arc lamp companies urged Edison to do the same, to protect his reputation and to maintain the public's respect. Hiram Maxim, yet another inventor in the race to perfect an incandescent lamp and electrical distribution system, downplayed reports of Edison's success as well as Edison's further improvements to his incandescent lamp. Adding insult to injury, he even managed to hire away Ludwig Boehm, Edison's chief glassblower, and by the end of the year was producing lamps whose only noticeable difference from the Edison's was the cross shape of its filament.

All the while, Edison defended himself in the nation's newspapers. A newsletter called the *Bulletin of the Edison Electric Companies* was started to keep stockholders apprised of the "truth" of matters surrounding Edison's lighting system. Edison also announced that he was starting work on a new invention, the electric train.

It was a sincere undertaking, and tycoon Henry Villard invested forty thousand dollars for its development. However, Edison also began work on the electric train during the summer of 1880 to divert attention from his lighting system, and for a few months the nation's newspapers and journals were supplied with a steady flow of articles on the electric train. Newspapermen made the now-familiar trek to Menlo Park and were given a ride on the electric train, which ran on tracks through the countryside. Articles on the experience were accompanied by drawings showing Edison at the controls.

By October 1880, sufficient progress had been made on the lighting system that Edison published an article titled "The Success of the Electric Light" in the *North American Review*. He addressed the time it was taking to introduce his lighting system, explaining that delays were being caused not because there were flaws in his original theories, but because of "the enormous mass of details which have to be mastered before the system can go into operation on a large scale." He concluded the article by revealing that his improved lighting system would be completed by December 1880, and that his ultimate goal was to "erect the first station in New York City."

As Edison prepared to unveil his electrical distribution system in New York City, he offered the following reasons as to why it would be cheaper than gas:

1. Because a specially designed building to serve as a power station does not have to be built. Any building will do, as long as it has adequate floor space.

2. Because depreciation of plant is much less.

3. The cost of labor is much less, since not as many men are needed to operate an electric plant and make repairs.

4. Because light companies can sell electricity for two uses— for light at night, and for power in the daytime.

As he had predicted, by the start of December, Edison's new and improved lighting system was completed. As it happened, the famed tragedian Sarah Bernhardt was making her New York City debut at the same time. She had always wanted to meet Edison since hearing of his famed phonograph and electric light. Learning of Ms. Bernhardt's desire, her manager, who was friends with a director of the Edison Light Company, arranged a visit after her final performance on December 4. Edison and his men waited at the laboratory. As the hour grew late, the men grew skeptical, and some suggested that she was not coming at all. They didn't know that the actress had been kept at the theatre by an enthusiastic audience that cheered her through twenty-nine curtain calls, and a crowd of supporters waiting for her outside.

The men were losing hope when they saw Edison's personal carriage making its way toward the laboratory. Edison stepped outside to greet her. Ms. Bernhardt extended a hand, which he took as he bowed at the waist and helped her out of the carriage. Edison led her inside, where he signaled Jehl to turn on the lamps scattered across the snow-covered landscape outside. Ms. Bernhardt peered outside, enraptured, as the lamps grew in brilliance. After a minute, she clapped her hands. Edison then led her through the entire complex as he had done countless visitors and reporters. Leaving the machine shop, she took Edison's arm to steady herself as they walked through the snow.

Upstairs in the laboratory, Edison demonstrated his model of the telephone. Ms. Bernhardt told him through her interpreter, Robert L. Cutting, who had arranged the visit, that she would have to order one for her home in Paris. At last they reached a table on which sat Edison's phonograph. Edison sang and talked into the instrument, and when his voice was played back, Ms. Bernhardt laughed and clapped her hands. Edison then stepped aside, and the famed actress stepped up to phonograph. She recited lines from Victor Hugo's *Hernani* and Jean Racine's *Phédre,* and when her voice was played back she was so taken by the invention that she wanted to take it home with her, and did not relent until Edison promised to manufacture one especially for her.

The hour grew late and Ms. Bernhardt took her leave, but not before she told Edison, "*C'est grand, c'est magnifique.*"

Edison kept his promise, and in due time sent Ms. Bernhardt her personal phonograph and had one of his telephones installed in her Paris home. For her part, the "incomparable Sarah" painted Edison two landscapes in oil. When they arrived at Menlo Park, the package was addressed to "The giver of light."

Now that the concept for Edison's lighting system was completed, a subsidiary of the Edison Electric Light Company named the Edison Electric Illuminating Company of New York was formed on December 17, 1880, to meet New York regulations for installing the system. To Edison's disappointment, the board of directors earmarked the company's one million dollar front money exclusively for construction and implementation—no money was budgeted for factories to build dynamos and the various other components. Major S. B. Eaton, an attorney and early president of Edison Electric Light, recalled Edison stating, "If there are no factories to make my inventions, I will build the factories myself. Since capital is timid, I will raise and supply it .... The issue is factories or death!"[1] Edison formed a partnership with Sigmund Bergmann and Edward Johnson to manufacture sockets, switches, fuses, fixtures, meters, and other devices, all invented by Edison. He also formed a partnership with Batchelor to create the Electric Tube Company and the Edison Machine Works. The manufacturing shop would produce Edison's oversized dynamos.

Three days after the Edison Illuminating Company of New York was officially organized, Edison and the board of directors hosted a demonstration of his lighting system for New York City officials at Menlo Park. Less than half of the New York City alderman joined the large contingent of city commissioners aboard the private railcar that transported the group to the New Jersey countryside. The Democratic mayor of New York City, Edward Cooper, who had taken a public stance in support of gas companies, did not make the trip. Edison led a tour of the laboratory complex, and on the first floor he demonstrated the ability of a one-horsepower electrical motor to operate two sewing machines and a lathe. He took a lamp, its filament burning brightly, and plunged it into a container full of water to ease fears that burying electrically charged lines underground would lead to the electrocution of citizens after a hard rain.

Edison then led the contingent to the second floor. The room was pitch black, then suddenly Edison's lamps came to life. Before the captivated officials lay a feast catered by Delmonico's, New York City's finest Italian restaurant. Waiters dressed in their finest, complete with white gloves, stood around tables placed in a semicircle with the organ on the open end. The party sat down to dinner, enjoying the never-ending stream of champagne. After dinner, Edison passed around cigars, and the champagne kept flowing. Edison then stood and took center stage. He thanked his visitors for joining him and produced a large map showing a square mile from Canal to Wall Street. The map designated potential customers and the route Edison would take in laying his electrical lines. He stressed the safety of his underground method, and in an indirect criticism of arc lights recently installed along a three-quarter mile stretch of Broadway, he spoke of the dangers created by the high-tension wires that system used.

J. C. Henderson, Henry Villard's chief engineer, followed Edison's presentation. He spoke of the success of Edison's lighting system aboard the SS *Columbia.* Grosvenor P. Lowery, one of the men responsible for getting Edison into the race for electrical lighting and an influential attorney in New York City, closed with a speech in total support of Edison and his system. With cigar smoke filling the room, Zenas Fisk Wilber, a chief examiner from the United States Patent Office, there to reassure the representatives of Edison's patent rights, lifted his glass and proposed three cheers for Edison. The New Yorkers left at 9:30 P.M. with cigars in their pockets and bellies full of champagne.

A day after the visit, the *New York Truth* published a cartoon criticizing the inebriated aldermen raising champagne glasses. The headline above the drawing read, "ALDERMAN AT MENLO PARK. EDISON GIVES SUCCESSFUL EXHIBITION OF HIS ELECTRIC LIGHT. The City Fathers Partake of a Collation, Swallow Innumerable Bumpers and Make the Most Scintillating Speeches." A day after that, the *New York Herald* reported that the aldermen's tour of Edison's laboratory was "a decided success, especially successful was his guests' capacity for champagne."

On January 8, the New York City Board of Aldermen voted to grant Edison permission to install his lighting system. Consent, however, had its price. The aldermen set the cost for laying electrical lines would run a thousand dollars a mile, and the company would have to turn over three percent of gross profits to the city after five years. The conditions had no precedent; gas companies were charged no added fees, and paid only property taxes. The fees, however, did not stand, thanks to pressure placed on aldermen by the Illuminating Company's board of directors, some of the most wealthy and prominent men in New York City. The rate was reduced to $52.80 a mile and the issue of sharing profits was dropped. The measure passed, and when the mayor vetoed the measure, the alderman overrode him nineteen to two.

On top of Edison's efforts to secure permission and begin the installation of his lighting system in New York City, he applied for fifty patents relating to his lighting system alone: five for auxiliary parts, six for dynamos, thirty-two for incandescent lamps, and seven for his distribution system. However, before the close of the year, yet another project would vie for Edison's attention: an offer to participate in the inaugural International Electrical Exhibition in Paris during the summer of 1881. George Gouraud, his London agent, wrote that a commissioner of the French government had requested that Edison exhibit all of his electrical inventions. Believing it to be advantageous for Edison to take part in more ways than one, Gouraud added, "That not to be there in force would render the Exhibition incomplete and most prejudicial influences might thereby de drawn."

ALDERMEN AT MENLO PARK.

EDISON GIVES A SUCCESSFUL EXHIBITION OF HIS ELECTRIC LIGHT.

The City Fathers Partake of a Collation, Swallow Innumerable Bumpers and Make the Most Scintillating Speeches.

This headline and cartoon criticizing the visit of New York City aldermen to Thomas Alva Edison's Menlo Park laboratory appeared in the New York Truth *on December 21, 1880.*

Edison therefore dispatched Batchelor, Johnson, Jehl, Moses, and Hammer to Paris in early February 1881 to make preparations. He remained behind to set up a headquarters in New York City and supervise manufacturing of the components for his lighting system. Joining him in his funding efforts was Samuel Insull, an Englishman who had been an Edison believer ever since reading an article in *Scribner's Magazine* titled "A Night with Edison." A wizard himself in business and finance, Insull brought order to Edison's enterprises and found the cash necessary to manufacture components as well as form additional companies.

Edison now oversaw the manufacturing of what would be, at the time, the largest dynamo in the world. Upon completion it would be shipped to Paris to supply the power to light his exhibit. Edison also selected the site on which to build his first central power station. For his headquarters and showroom, Edison selected a mansion at 65 Fifth Avenue. The ornate, four-story structure with well-furnished rooms perfectly announced the growing prominence of the thirty-four year old inventor and his company. Before long, a power generator was installed and Edison lamps placed throughout the residence. Edison exclaimed to a friend, "We're up in the world now! I remember ten years ago—I had just come from Boston—I had to walk the streets of New York all night because I hadn't the price of a bed. And now think of it! I'm to occupy a whole house on Fifth Avenue." Crowds gathered during the day to catch a glimpse of the remarkable Edison, and, at night, to witness the brilliance of his incandescent lamps.

Finding a location for his central power station was not as easy as finding his headquarters. Real estate was costly; even near the waterfront, buildings sold for roughly seventy thousand dollars apiece—a far cry from the ten thousand dollars Edison had in mind to spend. This eventually led him to 255-57 Pearl Street, a site that did not completely meet his expectations, yet was affordable enough that he was willing to alter the layout of the machinery to be placed inside.

While Edison began installing his lighting system in New York City, representatives from the various electrical concerns in Paris were negotiating with exhibition officials to light a prominent area inside the venue where the event was taking place. In the end, Edison was selected to provide lighting for the grand staircase and a number of exhibit rooms; Maxim's incandescent light company was awarded the main hall; the separate enterprises of Joseph Swan and Fox-Lane were given exhibit rooms, while the entrance hall-way was to be lit by Jablochoff arc lights.

Edison's exhibit consisted of a number of Edison lamps leading up the staircase, with an illuminated "E" at the top that opened to reveal Edison's name spelled out by shining lamps. The exhibit required a total of seven hundred lamps with an additional three hundred for the exhibit rooms. But Edison did not limit the demonstration of his system. Unlike his competitors, when each day's festivities came to an end, power was diverted to Edison lamps used to light a café on the Champs d'Elysees, where diners sat enjoying their wine and conversation late into the night. Offices were acquired away from the exhibition, which gave Edison's men an opportunity to network with parties interested in the Edison system.

Edison's system proved superior to his competitors', so much so that even William Preece, England's leading electrician, who had at one point called Edison's attempt to subdivide light an absolute *"ignis fatuus,"* could not help but admit as much:

> *The completeness of Mr. Edison's exhibit was certainly the most noteworthy object in the exhibition. Nothing seems to have been forgotten, no detail missed …. Mr. Edison's system has been worked out in detail, with a thoroughness and mastery of the subject that can extract nothing but eulogy from his bitterest opponents. Many unkind things have been said of Mr. Edison and his promises; perhaps no one has been severer in this direction than myself. It is some gratification for me to be able to announce my belief that he has at last solved the problem that he set himself to solve.*

Exhibition officials agreed, awarding Edison the top prize while Swan, Lane-Fox, and Maxim were honored with medals in the class below. So successful was this and other exhibitions in the years to come that Edison eventually organized installation companies in France, England, Italy, Holland, and Belgium.

While the prestige of Edison's lighting system was growing overseas, Edison and his men dug fifteen miles of trenches through the New York City streets. Electrical mains, feeder lines, and wiring to each building and home were laid in place. Wiring was then routed and mounted in every structure to be supplied with electricity and light. The Pearl Street central power station was outfitted with four oversized boilers, six 240-horsepower Porter-Allen steam engines, and three of an expected six improved Jumbo dynamos, the nickname given Edison's dynamo in London, where P. T. Barnum's elephant of the same name was a celebrity.

Edison's employees lay electric cables to supply New York City buildings with light from the Pearl Street generating station. The drawing was published in the June 24, 1882 issue of Harper's Weekly.

In addition, switchboards and control panels were set in place. On a top floor were stored an estimated one thousand electric lamps to be screwed into sockets once the system was ready. As if this wasn't enough, Edison and his crews also placed a number of independent lighting systems in the homes of prominent New Yorkers.

In the midst of installing his lighting system, Edison moved his family from Menlo Park to New York City, then, when his wife, Mary, took ill in early 1882, he took his family to Florida. He was there from February to March, which slowed progress considerably. In what can be seen as a defining moment, he also moved his library and his laboratory to New York City.

The enormity of the work, as well as unexpected professional and personal setbacks, delayed the testing of the installation until July 6, 1882. Recalling the less than auspicious event, an Edison associate later proclaimed, "It was a terrifying experience as I didn't know what was going to happen. The engines and dynamos made a horrible racket, and the place seemed to be filled with sparks and flames of all colors. It was as if the gates of the infernal regions had suddenly opened up."

While men bolted from the shop, some of them running as far as two blocks, Edison and Johnson, who was visiting from London, shut off the engines. Edison found that the problem was caused by the engines' inability to synchronize. Edison connected the engines' governors with a single shaft, whose purpose it was to keep the machines running at the desired speed. This still didn't correct the "see-sawing" of the engines. As Edison later explained, the challenge was not overcome until he …

> got a piece of shafting and a tube in which it fitted. I
> twisted the shaft one way and the tube the other as far as
> I could and pinned them together. In this way, by strain-
> ing the whole outfit up to its elastic limit in opposite direc-
> tions, the torsion was practically eliminated, and after that
> the governors ran together all right.

It wasn't a permanent solution, but it would have to suffice for the time being. Over $480,000 had already been spent on the project, well over the $100,000 budgeted for the entire undertaking.

Newspapers were once again hounding Edison, asking why it was taking so long to get his lighting system online. Investors, whose stock had fallen from roughly $3,000 a share at the start of the project to $600 a share at present, also became concerned. They demanded results, and they wanted them now. However, the overwhelming overseas success of Edison's lighting system kept criticism from learned scientists, inventors, and scientific and industrial journals for the most part silent.

Not one to be rushed, especially by reporters and Wall Street capitalists, Edison later confessed that while he was making final preparations, "I kept promising through newspapers that the large central station in New York would be started at such and such a time. These promises were made more with a view to keeping up the courage of my stockholders, who naturally wanted to get rich faster than the nature of things permitted."

Finally, more than four years since taking up the question of incandescent lighting, Edison was ready to unveil his lighting system. The date was set: September 4, 1882. Edison later reminisced ...

> The Pearl Street station was the biggest and most responsible thing I had ever undertaken. It was a gigantic problem, with many ramifications. There was no parallel in the world .... All our apparatus, devices and parts were home-devised and home-made .... What might happen on turning a big current into the conductors under the streets of New York no one could say .... The gas companies were our bitter enemies in those days, keenly watching our every move and ready to pounce upon us at the slightest failure. Success meant world-wide adoption of our central-station plan. Failure meant loss of money and prestige and setting back of our enterprise. All I can remember of the events of that day is that I had been up most of the night rehearsing my men and going over every part of the system .... If I ever did any thinking in my life it was on that day.

At three o'clock that afternoon, the switch was thrown, and the world entered a new age. Overall, the event was anticlimactic.

Unsure of how his system would perform, Edison had kept the news quiet. A handful of reporters and a small delegation of Illuminating Company directors were the only ones present to witness it in person. Dressed in a Prince Albert coat, white cravat, starched collarless shirt, and white derby, Edison stood in front of the station and proudly proclaimed, "I have accomplished all that I promised."

The next day, the *New York World* published two stories regarding the event: One story described Edison's incandescent light, the other the placement of lamps in the offices of the *New York Herald*. Both stories were told in a total of three paragraphs. The *New York Herald* was a bit more generous, providing half of one column and a quarter of another; the story, however, titled "Edison's Illuminators," was buried in the back of the day's edition. The *New York Sun* printed Edison's quote and then proceeded with a hodgepodge of inconsequential information.

Not until evening fell was the drama of Edison's accomplishment felt in its entirety. *The New York Times*, which was outfitted with Edison lamps, under the headline MISCELLANEOUS wrote:

> *It was not until about seven o'clock, when it began to grow dark, that the electric light really made itself known and showed how bright and steady it is …. It was a light that a man could sit down under and write for hours without the consciousness of having any artificial light about him …. The light was soft, mellow, and grateful to the eye, and it seemed almost like writing by daylight to have a light without a particle of flicker and with scarcely any heat to make the headache.*[2]

So successful was the Pearl Street Station that by the end of the year, 130 plants were supplying electricity to 22,000 lamps. In 1883, this number grew to 246 plants and 61,000 lamps. Among early buyers of the Edison lighting system were the Iowa State Prison, the Government Printing Office in Washington, Rand McNally Company, Marshall Field's in Chicago, and Cyrus McCormick's machine works. The University of Missouri became the first center of education in the world whose students studied by the light of Edison's incandescent lamp. Dr. S. S. Laws, Edison's first employer in New York City, had ordered the lighting system on behalf of the university.

> *In 1917, thirty-five years after the opening of Edison's Pearl Street Station, The American Scenic and Historical Society and the New York Edison Company placed a bronze memorial tablet at the site in recognition of Edison's accomplishment. The tablet is still there today.*

Profits, however, were slow in trickling down to Edison. At one point, when financial ruin remained a real possibility, Insull, who was concerned about how a payroll would be met, asked Edison what they should do. On hearing the forecast, Edison asked, "Sammy, do you think you can earn a living again as a stenographer?—because if you do I think I can earn my living as a telegraph operator. So that we can be sure of having something to eat anyway."

For Edison it was never about the money; it was about keeping one's word, and inventing marketable products that sold. By inventing an incandescent lamp and installing his electrical distribution center in New York City, Edison had achieved the goals he had promised in October 1878. His victory, however, would be short-lived. A new challenge led by George Westinghouse, a name synonymous today with household appliances, was looming. Westinghouse's forces would question the effectiveness of Edison's electrical distribution system and offer another system up in its place. The challenge was custom-made for Edison, who was always up for a good fight.

Chapter 9

_____

Changing Currents

Alternating current's effect upon muscular action is so great that even at exceedingly low voltage the hand which grasps a conductor cannot free itself, and it is quite possible that in this way the sensitive nervous system of a human being could be shocked for a sufficient length of time to produce death.

—*Thomas Alva Edison*

Edison left his Newark, New Jersey, factory for Menlo Park in 1876 to escape the day-to-day responsibilities that kept him from inventing, his true passion. How ironic that his success at Menlo Park as an inventor led him to New York City, where the bulk of his time was spent as a laborer and businessman, and not as an inventor. Of course, Edison had little choice: He couldn't trust the installation of his lighting system to anyone else. Giving up full-time inventing was well worth the sacrifice, because if Edison's lighting system succeeded, he would never have to worry about money again.

However, circumstances didn't play out as Edison might have hoped. Soon after his lighting system went on-line in 1882, he grew disenchanted with the Edison Electric Light Company's directors for their unwillingness to market the system on a large scale. Edison brought up the matter time and again, to no avail.

Two years after its introduction, only twelve of Edison's lighting systems modeled on the Pearl Street station were in operation in towns, although the system was doing fairly well overall, with over one hundred sold to private citizens and businesses.

In 1884, Edison received permission from the company directors to lead the marketing and selling of his lighting system—they feared they would alienate him if they refused. Of course, this made time for inventing even more dear. More important, Edison's attention was distracted by the death of his beloved wife, Mary, who passed away on August 9, 1884, in their Menlo Park home, with Edison at her side. Her death so touched Edison that his daughter, Marion, recalled that she found him in the morning "shaking with grief, weeping and sobbing so he could hardly tell me that mother had died in the night."

Within two years of Edison taking over sales and marketing, Pearl Street–style lighting systems sales numbered fifty-eight, and sale of the system to private citizens and businesses grew to over five hundred. Sales were doing so well that the combined assets of Edison companies charged with supplying lamps, as well as components and machinery for lighting systems rose from a little over $1.5 million to $10 million in two years. With sales of his lighting system improving, Edison distracted himself from Mary's death by returning to inventing on a more regular basis. Wireless telegraphy for use on trains and further improvements of his carbon button topped his list. He also started to show an interest in ore milling, yet another area of experimentation that had captured his attention years earlier, but in which he soon lost interest.

Aside from immersing himself in his work, as he had at Menlo Park, Edison spent his nights with employees at his 65 Fifth Avenue headquarters, trading stories while enjoying a cigar. He paid frequent social visits to the home of Ezra Gilliland, a friend from his days as an itinerant telegrapher in Cincinnati with whom Edison was conducting wireless telegraphy experiments. A successful businessman from Boston who acquired his money as an engineer of telephonic devices, Gilliland and his wife made it their duty to find Edison a new wife, and often invited young women to dine with them and Edison. So long was the list of candidates that at one Fourth of July celebration, Edison telegraphed a message to Insull urging him to "come to Boston. At Gill's house there are lots of pretty girls."

> Edison hardly ever returned to Menlo Park after his wife Mary passed away. He moved all the tools and machinery to the Edison Machine Works in New York City in 1881, and moved the library and his personal laboratory in 1882. In a letter dated April 27, 1882, Francis Upton, Edison's gifted mathematician, who had assumed control of the Edison Lamp Company, wrote that because the men at Menlo Park were unsupervised, there was little work being done, and that it would be best to close down the facility and leave a watchman on the property.
>
> Today, a recreation of Edison's Menlo Park complex, as well as Sarah Jordan's Boarding House, where some of Edison's men lived, can be found at Henry Ford Museum and Greenfield Field in Dearborn, Michigan, and at Menlo Park, New Jersey, a monument and a museum are located on the original Menlo Park laboratory site.

The Gillilands finally succeeded in the summer of 1885, when Edison was reintroduced to eighteen-year-old Mina Miller, the daughter of a wealthy family from Akron, Ohio. Edison met Mina early in the year while attending the World Industrial and Cotton Centennial Exposition in New Orleans and was so taken by her that months later he wrote in his diary, "Saw a lady who looked like Mina. Got thinking about Mina and came near being run over by a streetcar. If Mina interferes much more will have to take out an accident policy." After a brief courtship, the couple was married on February 24, 1886. The union would last the rest of Edison's life and result in three children: Madeline, Charles, and Theodore.

Edison now entered a phase characterized by an inclination to do everything on a grand scale, regardless of cost. Apparently, time had done nothing to change Edison's propensity to disregard how much money he had; however, up until now he had limited his lavish spending sprees to items for the laboratory or machine shop. Suddenly, he was spending large sums of money on his own indulgence. For example, he ordered a home built for him and Mina in

Fort Myers, Florida. Across the street from this house he built a laboratory, which would employ four men throughout the year. He topped this by purchasing Glenmont, a palatial mansion in fashionable West Orange, New Jersey, where the Edisons resided after their honeymoon. He also had a new laboratory built less than half a mile away.

The West Orange laboratory would be everything that the Menlo Park laboratory had been, but on a grander scale. As Edison wrote in a laboratory notebook ...

> *I will have the best equipped & largest Laboratory extant, and the facilities incomparably superior to any other for rapid & cheap development of an invention & working it up into Commercial shape with models & special machinery. In fact there is no similar institution in Existence. We do our own castings forgings Can build anything from a lady's watch to a Locomotive .... Inventions that formerly took months & cost large sums can now be done 2 or 3 days with very small expense, as I shall carry a stock of almost every conceivable material.*

Glenmont, Edison's home in West Orange, New Jersey.

When completed in 1888, the main building contained sixty thousand square feet of space. There was a machine shop, an engine room, glass blowing and pumping rooms, chemical and photographic departments, rooms for electrical testing, stockrooms, and an office and library, which eventually contained over ten thousand volumes. Separate from the main building were four one-story structures containing a physical lab, chemistry lab, and a chemical storeroom. In one building were the pattern-making shop and metallurgical lab. A fence surrounded the complex, with a guard stationed at the entrance. Visitation was by appointment only; far different from Menlo Park, where guests were free to come and go.

The money spent on these projects was tremendous. The responsibility for coming up with funding for them fell on Insull, who remained Edison's financial manager even though he also served as the manager of the Edison Machine Works. So great was the strain that he wrote an associate that Edison would require additional funding if he expected to carry through with his plans for the West Orange laboratory. "The trouble is," Insull confided, "that Mr. Edison does not seem to have anyone with him who urges him to curtail his expenses on his new laboratory."

Foundations for the West Orange laboratory were poured in May and June of 1887. The method by which products would be developed and brought to market were announced in the September 17, 1887, issue of *Scientific American*. The article, "Edison's New Laboratory," clearly outlined Edison's unique plans for developing an invention. The process would begin with the submission of rough sketches to model makers, from which a working model would be created. All materials for producing the prototype would be on-site or quickly acquired. An army of men would also be on hand if needed to quickly complete the prototype. Improvements would be made, then the final piece would be used to produce patterns and castings from which to produce a full-sized machine. If the machine met with Edison's approval, it was then sent somewhere else to be manufactured. If an invention proved profitable, Edison would then set up his own company to manufacture and sell the invention. Edison's Machine Works at

Schenectady, New York, already employed eight hundred men, and the Edison Lamp Works at Harrison, New Jersey, where four hundred men turned out one million lamps per year.

Edison's new and improved laboratory provided him with the space and materials to develop a number of inventions simultaneously. The first invention to occupy Edison's attention at West Orange was the one that first brought him worldwide fame and recognition, the phonograph. As a matter of fact, he had turned his attention back to the phonograph even while his West Orange laboratory was under construction. However, a new threat to Edison's lighting system was taking up more of his time than any project. The threat was from a recent advance made in the technology that would allow for the use of alternating current to supply the energy for use in electrical distribution systems.

In 1883, the year after Edison's lighting system was installed in New York City, an English patent was awarded to Lucien Gaulard of France and John D. Gibbs of England for an AC transformer, which permitted alternating currents to be transmitted efficiently at high voltages and then stepped down to lower voltages for use in a consumer's home. The invention had its flaws, but it did point the way for others to develop a lighting system using alternating current.

Located in West Orange, New Jersey, a short distance from Glenmont, Edison's West Orange Laboratory was to be every-thing the Menlo Park facility had been, but on a grander scale.

In order for an electric transformer to work, a current has to rise and fall so that the magnetic field around a current-carrying wire will build and collapse as the voltage reaches the high point and returns to zero. This moving magnetic field is imposed on the iron core of the transformer by the primary windings. This field, in turn, induces a current in the secondary coils, which are also wound around the shared iron core. Alternating current has a rising and falling current; direct current has only steady current. The ability to raise or lower voltage is achieved by changing the ratio of windings in the primary and secondary coils. More windings in the secondary makes a step-up transformer used to send electricity on a long journey. More windings in the primary steps the electricity down for local use. This means that the voltage of a DC generator is limited to what it has been designed to deliver. For example, a DC generator capable of producing five hundred volts could travel a considerable distance, but certainly not the hundreds of miles an AC generator of the same size would be capable of sending through the use an AC transformer.

In a DC generator, a coil of wire turns between the poles of a magnet in the same direction at all times. This causes the current to move down a line only in one direction. In an AC generator a coil of wire is turned between the poles of a magnet. Halfway through each turn in the magnetic field, the coil becomes positioned for an instant at a right angle to the magnet. This causes the current to move quickly in one direction, and after it reaches its peak, turn back in the other direction until it reaches its peak yet again; this cycle is repeated in an endless chain.

The Hungarian team of Karl Zipernowsky, Otto Blathy, and Max Deri were the first to not only improve on the Gaulard-Gibb AC transformer, but to use it in a complete alternating current lighting system. Debuted at the Bucharest Exposition of 1885, the trio's lighting system created an immediate interest for its ability to send electricity a considerable distance and, once there, to decrease its strength for practical use.

Edison's reputation in the world of electrical lighting had grown to such an extent that, with this success in hand, Blathy was sent to the United States to offer the system to Edison. Before accepting the group's proposal, Edison had the system examined in Europe by Upton, who immediately wrote Edison advising him to obtain the rights to the system in order to keep a "dangerous enemy" in check. Satisfied, Edison paid five thousand dollars to the Hungarian team for a three-year option to purchase the American rights to the system for a total price of twenty thousand dollars. In the meantime, the use of the ZBD system, named for the inventors' initials, spread throughout Europe.

What concerned Edison about this new lighting system was that alternating currents could now be produced at a low voltage then routed through an AC transformer, where it was stepped up to the voltage level desired. If the voltage level was high, the current could travel for hundreds of miles and then be brought down to a safe level with another AC transformer at the end of the line or at any point in between. Edison had designed his electrical distribution system using direct current, with an ability to send out a maximum of two hundred fifty volts, a safe supply for domestic use and the highest level that would not burn out incandescent filaments. However, because Edison had designed his system in this way, the electricity generated by his system could efficiently travel only a short distance. Sending a direct current over longer distances meant using a much higher voltage.

Of course, Edison was aware of the dramatic shortcoming of his direct-current lighting system, but he had a number of reasons to use it anyway. He chose to use direct current because he found it safe, and because AC technology had not yet reached a level that it posed a threat to his system. Direct current had been used to supply energy to arc lamps, and had been the focus of inventors working to develop an incandescent lamp prior to Edison's entering the race; a tremendous amount of research and development had already been done, while little to nothing had been done in the area of alternating currents. All of the machinery then in use was invented with the idea that it would be powered by direct current, and Edison could not afford to take time to develop a system based on alternating current—and, until the breakthrough in AC current, he did not have to.

Even so, in doing without this improvement to his system, if Edison had tried to light the entire city of New York using direct current, it would have meant building a supply station every few miles. For this reason, his lighting system made inroads in mostly densely populated urban areas, or in the homes of the wealthy. With an alternating-current system, the entire city of New York could be lit from one power station, which could even be located outside of town. It's clear why alternating current eventually overtook direct current as the system of choice.

In purchasing the patent rights to the ZBD system, Edison made sure, as Upton had suggested, to keep a "dangerous enemy" in check. This wasn't the first time Edison was approached by someone hoping to interest him in the possibilities of alternating currents. In 1884, a young man by the name of Nikola Tesla came to New York City from Paris. While living in Paris, he had been employed by the Edison electric light company franchised to French entrepreneurs, where he had worked with Charles Batchelor. He met Edison at his 65 Fifth Avenue headquarters with a letter of recommendation from Batchelor, which read, "I know two great men and you are one of them; the other is this young man." Impressed, Edison took the time to talk to Tesla. The conversation went well until Tesla started talking about his ideas on alternating currents. At this point Edison grew angry, shouting, "Hold up! Spare me that nonsense. It's dangerous. We're set up for direct current in America. People like it, and it's all I'll ever fool with."

Tesla stood silent. He so respected Edison that he did not dare challenge his opinion. Apparently impressed with the rest of what Tesla had to say in regards to his experience with direct current, Edison sent him to repair an Edison isolated lighting system aboard the SS *Oregon*. Tesla worked through the night and successfully repaired the system. His abilities proven, Edison offered Tesla a position, which he accepted.

Soon thereafter, Tesla approached Edison with a variety of ideas on how to improve Edison's dynamo. Edison gave Tesla approval to proceed, adding that there was fifty thousand dollars waiting for him if the work was completed and proved beneficial. After almost a year working day and night beyond his normal responsibilities, Tesla's improvements were finished. When he showed the work to Edison and explained the benefits of his modifications, proving them without a doubt to be a step above the original, Tesla inquired about his fifty thousand dollars. Edison laughed and exclaimed, "Tesla, you don't understand our American humor."

Outraged, Tesla walked out the door, never to return. His time in Edison's employ, however, was not wasted. His reputation had grown such that a group of American investors were willing to provide him with the funding to start his own company. The group had one restriction: They wanted him to develop an improved arc light. Tesla agreed, but when his work was finished and he had produced a superior model, he was eased out of the company.

Bitter from twice being taken advantage of, Tesla, as Edison might have done under the same circumstances, worked as a day laborer for a year to support his experiments. His luck changed when his supervisor took him to meet A. K. Brown, the manager of the Western Union Telegraph Company. No stranger to the benefits of alternating current, Brown listened to Tesla's ideas. Convinced that Tesla was onto something, Brown eventually helped him form the Tesla Electric Company for the sole purpose of developing an alternating current lighting system.

Meanwhile, George Westinghouse, an American inventor who had made his fortune on his discovery of the air brake for railroad cars, had become interested in electric power. In 1886, he and several investors had founded Westinghouse Electric and Manufacturing Company, a company that would sell light systems powered by alternating current. Westinghouse was able to develop a alternating-current lighting system by purchasing the American rights to the Gaulard-Gibbs transformer, from which William A. Stanley, a Westinghouse consultant, had managed to develop an AC transformer different from Edison's. The Westinghouse Electric and Manufacturing Company opened the first commercial alternating-current system on March 6, 1886, in Great Barrington,

Massachusetts. Stanley was able to generate five hundred volts of electricity and send the electricity down the wire, where his transformer stepped the current up to three thousand volts and sent it down the line. After reaching its final destination, a second transformer then reduced the electricity back to five hundred volts, making it easy to regulate the current and safely use it both commercially and privately.

Shortly after the success of the Great Barrington plant, Westinghouse purchased the United States Electric Lighting Company, and with it the right to the use the incandescent lamp patents once belonging to Hiram Maxim. Westinghouse would now be able to market his alternating-current system on a large scale. This did not sit well with Edison, especially after 1887 when Westinghouse moved to introduce his system in New York City. Still, Edison did not take the challenge seriously, even though thirty-seven alternating-current systems had been sold. He knew that Westinghouse's system could not supply power to machinery that depended on direct current.

At the same time Westinghouse was attempting to enter the New York market, Tesla had completed two prototypes of his induction motor powered by alternating current, one of which was sent to the United States Patent Office, which immediately granted him rights to the invention. At the same time, Tesla worked on designing the necessary dynamos, transformers, and automatic controls to make his system practical. So revolutionary was his work that he was invited to present his findings to the American Institute of Electrical Engineers on May 16, 1888. Tesla's discourse was so impressive that Dr. B. A. Behrend stated afterwards that not since Michael Faraday's "Experimental Researches in Electricity" had he heard "a great experimental truth voiced so simply and so clearly …. He left nothing to be done by those who followed him. His paper contained the skeleton even of the mathematical theory."

Hearing of Tesla's work with alternating currents, and of the excitement his presentation had created, Westinghouse paid a visit to Tesla's laboratory. As legend has it, Westinghouse was so impressed with what he saw in the laboratory that he offered him one million dollars on the spot for control of the forty patents Tesla held in alternating current inventions. This has never been proven and no documentation of this offer exists, but Westinghouse Company records do indicate that Tesla was given sixty thousand dollars for the forty patents, five thousand dollars cash, one hundred fifty shares of stock, and a whopping $2.50 per horsepower of electricity sold. Tesla, however, never repeated the full benefits of this deal because when Westinghouse's company was in serious danger of going out of business years later, Tesla restructured his agreement with Westinghouse in order to help keep the company afloat.

A few months before this meeting, Henry Villard, a longtime Edison investor, had paid a similar unexpected visit to Edison. Villard came to Edison's New York City headquarters to offer Edison a deal on behalf of a group of international investors for the takeover of the Edison Electric Light Company, Edison Machine Works, Edison Lamp Company, Edison Industrial Works, and a few others.

Edison listened to the offer, which he felt might finally give him an opportunity to get rid of the "leaden collar of the Edison Electric Light Company …." When Edison presented the proposal to the Electric Light Company's board members, Morgan wanted no part in it, at least not yet. For the moment, Villard was left with no choice but to return to Europe to discuss a second proposal with his partners.

In the meantime, after learning of Westinghouse's acquisition of Tesla's alternate current patents, especially that of his "alternate current motor," Edison at last realized that he could no longer sit back and let Westinghouse's lighting system overrun the marketplace. Even Edison's salesmen complained that something had to be done, and fast, because they couldn't compete with the asking price for a Westinghouse system.

> *Tesla's AC motor was the way to break Edison's position as the supplier of electricity to the industry. With an AC motor, large amounts of power could be sold to factories to run their machines and not just lighting electricity. Production and manufacturing facilities could now be built near the labor, raw material and market sites and not just near running water or where you could have your own steam engine. In the past belts connected to an overhead drive shaft powered by steam engines were used to power each machine. Now each machine could have it's own electric motor. The layout of the factory could be more compact with out the need for long runs of overhead power shafts.*

To combat this challenge, Edison turned to the press. The "war of the currents" was under way. In the days that followed, a barrage of articles detailing the perils of alternating currents were published in a number of newspapers around the county. The Westinghouse camp fired back with counterclaims showing that their system was safe and cheaper to use than that of Edison's. The company also warned consumers not to believe everything that Edison was saying. In February 1888, the Edison company released a red-covered pamphlet titled "A Warning from the Edison Electric Light Company," which in one section read:

They cannot make it safe.

They cannot make it reliable.

They cannot make it run twelve 16-candlepower lamps per horsepower.

They cannot make its lamps even.

They cannot make its lamps last a reasonable time.

They cannot make it sell by meter.

They cannot make it run motors.

In describing the Westinghouse lighting system, ironically enough, the pamphlet used the phrase *ignis fatuus*, the same idiom used by William Preece in 1878 to criticize Edison's ability to subdivide electric light. The Edison company then lobbied state legislatures to limit electric circuits to eight hundred volts, which would leave Westinghouse lighting systems practically useless. This strategy did not gain support; Westinghouse threatened to file a lawsuit on the grounds that elected officials were conspiring with

Edison to harm his right to do business. All the while, Edison invited reporters to his West Orange Laboratory to witness the electrocution of dogs and cats with alternating current.

With the year 1888 drawing to a close, Villard and his associates presented their revised proposal to Edison and stockholders of the Edison Electric Light Company. By January 1889, the offer was accepted; the Edison Lamp Works Company, the Edison Machine Shop, Bergmann and Company, and the Sprague Electric Railway and Motor Company were joined with the Edison Electric Light Company to form the Edison General Electric Company, eventually known as General Electric. In the end, Edison sold his stake in the industry he had single-handedly founded for $1,750,000 in cash and stocks. Bergmann collected $1,000,000, which he used to establish an electrical company in Germany. Johnson retired in luxury to an estate in Connecticut, and Insull earned $75,000.

Now that Edison had the funds to do as he pleased, he could've turned his back on the "war of the currents." What difference would it make if alternating current won and direct current went the way of the dinosaur? Perhaps the answer is that Edison, whether he liked it or not, was a businessman as well as an inventor. He was a capitalist who, like the owners of the gas companies he had once threatened, was willing to do anything to save an industry that he had nursed to maturity. Then again, the answer may be that Edison was not the jovial Wizard of Menlo Park, but a proud, ambitious fighter who would stop at nothing to come out on top.

One thing is certain: Edison was not motivated by money, otherwise he would have taken the cash and returned to the sanctuary of his West Orange home and laboratory. Battles in the "war of the currents" raged on throughout 1889 and culminated with an article Edison wrote for the November 1889 *The North American Review*, titled, ironically enough, "The Dangers of Electric Lighting," in which he wrote ...

> *The electric-lighting company with which I am connected purchased some time ago the patents for a complete alternating system, and my protest against this action can be found upon its minute book. Up to the present time I*

have succeeded in inducing them not to offer this system
to the public, nor will they ever do so with my consent.
My personal desire would be to prohibit entirely the use of
alternating currents. They are unnecessary as they are
dangerous.

Westinghouse responded to Edison's biting criticism the following month in the same journal. In his article, titled "A Reply to Mr. Edison," Westinghouse addressed every issue Edison's article raised, in great detail and in terms laymen could understand. In closing, Westinghouse pointed out that for alternating-current systems were out-selling Edison's by a five to one margin.

Defeat seemed imminent, but Edison and his ranks had a plan that in just a few minutes would wipe away all of the progress Westinghouse and his camp had made in convincing the public that alternating currents were safe, and were outselling Edison's. The plan was simple: Have the first person ever electrocuted put to death with alternating currents generated by Westinghouse dynamos. The idea had grown out of the June 4, 1888, passage of legislation in New York making the electric chair the preferred method of execution. However, since AC and DC designs of the electric chair were being considered, a committee had to decide which form to use. Edison vigorously lobbied for the selection of alternating current, knowing that the publicity following the execution would destroy public confidence in Westinghouse's system.

To assist with his plan, Edison hired an inventor, Harold P. Brown, who had authored a letter printed in *The New York Post* describing the death of a young man after he came into contact with an exposed wire running on alternating current, to design an electric chair for use with alternating current. Brown's assistant was Dr. Fred Peterson, who happened to be the leader of the deciding committee. In this powerful position, Peterson was able to sway the opinion of committee members in favor of AC current. The fact that Peterson was still on Edison's payroll when the committee made its official announcement must not have hurt.

Brown secretly purchased three Westinghouse dynamos and sold them to authorities at the Auburn State Prison, commonly known as Sing Sing. Now all that was needed was a prisoner.

The crime of the first man ever executed by electric chair was rather commonplace. Late on the night of March 26, 1888, William Kemmler, who lived in an apartment in the poor part of Buffalo, New York, returned home from a drinking spree in a quarrelsome mood. His common-law wife, Tillie Ziegler, was waiting for him in the same condition. A fight erupted, and Kemmler silenced his wife with an axe. Caught red-handed, he never showed remorse. Kemmler's trial started on May 6, 1889, and ended four days later with a conviction. He was sentenced to death by electrocution during the week of June 24, 1889.

As Brown conducted public demonstrations of a Westinghouse dynamo at West Orange by electrocuting dogs, cats, and horses, among other unfortunate creatures, Kemmler's lawyers filed a series of appeals—paid for by Westinghouse—arguing that the means of execution was "cruel and unusual punishment." A hearing was conducted in which the leading men in the science of electricity testified—including Thomas Alva Edison. Questioning him was Deputy Attorney General Poste of New York, who, after inquiring as to Edison's background and his knowledge of alternating current, finally asked, "In your judgment, can an artificial electric current be generated and applied in such a manner as to produce death in human beings in every case?"

Edison responded, "Yes."

During cross-examination, W. Bourke Cockran, one of Kemmler's attorneys, asked Edison, "What would be the effect of the current on Kemmler in case the current was applied for five or six minutes? Would he be carbonized?"

"No," Edison answered, "He would be mummified. All the water in his body would evaporate."

When asked to state for the record whether he believed, or knew based on fact, that one thousand volts of one-ampere current was ten times the amount need to execute someone using a Westinghouse dynamo, Edison stated, "From belief. I never killed anybody."

Kemmler's execution was set for five o'clock in the morning of August 6, 1890. The judge invited twenty-one individuals to witness the execution. Edison was extended an invitation, but he did not accept. At four o'clock on the morning of the execution an estimated five hundred people stood outside the Auburn State Prison. Kemmler was escorted to the death chamber and took his seat in the electric chair. As the domed cap through which the current would enter his body was strapped on his freshly shaven head, Kemmler turned to the prison's warden and said, "Now take your time and do it all right, warden. There is no rush. I don't want to take any chances on this thing, you know."

Preparations finished, the warden and his associates stepped back. Kemmler nodded his head. Feeling that the device on his head was loose, he said, "Warden, just make that a little tighter. We want every thing all right, you know."

The warden did so, then took his place at a safe distance saying, "Good-bye, William."

The event was described the next day on the front page of *The New York Times*, under the headline, "Far Worse Than Hanging." The agony suffered by Kemmler as the alternating current ran through his body was described in great detail. At 6:43 that morning, the attending physician pronounced Kemmler dead. The men in the room breathed a sigh of relief, "the great strain was over." Then someone in the room noticed that Kemmler's chest was lifting and falling. Men cried out for the current to be turned on once again. Warden Durston, who was already removing the domed hat from Kemmler's head, quickly reversed his actions. Upon examination of the body, the doctor turned to the warden and asked that the current be turned on once again without delay.

"Again," *The New York Times* reporter wrote, "the body of the unconscious wretch in the chair became rigid as one of bronze. It was awful, and the witnesses were so horrified by the ghastly sight that they could not take their eyes off it."

Exactly how long the current was kept on the second time is not known, but this time when it was turned off there was no doubt that Kemmler was dead. When asked to comment on the botched execution, Westinghouse responded, "I do not care to talk about it. It has been a brutal affair. They could have done better with an axe."

But the executions did not create the negative response Edison sought. Electrocution became the standard in New York and soon spread to other states. As Robert Silverberg wrote in his Edison biography, *Light for the World*, "... Edison had gone too far now to back down. All his prestige was pledged to direct current. Out of bitterness and testiness he had elevated his original shortsightedness to the status of an inflexible policy; it was the worst mistake of his career."

In the end, Edison's campaign against alternating current might have swayed the opinions of laypersons, but those in the industry had no doubt that the future would be powered by alternating current because of the tremendous savings the system offered.

> *Alternating current made possible our modern system of centralized power plants with large AC generators sending power over long distances. This is the root of the current problem in California, where large numbers of people depend on power made far away. If Edison had prevailed, local power production and consumption would be the norm. With the development of small, natural gas-powered fuel cell systems, something much more like Edison's pattern is emerging. There are some very high-voltage DC lines in the world. For example, in Russia, there are huge copper plates buried in the ground to put the return path through the earth so there can be a complete circuit. That means there are rivers of electricity flowing through the ground.*

In the years that followed, Edison General Electric merged with Thomson-Houston, a competitor that had switched to alternating current systems in the early years of its introduction: The resulting company was known as General Electric, which specialized in the sale of alternating current systems. Edison was granted a seat on the board of directors. He attended one meeting in August 1892 and never went back, later stating, "I may not be held responsible for the acts of an organization in which my voice is but one amongst a great many. I will not go on the board of a company that I don't control."

Edison's role in the industry he had founded was at an end. Yet when the dust cleared, the forty-five-year-old Edison seemed no worse for the experience. His success had provided him with what he always wanted: a laboratory and home that were second to none. Edison had always pushed himself forward, leaving the trappings of his life behind him once they had served their purpose. Now, he was settled. He would spend the rest of his life at the West Orange Laboratory and his Glenmont mansion, with his wife Mina and their children.

During the "war of the currents," another war had been building to a climax, this one over the invention that had transformed Edison into a wizard, his phonograph. Like the one waged over Edison's lighting system, this war was started when Edison felt threatened by someone trying to further perfect an invention that he had originated. Not one to back down from a fight, unless the price was right, Edison stood ready to defend what was his, and his alone.

Chapter 10

The Rebirth of Edison's Phonograph

I have more respect for a fellow with a single idea who gets there than for the fellow with a thousand ideas who does nothing.

—*Thomas Alva Edison*

While the "war of the currents" was in its early stages, Edison's creative energy was centered primarily on the invention that first made his name a household word: the phonograph. Left idle for over nine years, the phonograph was all but forgotten by Edison, whose time had been consumed with his lighting system. When he did return to it in 1886, it was because others had approached him asking for permission to sell an improved model called the "graphophone."

The graphophone had been "perfected" at Alexander Graham Bell's Volta Laboratory, a facility made possible by the fifty thousand francs awarded Bell in 1880 by the French government as part of the "Volta" prize for his invention of the telephone. There were only two noticeable differences between the phonograph and the graphophone, nurtured by Bell's cousin, Chichester Bell, a chemist, and Charles S. Tainter, a technician. The most obvious alteration was the surface on which a recording was made. On Edison's model, a long rectangular piece of tin foil was wrapped around a brass cylinder and a stylus "indenting" sound onto the tin foil made a recording. On the graphophone, the cylinder was cardboard, with coats of wax on which the stylus "engraved" the sound. A second difference was that on the phonograph, the stylus was always in contact with the recording surface, while on the graphophone, the stylus only "engraved" onto the wax cylinder when the sound caused it to do so.

The differences were slight, but significant enough that the United States Patent Office issued Chichester Bell and Tainter a patent in May 1886. There was little Edison could do to challenge the patent; his British patent on the phonograph had expired in 1885, and court practice at the time was to terminate American rights when European rights expired. Characteristically, when Edison heard of the patent for Bell and Tainter's graphophone, he chose to settle the matter by competing with the graphophone in the marketplace. He selected Ezra Gilliland, who had introduced him to his second wife and with whom he had been conducting wireless telegraphy experiments, to assist him in developing an improved phonograph.

While waiting for their patent to be granted, Bell and Tainter formed the Volta Graphophone Company to manufacture their device, but once the patent was awarded, rather than begin production, they decided to present the graphophone to Edison in person, hoping to convince him to join their endeavor. The Edison name would bring prestige and credibility to the product—and the Edison Speaking Phonograph Company, formed in early 1878, still existed, if only on paper. Gardiner Hubbard, Alexander Graham Bell's father-in-law, owned stock in the company and was still waiting to see a return on his investment. Perhaps a reorganization of the old company into one formed by Bell, Tainter, and Edison was in order; then again, maybe the time had come to put an end to the company altogether. Either way, Edison had to be consulted.

From the outset of their discussion, Bell and Tainter told Edison that they knew that he was "the real inventor of the talking machine." Most of their work, they admitted, was nothing but "refinement of Edison's ideas." Now that they felt their work was finished, they wanted to present to Edison their results "without any public announcements that would indicate the creation of conflicting interests." If Edison examined their work and found something unsatisfactory, they would finance his experiments to correct the problem. When Edison felt the product was ready to be produced and marketed, Bell and Tainter would take up these costs, as well. If Edison agreed, he would receive fifty percent in all profits, and the name "graphophone" would be dropped in favor of "phonograph."

Edison flatly rejected the proposal. A few months later, Edison's English representative, Colonel George Gouraud, who Edison had met in April 1873, while in London to demonstrate the automatic telegraph, wrote Edison informing him that he had been offered a position as the head of the British arm of the Volta Graphophone Company. Gouraud carefully positioned himself as looking out for Edison's interests, negotiating with Volta Graphophone Company officials about the possible use of his name and about securing stock for Edison in the new company at no cost. Gouraud also mentioned that he had heard that Edison was "occupied in some experiments upon the Phonograph," and asked if this was true so that he could use the information while bargaining with Volta Graphophone officials. Edison was furious. In his one-paragraph response to Gouraud he wrote:

> Under no circumstance will I have anything to do with Graham Bell with his phonograph pronounced <u>backward</u> graphophone. I have better apparatus and am already building the factory to manufacture and I not only propose to flood England with them at <u>factory prices</u> but I shall come out with a strong letter the moment they attempt to float the Co. They are a bunch of pirates!

Edison's refusal to do business with Bell and Tainter was rooted in pride. After all, Edison had brought perfection to the inventions of others—not the other way around. The only reason the phonograph had not evolved into a marketable product was because he had not had the time to devote to the invention. Edison must have scared Gouraud into thinking that he had lost Edison's trust and friendship, because he immediately wrote that he would drop the whole affair "like a hot potato" if Edison gave him exclusive rights to market his new and improved phonograph in Europe. Edison did not respond. Two months later, Gouraud was in America; he did not return home until he had what he came for: exclusive rights to market the phonograph overseas.

As was his practice, Edison turned to the press, not only bringing attention to planned improvements for his phonograph, but also using the media to publicize his new West Orange Laboratory. A move no doubt meant to lure potential investors in future projects. *The New York Post*, one of several newspapers to feature stories on Edison's new laboratory and phonograph, praised the facility for being "the most perfect physical and chemical experimental laboratory in the world," and featured the phonograph as one in a number of projects that Edison was currently investigating. In discussing the phonograph, Edison stated that the invention had never been far from his thoughts. "When resting from prolonged work upon the light," Edison added, "my brain would revert almost automatically to the old idea." However, after concentrating on the phonograph for the previous eight months, he announced that he hoped to have five hundred improved phonographs ready to sell by January, stressing that the device was ideal for business purposes, but also mentioning the instrument as being perfect for recording music and books.

Edison leased a building in Bloomfield, just north of West Orange, where his phonograph could be manufactured. Gilliland was placed in charge of the endeavor, and granted the rights to sell the phonograph in North America. His salary would be fifteen percent of what he sold. Capital to support the endeavor was raised by the formation of the Edison Phonograph Company. The new company would be formed with patents granted for his new and improved phonograph. In creating this new company, the patent rights held by the Edison Speaking Phonograph Company—the original phonograph company formed ten years earlier—thus became obsolete. As a slap in the face to shareholders in the original company, whom Edison believed had supported Bell and Tainter's work in improving his phonograph, Edison offered them four thousand shares in the new company, which meant that not only had they paid for stock in the original company, for which they had never seen a return, but they were now being asked to pay yet again for stock in a new company. Knowing that Edison's treatment of Gardiner, Hubbard, and the rest of the original investors would bring bad publicity and not look good in the eyes of potential investors, Edward Johnson, Edison's trusted assistant, pleaded with him to reconsider the formation of the new company and meet with Hubbard and his associates to hammer out a new agreement, even form a new company, to bring peace to the situation. "Recognize," Johnson wrote, "the error committed in so ignominiously setting aside those who have had Pride, Hope and Faith locked up in the Phonograph for the past ten years ...."

Edison ignored Johnson's attempt at reconciliation. If the original stockholders wanted to take the matter to court that was their prerogative. If they wanted to buy stock in the new Edison Phonograph Company, they were free to do that as well. As far as Edison was concerned, he would continue down his chosen path.

Edison's new and improved phonograph was dramatically different from his original in a number of ways. On the original model, a recording was made on a piece of tin-foil wrapped around a brass cylinder. The brass cylinder had a continuous groove from one side of the cylinder to the other. To make a recording, a person spoke into a diaphragm. A stylus attached to the bottom of the diaphragm was set so that it came into contact with the tin-foil underneath, vibrating up and down with the sound waves of the person's voice. As the hand crank was turned, the stylus followed the continuous grove etched into the cylinder, where the vibration of the stylus left a series of indentations. If the tin-foil was removed from the cylinder, it would be impossible to realign the recording on the tin-foil with the groves etched into the cylinder. It also meant that if too many recordings were made on the same piece of tin-foil, it would wear out.

Edison changed his recording medium to tin-foil wrapped around a cylinder made of thick cardboard coated with a plumbago-stearite compound. He also adapted his phonograph so that the cylinder could be removed and played back on another phonograph. Further improvements called for a small DC motor powered by two wet cell Bunsen batteries to rotate the cylinder, eliminating the need for a hand crank, transforming the invention from a mechanical device to an electrical one. Finally, a foot pedal, when pressed, allowed the cylinder to automatically "rewind" itself, which allowed people transcribing messages to go back and hear it once again.

By March 22, 1888, Edison felt confident enough to invite a group of New York bankers to West Orange Laboratory for a demonstration of the model, hoping they would invest in his new enterprise. Not one to take chances, an hour before the demonstration Edison re-tested the instrument: It was ready. However, as his audience sat watching in Edison's fine library, the device did not work. The New York bankers left without hearing a single word from Edison's new and improved model. That afternoon Edison found that John Ott, a machinist who had been with him since his days in Newark, had replaced the diaphragm and stylus attached underneath with a different model. Unfortunately, Ott replaced the part with a diaphragm which contained the stylus from an older model, and the diaphragm to which it was attached was not pliable enough to vibrate when sound waves bounced off of it. Learning of what had happened, Edison tried in vain to get the New York bankers to come back for a second demonstration; they never did.

It was probably best that they didn't. For the rest of the spring, Edison made further modifications and improvements. From Bell and Tainter, he "borrowed" their idea of a cardboard cylinder coated with layers of wax, which allowed for a recording to be saved. He also added an original feature that allowed the wax to be "shaved" in order to make a new recording. This meant that the same wax cylinder could be used a number of times. From Bell and Tainter, he also "borrowed" the idea of what he referred to as a "floating" stylus. This meant that the stylus attached to the bottom of a diaphragm did not come into contact with the wax cylinder underneath unless made to do so by sound waves. He also replaced his battery-powered motor with an electric motor.

In April, while making these changes to his phonograph, Edison learned that Bell and Tainter had sold their Volta Graphophone Company to Jesse W. Lippincott, a millionaire from Pittsburgh who had made his fortune producing and selling glass tumblers. After purchasing the company from Bell and Tainter,

Lippoincott renamed the business American Graphophone Company. May brought word of Tesla's presentation before the American Institute of Electrical Engineers on the subject of his "alternate current motor." And the first of three children was born to Edison and his second wife, a girl they named Madelaine.

Lippincott's, American Graphophone Company wasted little time introducing its model in June 1888. Hearing the news, on June 11 Edison sequestered his top assistants in a room of his West Orange laboratory and informed them that they would not leave until they had brought his phonograph up to his standards. Word of Edison's round-the-clock endeavor to further perfect his phonograph soon reached newspaper reporters, who descended on the facility. However, they were not allowed inside, which gave the proceedings a flare of the dramatic.

> Throughout his life Edison returned to the phonograph in an effort to further perfect what he considered his most favorite invention. When asked in 1921, at the age of seventy-four, why he did this, he responded, "Many inventions are not suitable for the people at large because of their carelessness. Before a thing can be marketed to the masses, it must be made practically foolproof. Its operation must be made extremely simple. That is one reason, I think, why the phonograph has been so universally adopted. Even a child can operate it."

A few days later, Edison emerged and had his photograph taken with the perfected phonograph. The Edison Phonograph Company used the image of the exhausted Edison slumping next to his baby in their advertising campaign. The nickname "Napoleon of Inventors" was reborn—in the photograph, Edison looked a lot like the Little General.

Before going public with the invention, Edison and Gilliland demonstrated the phonograph on May 12 for the New York Electric Club. To prevent a reoccurrence of the fiasco with the New York City bankers, ten instruments were brought along. Twelve days later, the phonograph's ability to record music was demonstrated on the third floor of the laboratory. H. H. Rosenfield, a popular composer, played an organ and a piano. Both presentations were a success.

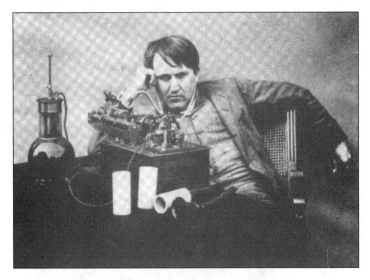

Edison as he appeared after working several days nonstop to perfect his phonograph at his West Orange Laboratory.

(© *Courtesy of Edison National Historic Site*)

Ready to introduce his "wonder of the ages" to the masses, Edison wrote an article titled "The Perfected Phonograph" for the *North American Review* of June 1888. Edison served notice to his competitors that he was prepared to fight for what was his, and pointed out, as he had done after installing his lighting system in New York City, that he was a man of his word.

Rumors, I understand, have been circulated to the effect that ... I allowed the phonograph to go adrift leaving its further development to chance and to the tender mercies of such interested persons, not connected with me, as might conceive that they were doing me a favor by claiming to having developed my idea. Those who have been taken in by these rumors would do well to inform themselves concerning the prolonged labor involved in carrying out important inventions.

As with the introduction of Edison's original phonograph eleven years earlier, newspapers around the country carried news of the newly perfected device. The *New York Herald's* headline read, "The Wizard Completes His Phonograph," and the *Philadelphia Ledger,* declared, "The Phonograph Perfected." Demonstrations were held at fairs and at exhibit halls. Some exhibits featured a recording of Edison's voice explaining how the machine worked. Most stories claimed that Edison had "been experimenting and perfecting the instrument" for the past ten years, and quoted Edison asserting that, "I don't want the phonograph sold for amusement purposes. It is not a toy. I want it sold for business purposes only."

In England, Gouraud demonstrated the phonograph on a daily basis at his office in downtown London, aptly called Edison House. The presentation featured a recording of Edison explaining how the instrument operated. Then came a speech from Prime Minister William Gladstone, then Robert Browning reciting his poem "How They Brought the Good News from Ghent to Aix." Just two lines into the poem, Browning stopped, apologized for forgetting the poem, then started again, but still could not remember the poem. He then apologized again, saying, "I am exceedingly sorry that I can't remember my own verses: but one thing that I shall remember all my life is the astonishing sensation produced by your wonderful invention."

Even before Edison completed his efforts, Lippincott had shown an interest in purchasing the Edison Phonograph Company in order to merge it with his company under the name North American Phonograph Company. In this way, he would control the patents for the phonograph and the graphophone, as well as do away with having to compete with Edison in the marketplace. Edison was interested since Bell and Tainter were out of the picture and would receive no benefits from the merger. At the same time, Edison stood a chance to make a great deal of money that could be used to fund his other ongoing projects. He had his close friend Gilliland and John Tomlinson, his new personal attorney, negotiate with Lippincott. After a number of meetings in the spring of 1888, Lippincott offered $500,000 for the enterprise, one-fourth payable within two months of signing the contract and the rest due within four months. Edison would also retain the right to manufacture the phonograph for fifteen years, with a five percent royalty on all units sold. Tomlinson presented the offer to Edison, stressing the financial freedom it would provide. Edison rejected it, insisting that the monetary compensation be raised to $1,000,000, keeping the right to manufacture the phonograph and the five percent royalty. Lippincott refused to budge. Tomlinson advised Edison that the offer was fair and honest, and that he should accept.

Ten days later, Edison agreed to the original offer, but what he did not know was that Gilliland had also sold Lippincott the North American rights to sell Edison's phonograph. Gilliland would receive $50,000 up front and $200,000 worth of stock options in Lippincott's newly formed North American Phonograph Company. Out of his share, Gilliland promised to pay Tomlinson $75,000 for serving as his attorney. In order to avoid potential lawsuits, Lippincott also paid the remaining stockholders in the original phonograph company $250,000 for their stock in the dormant enterprise. The day after the transaction was completed on August 31, 1888, Gilliland and Tomilson left for Europe with their families to promote Edison's phonograph. Before their departure, Tomlinson asked for, and received, $7,000 from Edison for expenses incurred while working on his behalf.

> When, two months later, it came time for Lippincott to pay Edison the first installment, he could not, because of a cash flow problem and the tremendous amount of money paid to Gilliland and the original stockholders. Trying to buy himself time, he paid Edison a visit. At first, he spoke only of his predicament, but soon revealed the sum of money he had paid Gilliland for the North American rights to sell the phonograph. It upset Edison that his trusted friend Gilliland had not told him of the transaction, and he was even more upset that Gilliland felt that the rights were his to sell. Though legally not true, Edison never felt it was ethical.
> On September 11, 1888, he sent a telegram to Gilliland in Europe informing him that he was no longer his European representative for the phonograph and that he was canceling his employment. He further advised Gilliland to turn over

> to him all monies paid to him by Lippincott. If Gilliland did
> not do so, Edison threatened a lawsuit.

Two days later Gilliland responded that he had always been loyal to Edison and that he was returning to America as soon as possible to clear the air.

Edison never did talk to Gilliland on his return, or ever again. Tomlinson was fired and his reputation suffered. Edison filed a lawsuit against the two men, but when they were able to show that they had done nothing to break their agreement with Edison, the case was dismissed. This episode proved to be a turning point in Edison's life and his relationships with employees he considered his equal, or otherwise, for the remainder of his life. As Edison's eldest daughter from his first marriage, Marion, later recalled, the episode left her father brokenhearted, to the point that he even stated afterwards that he "would never again trust anyone." Edison never again formed a close relationship with a business associate or in his personal life until he met Henry Ford in August 1896.

After all was said and done, Lippincott and Edison made arrangements for Edison to be paid the amount owed him, and even though he did not necessarily care to do business with Lippincott anymore, Edison had to manufacture his phonograph for the man based on the contract they had signed. Of course, Edison could have tried to fight the contract in court, but Gilliland's arrangement with Lippincott was perfectly legal. At least in manufacturing the instrument for Lippincott, Edison was making money, and able to ensure the quality of the product. Most importantly, he still had some control of the invention that he considered, more than any other, to be truly his.

To manufacture the phonograph, Edison constructed a building near his West Orange Laboratory. He employed hundreds of men, and even more when he leased a nearby building to produce wooden cabinets to house the device. Edison's plan for using the space around the laboratory for manufacturing inventions deemed worthy was becoming a reality.

Under Lippincott's management, subsidiary companies were established around the country to market both the graphophone and the phonograph primarily to businesses. The instruments were leased, not sold, at a price ranging from forty to sixty dollars a year. The phonograph outsold the graphophone fifty to one.

Edison's "perfected" phonograph was not, however, without fault. Businessmen complained that it needed constant adjusting and depending on a person's voice was sometimes not very clear. Of course, the problem lay in articulation and enunciation; nonetheless, Edison developed a hose-like device that connected to the diaphragm and had a funnel-like opening on the other end in which a person spoke. This greatly increased the focus of sound waves beyond the cone-like funnel that had been in use since the original phonograph was discovered. Edison, because of the proximity of his laboratory and manufacturing facilities, was able to quickly find solutions to such defects and introduce them to the market within a month.

Even with this ability to react to, and make modifications to the phonograph immediately, the instrument's use as a business tool never blossomed. Of the companies founded to lease them to businesses, only the Colombia Phonograph Company of Washington, D.C., forerunner of the Colombia Broadcasting Company, fared well, leasing instruments to governmental agencies.

The poor overall performance of the phonograph as a business tool left Lippincott in thousands of dollars of debt to Edison for phonographs that had already been delivered. Matters grew worse after Lippincott suffered a paralyzing stroke. Edison had little choice but to assume control of the company, the debt owed to him being secured by Lippincott's controlling stock.

In 1894, Edison placed the North American Phonograph Company in bankruptcy, which enabled him to purchase the rights to his phonograph. As part of the legal proceedings, the company was barred from doing business in the United States for two years while lawsuits against Lippincott were settled. This did not apply to sales overseas, where the phonograph's use for entertainment soared. It also did little to stop the appearance in 1895 of the Edison Spring Motor Phonograph in America.

As far as Bell and Tainter's graphophone was concerned, because of the way Lippincott had structured contracts with various dealers, the rights remained unclear until the Columbia

Phonograph Company gained control of the American Graphophone Company in 1896. The American Graphophone Company was the original company that Lippincott had founded after purchasing the rights to the graphophone from Bell and Tainter. Apparently, the company had remained solvent, at least on paper, and had maintained control of the patent rights to the graphophone. When this was discovered, Columbia Phonograph purchased the company and filed a lawsuit preventing Edison from using their patents. However, since the graphophone relied just as much on innovations introduced by Edison, the two companies agreed to license their patents to each other in December 1896. The following year, his two-year moratorium placed on his doing business in America over, Edison founded the National Phonograph Company, which could now "officially" manufacture the Edison Spring Motor Phonograph. This was followed by the introduction of the Edison Standard Phonograph in 1898, the first to carry Edison's trademark signature on the instrument's cabinet. Prices ranged anywhere from $20 for the Standard to $7.50 for the Gem, introduced in 1899.

> *Even before Edison realized that his phonograph's future lay in entertainment, he approved the manufacture of the world's first talking doll, containing a simplified phonograph. The cylinder on which the doll's words were recorded was mounted on a screw-threaded shaft turned by a hand-crank in the doll's back. An army of women recorded the dolls' words, day after day uttering "Little Bo-Peep," "Jack and Jill," or "Mary Had a Little Lamb" into a mouthpiece. At the peak of the dolls' popularity, over five hundred were produced a day, but by 1890 there were reoccurring problems with the phonograph inside. Edison and his associates were less concerned that the dolls went out of fashion than that so many had been sold: They feared that fathers, having seen them fail, would decide not to lease a phonograph for the workplace.*

The phonograph's transition from a business tool to a device for entertainment saved the industry and the invention. In what seemed to be a contradiction of his previous statements, Edison went on record saying, "It has always been my idea that one of the greatest fields for the phonograph was in the households for reproducing all that is best in oratory and music, but I have never got any one to believe it until lately."

To meet this expanding niche in the marketplace, Edison produced recordings of selected songs and stories, thousands of which were sold in the years to come. In order to make the recordings interchangeable, a standard for the cylinder had to be set. It was decided that the cylinder should be two inches in diameter and four inches in length. A recording was made on wax made sturdy by a liquid additive developed in the laboratory, which gave the wax a brown color. Recordings were then packaged inside a thin cardboard cylinder with an ornate label featuring Edison's signature.

One drawback to the phonograph was that each recording had to be individually created. An entertainer had to stand in front of a phonograph and sing the same song over and over. However, in 1901, a process was developed whereby molds could be cast of an original. These molds were coated with a protective layer of a thin, metallic substance. From these "stepped-down" originals, one hundred twenty to one hundred fifty recordings could be produced. By 1904 the process of recording was so economical that recordings sold for thirty-five cents apiece. The innovation was one of many that would follow in the coming years.

> At the outset of the recording industry, the diaphragm was unable to capture the nuances of certain instruments, such as a violin. Brass instruments did not have this problem, so early entertainment recordings were often of marching bands. A model of the phonograph that used a spring-driven motor was also introduced. It was a simplified version consisting mainly of a diaphragm with stylus and the rod that held a recording in place.

Aside from marketing recordings directly to the public, phonograph "parlors" were established throughout the country. For a fee ranging anywhere from a nickel to a quarter, a customer selected from over one hundred and fifty recordings, then listened to the piece through a set of "ear horns." The Pacific Phonograph in San Francisco generated profits by modifying instruments into coin-operated machines and placing them in public areas such as saloons. The process was patented by Louis Glass, the firm's owner, who sold the rights to Felix Gottschalk, secretary of the Metropolitan Phonograph Company in New York City. Gottschalk then founded the Automatic Phonograph Exhibition Company and, with Edison's assistance, further perfected the innovation.

Competitors introduced further improvements in the years to come, the most dramatic of which was Emile Berliner's "gramophone," the forerunner of the Victor Talking Machine, whose trademark was an attentive terrier named Nipper listening to "his master's voice." Berliner's invention differed because the stylus traveled laterally across a flat disk of hard rubber. The discs were cheaper to produce and easy to duplicate from a zinc master. Berliner had invented his gramophone in 1887, but it posed no threat to Edison's phonograph until the early 1900s when improvements made it possible for the device to record programs of more than four minutes, almost double that of Edison's phonograms. The revolutionary design became the industry standard—except for Edison, who did not follow suit until 1913, twenty-six years later.

The inventor who never thought of himself as a businessman had regained full control of his phonograph and the company that sold it. Before all was said and done, he even marketed two instruments for use in the workplace: the transophone and the telescribe. The transophone featured a button that automatically rewound the device when a secretary or clerk was trying to transcribe a recording and the telescribe allowed telephone conversations to be recorded.

The rebirth of Edison's phonograph brought attention to Edison and to his newly established West Orange laboratory just as it had his laboratory in Menlo Park. In time, the invention and the entertainment recordings manufactured by Edison would bring him untold riches, and give the public a form of entertainment that lasts in one form or another to this day. For the moment, Edison would turn his full attention to the question of iron-ore milling. On the second floor of his laboratory, secret experiments were being conducted for a new invention that would rival even the phonograph. However, Edison would spend the coming years in the mining business.

Chapter 11

Edison's Greatest Folly

*Spilled milk dont interest me. I have spilled lots of it, and
while I have always felt it for a few days, it is quickly
forgotten.*

—*Thomas Alva Edison*

Throughout the period when Edison was involved in the "war
of the currents" and the introduction of his improved phonograph, he had been conducting research and developing a plan for
his next project involving the mining and milling of iron ore. As
with a number of Edison's projects that were left to sit idle, this one
too had been left unfinished.

He had first become interested in iron ore in the early 1880s
when he discovered that the cost of iron ore used in manufacturing his dynamos was exceedingly high. Companies were forced to
pay a high price for iron ore because by this time the eastern iron
mines were nearly depleted, and regional mills that depended on
these mines now had to rely on the mines of northern Michigan,
where the Marquette Iron Range had been in service for thirty
years, as well as the new mines on the Menominee Range.
However, shipping Michigan iron ore to eastern mills was considerably more expensive than shipping it to newly opened mills west
of the Alleghenies, and long-standing eastern companies were
finding it increasingly hard to compete.

In 1810, an estimated one thousand tons of steel were manufactured in the United States. By 1850, production rose to a modest six thousand tons a year. With the invention of the Bessemer process which used a blast of air to burn impurities out of molten pig iron and the development of the Lake Superior iron-ore ranges, the United States became the leader in world steel production. In 1900, 556 pounds of steel were manufactured for each individual in the United States. By the 1960s, this number rose to 1,275 pounds per person.

As Edison developed and installed his lighting system in New York City, he kept looking for a solution to the high cost of iron ore. Edison had always found breakthroughs that others missed. Continually observing the world around him and paying close attention to his experimental work His exploration of iron ore would prove no different.

On a fishing trip with his men in the spring of 1880, Edison noticed black particles stretching for miles along a section of beach located in Quogue, Long Island. Gathering a handful of the material, he returned to his laboratory and found that the particles were magnetic iron. Edison's worries were over—there were "hundreds of thousands of tons" of iron ore waiting to be harvested on that sandy Long Island beach!

In his caveat for the invention for harvesting this iron ore, dated April 3, 1880, Edison claimed that he had "invented a new and useful Improvement in the Magnetic Separation of Substances." Edison wrote that it would separate magnetic particles from nonmagnetic particles with a simple, cost-effective method. A large amount of material would be dumped down a hopper, streaming past a magnet just strong enough to draw the magnetic particles into one container, while the nonmagnetic particles fell into another. Edison had conducted various experiments in 1879 using magnets to separate platinum from a variety of ores in the hope of finding an economical way to extract the material from the earth and use as a filament. Over the year that followed his failed experiments with platinum, Edison continued to experiment with removing metals such as gold, silver, and lead from a variety of ores and rocks. He hadn't considered registering a patent until he came across the iron-ore particles on the beach. Once his caveat was filed with the patent office, he founded the Edison Ore-Milling Company to use what he aptly named, the "iron-ore separator."

It took Edison approximately a year to make adjustments to the invention. Most changes focused on creating an effective magnetic field that separated the iron ore from rocks . Finally ready in the spring of 1881, Edison set up a small plant on the Long Island beach to test out his theories on a much grander scale. By October, it was decided that a commercial plant would be opened in Quonocontang Beach, Rhode Island. While productive, the plant never did build up a clientele; most of the furnaces owned by interested companies were not able to produce the heat needed to smelt the tiny particles being recovered. Having spent a relatively small amount of money on the project, and with work on his lighting system taking up much of his attention, Edison let the venture slip into dormancy.

Between 1880 and 1885, Edison continued designing a variety of crushing and separating machines. He concluded that the only economical means by which his vision of iron-ore separation could occur was on a colossal scale. Research had also shown that it was cheaper to quarry low-grade ores than mine high-grade veins. Of course, this meant that thousands of tons of material would have to be handled on a daily basis, which called for holding down costs as much as possible.

To this end, Edison designed a totally automated system. Visiting plants of soon-to-be competitors, Edison noticed that men were required to carry out almost every aspect of the process, from blasting the rock off the side of the mountain to loading material on railroad cars for shipment to the refinery. Under Edison's system, dynamite would rip huge chunks of rock from the earth. The gigantic boulders would be loaded by a giant steam shovel onto a railroad car that transported them to the crushing mill. Once there, the stones would drop onto two gigantic rollers powerful enough to reduce the piano-sized boulders down to rocks the size of a man's head. A series of steps would reduce the rocks to a fine powder, then drop it in a stream through a magnetized field. The magnets would extract the iron ore and allow unwanted material to fall through, where it would be gathered and sold as fill-dirt. The iron-ore particles would then be formed into briquettes with a consistent iron-ore content. The briquettes would be loaded onto a railroad car by a conveyor belt.

Thus far, Edison's career had followed a natural progression. His job as a candy butcher led him to selling newspapers; from newspapers he turned to publishing and a deeper understanding of telegraphy; his years as a telegrapher prepared him for his move to Boston and New York City, where success made possible his Newark factory, which provided him with the income to establish his Menlo Park laboratory. At Menlo Park, his continued work in telegraphy, specifically with his embossing telegraph repeater, led to the invention of the phonograph. The phonograph laid the foundation in Edison's mind for a project he would turn to years later, the motion-picture camera. Of course, the progression of Edison's career was made possible by his constant willingness to reinvest his earnings in his profession, resulting in greater monetary gains at each level. Edison had reached the pinnacle in 1889 when, for all practical purposes, he was bought out of the electrical industry in exchange for $1,750,000 plus stock in the newly formed Edison General Electric. The stock and money would have made for a nice retirement, but the forty-one-year-old Edison would use the money, at least a large percentage of it, as he always had: to support his work and his continuing self-education. Edison was now free to pursue his iron-ore research. So enthused was Edison about his newest undertaking that he confided to a friend: "I am going to do something now so different and so much bigger than anything I've ever done before that people will forget my name ever was connected with anything electrical."

Prior to this time, Edison's ability to implement his ideas regarding iron-ore milling was limited by cost and time. With the sale of his electrical concerns, however, he had both at his disposal. If he could interest others in investing in his new enterprise so much the better. He returned to the project prepared to test theories that had fermented on paper for years. Edison surveyed the state of the industry and discovered that conditions were just as bad as they had been in the early 1880s. This was all he needed to know; he determined to undertake the venture in an effort to reduce the price of iron ore for manufacturers east of the Alleghenies—and add to his fortune.

Edison's plans called for the licensing to mining companies of his iron-ore separator manufactured by an Edison owned plant. To reduce competition amongst licensees, the rights to regions across the United States would also be licensed. Walter Mallory, a friend of the Millers, whom Edison had met years before, led the first group of investors in securing the rights to Michigan, Wisconsin, and Minnesota. To fund the project, the Edison Iron Concentrating Company was organized. Investing in Mallory's undertaking were Edison; his father-in-law, Lewis Miller; his brother-in-law, Ira Miller; and Mallory's father. The first order of business was for the company to construct a pilot plant, to identify potential problems with Edison's designs before building a full-scale plant. In surveying potential sites, Mallory and his group erected their plant in Humboldt, Michigan, and construction was started in the fall of 1888.

While work continued on the Mallory plant, on December 27, 1888, Edison formed the New Jersey and Pennsylvania Concentrating Works (NJPCW) with capital stock of thirty thousand dollars, an amount that would grow considerably as the venture went from bad to worse. Not wanting to do business with Wall Street investors because of their incessant cries of wanting things done their way, Edison turned to investors whom he knew personally. Edison contributed ten thousand dollars, while Robert and Walter Cutting, two brothers who had invested in his lighting company come in for five thousand dollars each. Making up the difference was Charles Batchelor, Samuel Insull, Alfred O'Tate, Joseph Hutchinson, and Harry Livor. Selected as the site for their pilot plant was Bechtelsville, Pennsylvania, where work was started on March 1889.

Meanwhile, the month before, the Mallory plant was placed into operation after several months of construction. From the beginning, problems arose in a number of the steps in the process. For example, the magnets were not strong enough to attract a sufficient amount of iron-ore particles, and the blowers designed to aid in the process of separating the dust from the iron-ore particles were too strong. Not only were they blowing dust everywhere, which made the machine hard for men to operate, they were also blowing away a considerable amount of usable iron ore! Also creating a challenge was the hopper into which the material to be separated was first dropped. The opening of the hopper was too large for the amount of material they could work at any one time. This problem was easily corrected; however, the others took Mallory a considerable amount of time and correspondence with Edison to get things in working order. Even so, when improvements were complete and a chemical analysis was made of the iron ore, the test revealed a concentrate lower than sixty-five percent, the amount needed to make the material attractive to buyers. Edison told Mallory to close down the plant for a month and to send samples to the laboratory for testing.

The Bechtelsville plant was in operation by July 1889. There were again problems with the magnets, but once they were corrected, early chemical analysis of the iron ore showed the required concentrate to be marketable. Based on this early success, board members decided to increase the capital stock in the company to one hundred thousand dollars, and Edison independently commissioned "a great magnetic survey" to uncover new deposits of low-grade iron ore. Used in the undertaking was a magnetic needle invented by Arthur Kennelly that was sensitive enough to reveal even the smallest iron-ore deposits when moved over the ground. An immense section of land from Lower Canada to North Carolina was selected for the survey. Detailed records were kept so that when the survey was complete, Edison had an exact account of deposits in every state they had covered.

Edison decided to concentrate on a site outside of Ogdensburg, New Jersey, a town named after his great-grandmother's side of the family. The region was selected not only because it was relatively near his home and laboratory, but because after having had an opportunity to study the results of the survey, Edison estimated that in the three thousand acres immediately surrounding the site there were over two hundred million tons of low-grade iron; enough to supply United States manufacturers for over seventy-five years. After these facts were presented to the board members of NJPCW in July 1889, it was agreed that a full-scale plant would be built there. To finance construction the company's capital stock was raised another one hundred fifty thousand dollars. Plans called for Edison to be on hand most of the time during construction. However, once the plant was finished, the project superintendent, Harry Livor, would take over day-to-day operations. Construction would eventually take from August 1889 to March 1890.

In the months following the July 1889 opening in Bechtelsville, operations were running well. However, by November, Livor reported that the iron-ore concentrations were starting to drop to unacceptable levels. In late January, he wrote Edison stating that the situation was not improving and that the only solution he could offer was to dig deeper in the hope that the iron ore found there would meet expectations. On hearing how desperate the situation was becoming, Edison immediately rushed to the site. He found that Livor's recommendation was probably correct, but the cost would be so great that he decided instead to put Bechtelsville's resources to work at Ogdensburg and closed the plant.

In Humboldt, the milling operations were doing well after Edison figured out that the iron-ore particles found there were so fine that the only way to separate them from the dust was for the material to stream past a series of magnets, not just a single large magnet as had been used in Bechtelsville. After two months, Mallory and his partners were satisfied with the plant and decided to build a full-scale plant; it was starting to gain the interest of regional iron manufactures. They shared their optimism with Edison, but he advised them to wait until the Ogdensburg mine had been open for a while, so they could learn from the experience.

After seven months of construction, the Ogdensburg milling plant, expected to be the centerpiece of Edison's iron-ore operation, was completed in March 1890. Experienced men were soon hired, as well as Italian and Hungarian laborers just disembarked from immigrant ships. Edison noticed that turnover was high due to the poor housing conditions, and told an associate, "If we want to keep the men here we must make it attractive for the women—so let us build some houses that will have running water and electric lights, and rent at a low rate." Edison designed a house, and fifty units were soon built with the proper amenities. The homes were then used in advertisements, to draw the best workers possible and create a pool from which openings could be filled. In three days of advertising, over six hundred and fifty applications were submitted. After that, Edison had no trouble finding men. Before long the enterprise had so taken over the landscape that the area was simply dubbed Edison.

The Ogdensburg site consisted of the largest steam shovel in America and a gigantic traveling crane spanning two hundred ten feet. Conveyor belts were everywhere, held up by metal or wood frames. Odd-shaped buildings dotted the area, housing a vertical dryer, an air separator, and the briquetting plant. Electrical wires carrying power from dynamos to machinery were strung everywhere. Little narrow-gauge locomotives carried boulders from the blasting site to the worksite. The centerpiece, however, was the building housing the gigantic rollers used for breaking up the piano-sized boulders, the starting point of the entire automated process. If anything went wrong with the rollers, the entire system was brought to a halt.

Edison's iron-ore milling operation near Ogdensburg, New Jersey, the site of his grandest experiment and enterprise.

Of the workmen, Thomas A. Robins, an industrial product salesman visiting the site in the hope of selling vulcanized rubber for use on the conveyor belt system, stated that they "look like millers, so coated do their clothes become with the flying white particles, and everyone wears a patient mask with pig-like snout."

Critics, experts, and newspapermen were waiting to question Edison's unconventional methods or add to his mystique. Jonathan Glidden, an experienced mine owner, expressed his concerns over Edison's methods to Lewis Miller, perhaps trying to steer his old friend away from getting into any more financial obligations with Edison. In a letter to Lewis, Glidden wrote that Edison's plans for handling immense quantities of material were unrealistic, and that a man of Edison's genius sometimes had to place his theories into practice before he could see they were wrong. Miller, who had yet to see a return on his original investment, never had to consider this advice. On December 3, 1890, the Humboldt plant burned to the ground. Due to persistent problems with machinery and the low-grade iron ore being extracted there, it was never rebuilt.

Newspaper reporters visited the site and wrote that Edison was using his claim of extracting iron ore to cover up his real purpose: extracting gold from the earth by a new method known only to him and his men who were sworn to secrecy. Even Edison's closest associates sang a familiar tune; Samuel Insull wrote O'Tate, "There is no doubt that we are going to make a great deal of money in concentrating iron ores …. I am sure we have got an extremely good thing."

By April 1891, the Ogdensburg plant was completed and running at full capacity. One hundred tons of iron-ore briquettes were delivered to Bethlehem Steel and the Pennsylvania Steel Company to judge the consistency and quality of the low-grade ore being produced. The Cambria Iron Works and Lackawanna Iron & Steel Company expressed an interest in placing an order, but would not commit until others were willing to take a chance on the material. Satisfied with results, by May, John Fritz, the manager of Bethlehem Steel, ordered one hundred thousand tons with the approval from the company's board of directors. However, when early shipments arrived and Frits conducted another test, he found that phosphorous levels were beginning to climb. He further discovered that the briquettes were falling apart in transit, and that particles were breaking off the briquettes and flying up the chimney when they were cast into the blast furnace. When word of Fritz's findings reached Edison, he cautioned Livor to "be careful or we will be ordered to stop shipping." He also set to work on solving the binding problem with the briquettes.

To learn why briquettes were breaking apart, Edison inspected the plant from top to bottom. He had planned to only make occasional visits, but he was the only one who knew enough about the overall system to make the necessary changes. He would have to be on-site every day, which he welcomed, even if it did take him out of the laboratory. He declared that he would stay at the plant "if it took him six months." It would take much longer, especially after Harry Livor resigned. Edison then took charge of daily operations. He worked as hard and as long as his men and asked nothing of them that he was not willing to do himself. This nearly cost him his life at least twice. Once, a steel rod shot from its place and came inches from his face. Another time, Edison and a co-worker were buried under sixteen tons of iron ore inside a dryer tower that they were inspecting. His commitment and dedication earned the men's respect; they, too, called him the Old Man, just as his Menlo Park associates had done years before.

After working on-site for months, Edison concluded that the briquettes were breaking apart due to the contamination of the iron ore with dust and unwanted minerals. His solution was drastic: the structures housing the crushing mill, the intermediate crushing rollers, the conveyor belt system, and the machinery to press the iron ore into briquettes would have to be torn down and rebuilt. The investors were startled, even though most of the working capital was Edison's. Batchelor, one the largest stockholders, urged fellow investors to follow Edison's recommendations. In a show of confidence in the venture and Edison's judgment, Batchelor purchased nineteen additional shares in the company.

After considerable discussions and more than one threat of a lawsuit, investors finally granted an astounding two hundred fifty thousand dollars in additional working capital. Edison tore down and rebuilt. He introduced additional crushing rollers that broke pieces of rock down to a finer material before streaming past magnets. He also added a new method for spraying the iron ore with water to refine it further, and he created a method by which the iron ore was completely dry before moving on to the pressing process. Edison was joined by Batchelor, who worked with Owen Conely, the plant's new superintendent, and Edward Thomas, the plant's first mechanical engineer, to get the plant up and running. Batchelor also conducted experiments regarding phosphorous content in briquettes. Based on Batchelor's research, the iron ore, once separated and dried, was then washed, and run through a series of screens, resulting in a considerable decline in phosphorous content. Edison designed the machinery to make this possible. With these new methods in place, Edison was finally able to deliver a large shipment to the North Branch Steel Works in February 1892.

During the journey to North Branch, the briquettes once again started showing signs of flaking. Edison dropped everything and focused on the problem. By April 1892, he had developed a new system for binding the iron-ore particles together in brick-size chunks. In May, a test run produced mixed results. An analysis showed that the problem lay with the automatic mixers' inability to combine ores in just the right amount with the binding resin that Edison had developed prior to the start of the entire project. It took months for the problem to be corrected—and then a new problem surfaced. The bricking plant dryer was not doing its job. The only solution was to build a new one. Making matters even more complicated was that during this time, the plant was also shipping over seventy tons of iron-ore concentrate per day to Bethlehem Iron Works, its only remaining regular customer. Breakdowns occurred without warning, and the whole interdependent system would come to a complete halt. By November, Edison concluded that it was time to halt operations. With the depression of 1893 looming, it was the right decision.

Over the next few months, Edison revisited every aspect of the mill. He became convinced that everything worked fine except for the gigantic crushing rollers that began the entire process. He experimented with a variety of rollers, but didn't have the time or the resources to conduct experiments on a grand enough scale to know if it would work.

Edison seated in front of the ore-processing plant's office. His attire serves as a testament to his willingness to be involved in the work at hand.

Throughout 1893 and the spring of 1894, a number of buildings were once again torn down and reconstructed to new, improved standards. Conveyor systems, screens, the bricking plant, dryers, washing stations—almost everything was taken down and replaced. If all went according to plan, the mill's capacity would rise from one to five thousand tons of material a day.

Though some historians have long credited Chicago's meat-packing industry with inspiring Henry Ford's moving assembly line, Ford insisted in his book, Edison as I Knew Him, that inspiration for his system of mass production came from Edison's Ogdensburg operations after he was shown the site and plans for the project years later. Ford further noted in his book that articles on Edison's progress in the venture during the 1890s also helped to keep the idea alive in his mind.

By April 1894, the plant was ready for another trial run. Rock was blown from the quarry and sent to the crushing mill. The giant crushing rollers were started; one spun in one direction, the other in the opposite direction. Once they reached their maximum speed, the power was turned off, letting kinetic energy break the rocks apart. The first load was dumped onto the rollers. The spikes in the rollers reduced the rock to manageable pieces that moved to the next in a series of rollers, reducing in size at each stage. At long last, the mill seemed to be on the right track. Exuberance grew with each passing hour—it seemed too good to be true!

It was. A few hours later, cracks appeared in the crushing mill's foundation. Suddenly, the machinery gave way. It jarred violently, tilted, then came to a complete stop. The structure would have to be torn down and erected once again. Edison's ignorance in the field of engineering had cost him dearly.

Ever the optimist, Edison immediately put up the money from his own pocket to finance the cost to rebuild the mill, as well as financing additions to the site. By 1895, buildings stood as high as seven stories. Thirty-one conveyor belts transported material from one process to another, and six elevators dried material as it passed through. There were four stock houses, shafts, pulleys, hoppers, and locomotives hauling material back and forth. Edison proudly exclaimed, "We are making a Yosemite of our own. We will soon have one of the biggest artificial canyons in the world."

The harsh reality, however, was that the plant was still not efficient. Breakdowns still haunted the operation, and orders did not come close to matching the twelve hundred dollars a day it cost to keep it working. Not that it mattered; as one disgruntled employee put it, "The machinery don't work half the time anyway."

Unable to meet the August 1895 payroll, and with company debt mounting, Edison had no choice but to close the plant briefly. So far two million dollars had been invested in the project: $1.25 million from Edison's pocket. Edison tried to interest stockholders in investing additional capital in the venture. They refused. Edison was on his own. Over the next few years he would invest an additional seven hundred fifty thousand dollars of his own money in the project.

With Edison's funds pouring into the project, operations resumed immediately, Edison at long last hit his stride, thanks in large part to a managerial system that allowed areas to be managed by an individual. If anything went wrong, the manager reported the problem to the superintendent who then sent in a team of specialists trained to fix the problem quickly and efficiently.

While the plant was running smoothly, Edison returned to the laboratory, where in November 1895 he became interested in x-ray technology after the discovery of the rays by German physicist W. K. Roentgen. So intense were Edison's efforts that a few weeks after beginning his work, he sent a fluoroscope and tungstate-of-calcium screen to Michael Pupin of Columbia University. Pupin used the instrument to x-ray a patient with a bullet wound to his hand and immediately performed surgery to remove the foreign materials. This was the first medical procedure to use x-ray technology in the world. Soon afterward the newspapers began reporting every detail of Edison's work with x-rays on a daily basis. This in turn created excitement and hundreds of people started writing the inventor with suggestions and questions about the machine. The Wizard had captured the nation's imagination once again.

Darkening the success of his x-ray machine and the operations at the Ogdensburg plant was the death of Edison's father, Samuel, on February 26, 1896. Edison attended the funeral in Norwalk,

Ohio, the town where Samuel had settled years before after taking up residence with an eighteen-year-old girl. Edison went to the funeral, then quickly returned to his work.

During the early years of x-ray experimentation, almost no one in the scientific community exercised caution in their investigations. At the Electrical Exposition of 1896 at the Central Palace in New York, visitors used Edison's x-ray machine to look at the bones in their hands, feet, and even their brains. Reports of vomiting, nausea, and diarrhea followed, but not until November 1896 was radiation poisoning discovered by the military after a wounded soldier was x-rayed a number of times to locate and remove a bullet near his spine. Edison witnessed the ravages of radiation sickness firsthand after a laboratory assistant, Clarence Dally, was poisoned and ulcers began appearing on his skin. Dally suffered for years from the exposure and died after a series of amputations. To Edison's credit, as soon as he saw the dangers involved, he dropped the matter entirely.

At the Ogdensburg plant things were only getting better. A few minor orders had been placed by steel manufacturers, and a large order was received from the Bethlehem Steel Company. In placing the order the company's manager, John Fritz, stated, "Mr. Edison, you are doing a good thing for the Eastern furnaces .... I am willing to help you."

So confident was Edison growing that even after he closed the plant again in the summer of 1897, he invited the press to tour the facility in October. One of the industry's leading journals, *The Iron Age*, wrote that Edison's "genius as an inventor is revealed in the many details of the great concentrating plant .... But to our mind, originality of the highest type as a constructor and designer appears in the bold way in which he sweeps aside accepted practice ... and attains results not hitherto approached."

It seemed to prove once again the Wizard of Menlo Park's ability to overcome any challenge. Crowds flocked to catch a glimpse of the legendary Thomas Alva Edison. The truth, however, was that the plant was still continually halted, and with prices at $3.50 to $4.00 a ton for low-grade iron ore, Edison could not survive, not when he counted on prices to be around $6.00 to $7.50 a ton to make a profit.

Even in the face of this dismal prospect, during the autumn of 1898, Edison ran the mill at full capacity to fill the Bethlehem Steel Company's order, as well as "bit" orders from smaller companies. As the holidays neared, one of Mina's sisters passed away. In a letter expressing his regrets for not being at her side, Edison wrote that he was getting little sleep because he had to look after every aspect of the plant. A "great blizzard" had left snowdrifts piled everywhere, making it impossible to enter most of the buildings. Everything was frozen, leaving men stranded at home. The plant had been shut down for four days. He apologizes to Mina for not attending her sister's funeral, explaining that he simply could not shut down the plant at what he referred to as "a most critical time technically and financially." In closing, Edison confided that if he had "an intelligent assistant I could have come .... I expect that until the whole thing is systematized and the men well trained, it will be impossible to find a man."

Charles Batchelor, back from a trip to Europe with his family, returned to the site on a part-time basis to aid Edison as much as possible. He served as an inspector and researcher, and as a liaison between Edison and his men. One day in the winter of 1898, Batchelor arrived at the site, went directly to Edison's office, and handed him a newspaper clipping. Edison read it as Batchelor stood by. The story told of recent developments in the Mesabi Range in northeastern Minnesota, a chain of hills rich in high-grade iron ore. So plentiful was it that open-pit mining was used to extract the material. The site had been mined since 1890, but had not posed a threat to low-grade iron-ore producers because of the cost of transporting it east. This was about to change. John D. Rockefeller and W. H. Oliver, two of the wealthiest men in America, had recently bought a bulk of the Mesabi Range acreage, planning to initiate mining on a grand scale and reduce the cost of transportation by establishing "ore trains" to transport the material to Lake Superior, where great ships could then make the ore available to industries all over the world. In reaction to the news the price of iron ore had dropped to $2.65.

Edison laughed and gave the clipping back to Batchelor. "Well, we might as well blow the whistle and close up shop."

By now, Edison had spent two million dollars of his own money on the enterprise. The company was thousands of dollars in debt. He knew the end had come; however, he continued production at a loss until every order was met. In December 1898, in the midst of a harsh winter, employees walked off the job because of a lack of housing. Over the next year the plant remained closed. During a portion of this time Edison had additional housing units built for his employees, and he attended the funeral of his father-in-law Lewis Miller in Akron, Ohio. The plant reopened in 1900, but because of the overabundance of ore at Eastern blasting furnaces and a depression, the "Ogden baby," as Edison fondly called the works, was closed for the last time in September of that year.

Although the financial disaster might have crushed the spirits of many an entrepreneur, it had little effect on the ever-optimistic Edison. The experience would be of use somewhere, sometime. He concerned himself with paying off the company's debts. On a visit to the site to dismantle the mills and dispose of the machinery, Edison confided to Walter S. Mallory, the plant's last superintendent and the heir to Batchelor's role as Edison's right-hand man, that he was not concerned about his future, that he could always land a seventy-five dollar a month job as a telegrapher. However, as far his obligations to creditors went, he told Mallory, "No company I was ever connected with has ever failed to pay off its creditors." In the coming years Edison paid off every account with a claim against the company.

Two years later, during the boom times of 1902, when Edison and Mallory were returning to Glenmont from a day trip to New Village, New Jersey, Mallory called Edison's attention to the General Electric stock quotes. Edison asked, "If I hadn't sold any of mine, what would it be worth to-day?" After a few minutes, Mallory replied, "Over four million dollars." Edison sat silent for fifteen or twenty seconds. With his right hand, he pulled at the eyebrow over his right eye as he was apt to do when deep in thought; then his face lit up, and he said, "Well, it's all gone, but we had a hell of a good time spending it."

In deciding to undertake the development of his iron-ore separator as the centerpiece around which an entire industry would be built, Edison did not follow his own pledge never to make something that wasn't wanted or necessary. Edison found investors who wanted to put his invention to work for them, and he knew a market existed in the east for the low-grade iron ore that he was going after. However, he continued to push forward with the invention even after pilot plants showed serious problems with the machine. Instead of taking the time to research and develop solutions, Edison pushed forward, constructing a full-scale plant in Ogdensburg. Once again, investors were willing to stand by him, but in the end it was Edison's money that kept the project from faltering, as one challenge after another cropped up. Most importantly, after the failure of his pilot plants, no one in the industry wanted anything to do with Edison's invention. At that point, Edison ignored his original goal of leasing machines and land to those interested in the invention, but after it proved to be ineffective no one wanted it. While some companies such as Bethlehem Steel were willing to take a chance, they were the only ones. In accordance with his pledge, Edison should have stopped production once he realized that he had a product no one wanted, especially once the price of iron ore was reaching levels so low that he could not stay in business.

Ironically, most of the dismantled remains of Edison's biggest failure became the beginning of a profitable business venture. Edison and Mallory were visiting New Village, New Jersey to check on yet another Edison enterprise. This one was spawned in 1898, when cement rock was found a mere forty-five miles west of his home and laboratory. On hearing the news, Edison bought eight hundred acres below the strike. After closing his "Ogden baby," much of the machinery and techniques were placed into service at the cement plant.

The cement industry gave birth to Edison's idea of affordable housing for the working classes. He conceived a plan to use two sets of molds and free-flowing cement to form a six-room house complete with floors, roof, walls, stairways, doors, windows, and conduits for electrical and water service. Edison figured that the total cost of each house would be twelve hundred dollars. He had several houses constructed in the West Orange area, but critics found them drab and monotonous, and they never caught on with the public. Not until the housing shortages several decades later did the housing industry return to the idea of prefabricated housing and construction methods similar to Edison's. Not that the failure of the cement housing venture mattered; by 1905, Edison's cement plant had become the fifth largest in the country, an unexpected benefit of recycling the failed iron-ore works. Edison's greatest folly revealed a man who struggled against admitting defeat; however, it was an example of Edison's fighting spirit and belief that whatever he undertook always provided a learning experience.

By 1905, Edison was fifty-eight. He knew the business of inventing, and if anything, the business had taught him that in order for an inventor to survive, he'd better always have another invention in the wings. For this reason, Edison kept a number of projects under research and development. One was showing particular promise as Edison's work at Ogdensburg was coming to a grinding halt. Research and development of the device had been secret from everyone but Edison and two assistants aiding his efforts. The instrument would so revolutionize the entertainment industry that people of Edison's time would soon forget that Edison had ever been involved in milling and mining.

Chapter 12

Focus on the Future: Edison's Kinetograph and Beyond

*… Whatever part I have played in its [the motion pic-
ture's] development was mainly along mechanical lines.
The far more important development of the motion picture
as a medium for artistic effort and as an educational factor
is in your hands. Because I was working before most of
you were born, I am going to bore you with a little advice.
Remember that you are the servants of the public, and
never let a desire for money or power prevent you from
giving the public the best work of which you are capable.*
—*Thomas Alva Edison*

While the phonograph was in its early stages and the challenge of alternating current was growing, early experiments
were conducted at the new West Orange laboratory on an invention that would come to be known as the kinetograph: the forerunner of the motion-picture camera. The project was not a
priority like perfecting the phonograph, finding suitable filaments
for incandescent lamps, and Edison's iron-ore project, but Edison
was drawn to the concept of pictures in motion and kept coming
back to it.

Edison's work on the kinetograph was inspired by someone bringing the need for the instrument to his attention. Eadweard Muybridge, a noted British photographer residing in San Francisco, had gained fame for his series of photographs showing that a horse in full gallop had all four feet off the ground, published in the book, *The Horse in Motion,* and featured in the October 19, 1878, issue of the *Scientific American.* A second article a year and a half later described Muybridge's "zoogyroscope," a device that used spinning mirrors and a oxyhydrogen lantern to project on a screen an animal in movement. Of the "zoogyroscope," the *Scientific American* wrote, "Nothing was wanting but the clatter of hoofs upon the turf and an occasional breath of steam from the nostrils to make the spectator believe that he had before him genuine flesh and blood steeds."

Muybridge visited Edison at his laboratory in late February 1888, following a lecture and a demonstration of his improved instrument, now called the "zoopraxiscope," before the New England Society in Orange, New Jersey. Muybridge demonstrated his instrument to Edison, explained his plans for incorporating his device with the phonograph in the hope of arriving at a talking motion picture, and asked for Edison's assistance. Edison agreed and according to Kevin MacDonnell, Muybridge's biographer, "Edison was enthusiastic and offered to record the voices of people such as Edwin Booth and Lilian Russell, while Muybridge made moving pictures of their gestures and expressions." Muybridge agreed to send Edison a set of photographs showing a variety of animals in movement for use in his experiments.

The motion-picture camera has its roots in ancient times. Around 65 B.C.E., the Roman poet Lucretius discovered a phenomenon called the "persistence of vision," which occurs in the human brain when an image is presented to the mind's eye before the previous image fades away. (At least twenty-four pictures per second must flash by for pictures to appear to be in motion.) Two hundred years later, Ptolemy, the Greek astronomer experimentally proved its existence. In 1824, Peter Mark Rôget, author of the famous thesaurus, presented a paper on the subject to the Royal Society in London. Two years later, Henry Fitton, an English scientist, developed a toy that explained persistence of vision, consisting of a coin with long pieces of string attached to each side. On one side was a picture of a bird, on the other, an empty birdcage. When the coin was spun using the strings, the bird appeared to be in the cage. The toy, called a thaumatrope, became popular with the English.

Joseph Antoine Plateau, a Belgian scientist, invented the phenakistoscope, the first device to give a series of pictures the appearance of movement. Plateau placed two rotating disks a few inches apart on a rod. Along one edge of a disk he painted pictures. Each picture varied slightly as the subject completed a motion. A series of slots were then cut on the other disk radiating out from the center. When the disks were spun on the rod, the picture viewed through the slots appeared to be moving. In 1860, Pierre Habert Desvignes of France developed a more famous variation of Plateau's device called the zoetrope. The zoetrope used the same basic idea as the phenakistoscope, except that slits were cut onto the side of a hollow cylinder, while the pictures to be viewed were painted inside in between the slits. When the cylinder was laid flat and spun, the pictures inside appeared to move when viewed through the slits on the side. John Barnes Linnet then patented the kineograph process, whereby a series of pictures of a moving image were drawn on the pages of a book. When the pages are flipped, the image appears to move. Linnet's simple invention would be followed by the Muybridge's work. His photographs of a horse in motion were the first to capture motion in photography.

The idea of using the phonograph as Muybridge proposed was not new. In the months after the phonograph was made public in 1877, English inventor Wordsworth Donisthrope suggested that the phonograph could be combined with a strip of photographs showing actors in a drama and shown on a screen complete with movement and voice. An 1877 *Scientific American* article introducing "The Talking Phonograph" observed, "It is already possible by ingenious optical contrivances to throw stereoscopic photographs of people on screens in full view of an audience. Add the talking phonograph to counterfeit their voices, and it would be difficult to carry the illusion of the real presence much further." In an interview with the *New York Sun* on February 22, 1887, Edison stated that he foresaw a day when the "pictures and gestures of [an] orator, as well as his voice, could be exactly reproduced, and the eyes and ears of the audience charmed by the voice and manner of the speaker. Whole dramas and operas can be produced in private parlors."

Characteristically, in the months after his initial meeting with Muybridge, Edison put himself through a crash course in photography. Though Muybridge dropped the project months later due to concerns about the phonograph's lack of volume, Edison continued his research. He found that relatively little had been accomplished in the field and that nothing existed to take commercial advantage of the medium's possibilities. That was all Edison needed to know. He appointed as his primary assistant William Kennedy Laurie Dickson, who had also assisted him in his iron-ore separation trials. An immigrant from Britain, Laurie had come to America, like many others on Edison's staff, to work for and learn from him. He had proven himself a leading experimenter, and was a proficient photographer of Edison's facilities, and his family. Edison and Dickson developed a motion picture device clearly influenced in concept and design by the phonograph. The concept called for a long photographic cylinder made of plaster on which pictures one sixteenth of an inch square were photographed in rapid succession by turning the cylinder, in much the same way sound was recorded on the phonograph. Once the pictures were developed, the cylinder would then be placed back in position. When the cylinder was turned, a person looking through the eyepiece of a microscope attached to the instrument would see the subject in the minute photographs appear to be moving.

By October 1888, Edison filed a caveat with the United States Patent Office that not only specified the work that he was conducting with Dickson, but also the overall concept he had in mind: "I am experimenting upon an instrument which does for the eye what the phonograph does for the ear, which is the recording and reproduction of things in motion, and in such a form as to be both cheap, practical and convenient."

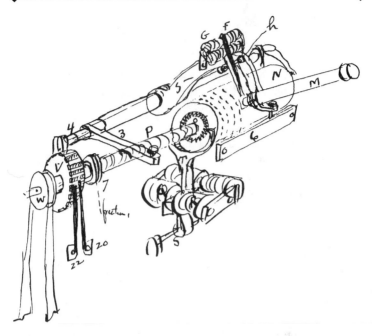

In Edison's original concept for his motion picture camera, photographs were "recorded" on a cylinder. A person could see the moving pictures with a microscope.

(© *Courtesy of Edison National Historic Site*)

The rest of that year and 1889, Edison spent the bulk of his time on his new and improved phonograph, trying to perfect the stop-and-go action of the cylinder. When Dickson's time was not occupied with iron-ore separation, he tested photographic cylinders in a variety of materials including metal and glass. He got the best results by wrapping photographic paper around an aluminum cylinder, in much the same way that tin-foil had been wrapped around the phonograph's brass cylinder. However, the curvature of the cylinder caused the top and bottom of the photographs to be out of focus. Dickson designed a cylinder consisting of a number of planes, so the photographs could be taken on a "flat" surface. Edison and Dickson also worked on a means of illuminating the photographs with a bright light when viewed. They also decided that photographs needed to be enlarged from one sixteenth to one quarter of a square inch, a tedious process that took up a great deal of their time.

While in the midst of this and all his other projects, Edison decided to attend the Paris Exhibition in August 1889, where a number of his inventions were on display. Accompanied by his wife and his eldest daughter from his first marriage, the Edisons were greeted and pampered by French officials. Edison journeyed overseas on a number of occasions, each time endearing himself to Europeans through countless published interviews portraying him as an energetic and fascinating man, quite different from his stuffy European counterparts who preferred to associate with nobility rather than the common man. Edison always made himself available to the press, forthrightly voicing his opinion on any subject with answers that were direct and sincere, never contrived, revealing a personality the equal of the great American writer Mark Twain.

On this visit to Paris, an exclusive interview with R. H. Sheard of the *London Pall Mall Budget* captured his wit and unique perspective. When asked to compare his work ethic with that of Parisians, Edison responded, "What struck me so far chiefly is the absolute laziness of everybody over here. When do these people work? ... People here seem to have established an elaborate system of loafing ...." Speaking of Parisian cuisine, Edison stated, "[T]hey put rolls and coffee on the table for breakfast. I thought that that was a very poor breakfast for a man to do any work upon .... But I suppose one gets used to it." Finally, when asked if it was possible to create a machine that could read a man's mind, Edison reflected for a few seconds, smiled, then said, "Such a machine is possible, but just think if it were invented. Every man would flee his neighbor, fly for his life to any shelter."

Edison's personality captivated the European public, but it would have meant nothing without the inventions on which his reputation was built. Since his first international exhibition in Paris in 1881, Edison's reputation had grown to where he was now the main attraction. Edison knew the importance such exposure meant to him and his inventions, and he tried to be represented at such events no matter where they took place or how much it cost. Edison's display at the Paris Exhibition cost approximately seventy-five thousand dollars and featured twenty thousand individual incandescent lamps in the shape of a light bulb. On either side of the "lamp of lamps" the American and French flags were configured out of colored lamps. Underneath this impressive array of lights were a number of Edison inventions in telegraphy, telephonic, phonographic, lamp manufacture, electrical separation of metals, and electric meters. There was also a complete lighting system in operation, and the original "Jumbo" Edison dynamo used in the 1881 Edison exhibition.

Edison was never truly away from his work, however. While he was in Paris, he met a number of distinguished photographers during a dinner celebrating the life of the great French photographer, Louis Jacques Mandé Dagger, the inventor of the daguerreotype process. Edison met Étienne Marey, renowned for his photographs of people and animals in motion. Invited to Marey's studio, Edison noted that Marey's camera "was capable of producing sixty frames per second on a roll of paper-based photographic film."[i] Edison had considered Marey's approach previously, and had even mentioned in his original caveat for the kinetograph that "a continuous strip could be used," but had dismissed the idea early on, citing "many mechanical difficulties." Marey discussed his method of photography with Edison, and presented him with a book he had written explaining the process in detail, *Physiologie du mouvement* (physiology of movement).

The visit to Marey's studio had a profound impact on Edison. Marey's machine and filmstrips reminded Edison of his automatic telegraph, and he turned to this earlier invention to perfect a camera that captured motion. From the automatic telegraph he borrowed the idea of electrochemical paper, sprockets on the paper, and double-toothed wheels to guide the strips through the machine. To control the rate at which it photographed and viewed the film, Edison used the polarized relay also from the automatic telegraph.

As far as many experts in the industry are concerned, Edison's greatest contribution to motion-picture technology is the use of perforations on the sides of the film to help guide it past the shutter. The Edison-Dickson perforation soon became an industry standard, and the perforations are called "American Perforations" to this day around the world.

On his return from France, Edison took up work on his radically revised kinetograph in a new building constructed under Dickson's supervision while he was away. He explained his new concept to Dickson, who had been busy working on a new method of projecting images onto a screen based on the findings of a German inventor named Ottomar Anschütz, who had invented a projector he called the tachyoscope. The instrument "used a metal disc with a glass periphery on which was mounted a series of pictures. As the disc rotated rapidly, each picture was illuminated by the bright light of a Geissler tube and projected on a screen, giving the illusion of motion."[2] Dickson even managed to synchronize the human voice recorded on a phonograph so that the images on the screen appeared to be talking.

Perhaps to throw off competitors, in early February 1890 Edison leaked news of the device to the press. The news created a sensation, especially overseas where the Paris Exhibition had recently renewed interest in Edison and his work. Not all the reports were favorable. The London *Pall Mall Gazette* reported, "Mr. Edison has added a new horror to existence. He attaches an instantaneous photographic camera to his phonograph, plants his two lethal instruments in front of an orator, and sets them to work. The phonograph records every syllable that fall from his lips, every 'hem' and 'er' and mispronunciation ...." Although the excited, elaborate descriptions of the new device were based almost entirely on hearsay and hyperbole, it didn't matter. To the public, no invention seemed beyond Thomas Alva Edison's reach. Nonetheless, newspaper accounts were premature. Completion of the kinetograph was delayed because he and Dickson spent the summer of 1890 in Ogdensburg, New Jersey, working on the extraction of iron ore.

When they returned to the project in the fall of 1890, William Heise and John and Fred Ott joined them. These men had been with Edison since his Newark days, working with telegraphic instruments. Charles Kayser, a machinist who manufactured the various parts of Edison's kinetograph, also joined the group. Edison's efforts were also aided by recent advancements in celluloid film by George Eastman, the inventor of the rapid-action "Kodak," who had developed a durable, light, and flexible film that could be rolled around a spool. In discussions with Edison, Eastman agreed to produce the film in strips approximately fifty feet long. Dickson later wrote that Edison, on seeing the film, exclaimed, "That's it—we've got it—now work like hell!"

> One of the chief actors in the films of Edison's assistant William Dickson was an Edison mechanic named Fred Ott. According to fellow associates, Ott was quite a comedian, whose signature gag was a sneeze that he could reproduce on demand. When Dickson put Fred in front of the camera, he froze. But, after several attempts, Fred Ott finally managed his famous sneeze and the first filmed close-up was born.

Throughout the winter of 1890 and the spring of 1891, Edison and his assistants focused on perfecting the kinetograph using Marey's reel-to-reel method. They made attempts to combine the device with the phonograph, but finally dropped the idea when it became evident that current technology would not allow the two instruments to work in unison. However, advances were made on the kinetoscope, which would be used to view a finished strip of film. At this time Edison found that projecting the images on a screen only heightened the already jerky action of the film. Since Edison's primary goal was to make the project a commercial enterprise, he decided that, for the time being, completed films would not be exhibited on large screens, but would be viewed one at a time using the coin-operated method popular with phonographs. The kinetoscope was designed with a "peep-hole" at the top of a cabinet housing the rollers, motor, and light.

Edison demonstrated the kinetograph and the kinetoscope in the spring of 1891 at the West Orange Laboratory for members of the National Federation of Women's Clubs (after they dined as Mina's guests at Glenmont). Also present were reporters for the *New York Sun* and *New York Herald,* who wrote that Edison stated he was on the right track, but at least two years away from introducing perfected models commercially. Even so, by June 13, 1891, Edison apparently felt that the time was right. He granted *Harper's Weekly* exclusive rights to publish a detailed description and drawings of the instrument. George Parsons Lathrop, son-in-law of Nathaniel Hawthorne and a future Edison biographer, wrote that the kinetograph "performs the same service in recording and then reproducing *motion* which the phonograph performs in recording and reproducing sound." Edison responded, "All I have done is to perfect what had been attempted before …. It's just that one step that I have taken." In response, Lathrop wrote, "Yes, that is all. But in science and invention the clever old maxim does not hold true that 'it is the first step which costs.' Not the first, but the last—the conclusive and triumphant step—is the one that costs and that counts."

Lathrop's observation was full of the accepted characteristics of the Edison legend; Edison saw things that other inventors did not; he was humble; he never gave up; he was patient; he tackled a number of projects at the same time, and his inventions were beyond the realm of the common man.

In July 1891, Edison filed for a patent on both the kinetograph and the kinetoscope. After being advised by lawyers that the foreign patents would cost one hundred fifty dollars, Edison decided that it was not worth the effort. He only filed for patents in the United States, which meant that anyone overseas could manufacture the kinetograph or the kinetoscope, file a patent for it in Europe, and then make the instruments available for sale in the United States.

Dickson returned to the laboratory as often as his work at the mine permitted to make further modifications to the kinetoscope in hopes of exhibiting it at Chicago's World Fair. Exhausted by the demanding schedule, Dickson fell ill in late January 1892. Edison sent him to Florida to rest and relax, and the deadline for the Chicago World's Fair came and went. For the time being, the kinetoscope and kinetograph would lie dormant.

Dickson returned from Florida in March and joined Edison at Ogdensburg, then departed to the laboratory in early 1893. Construction soon started in the laboratory compound on an odd-shaped structure covered in tarpaper and painted black inside and out, built on a platform that allowed it to be rotated to take advantage of the light of the sun. In the roof was an opening that could be opened or closed tight to block out the elements. It would become the world's first motion-picture studio, affectionately referred to as the "Black Maria."

This odd-shaped structure, affectionately known as the "Black Maria" to Edison and his staff, was the world's first motion-picture studio.

(© Courtesy of Edison National Historic Site)

Over the next three years, modifications to the kinetograph continued, and a variety of entertainers, showmen, and sportsmen came to have themselves "recorded" by Edison's kinetoscope. Among them were Buffalo Bill Cody, the dancer Carmencita, the strongman Eugene Sandow, the Gayety Girls, Japanese dancers, French ballet girls, and knife throwers, as well as the boxers Corbett and Courtney. Animal trainers brought dogs, bears, trained lions, and monkeys to perform before Edison's contraption.

In 1896 John Rice and May Irwin were asked by Edison to recreate a stage kiss from a play they were performing on Broadway. On film the couple spent a great deal of time puckering up for the kiss, and then delivered a very brief smack on the lips. This kiss, which today seems like the most innocent of images, caused quite a stir in its time. Moralistic citizens flooded the papers with complaints about the lewd event, and reformers cried out to politicians to implement censorship regulations.

In the meantime, Tate and Thomas Lombard, a Lippincott associate who had joined Edison's staff after Lippincott's death in 1891, managed to interest investors Frank Gammon and Norman C. Raff in purchasing twenty-five of Edison's kinetoscopes. They also formed a partnership with the two men in an effort to purchase and market the invention exclusively. Tate presented the group's proposal to Edison on February 13, 1894. The group financed the completion of all work on the camera and paid Edison's employees their wages during this time. They decided to take on Edison's agreement with Dickson to pay him a percentage of profits. Edison himself gained a ten thousand dollar bonus and guaranteed royalties of ten thousand dollars a year. The group would buy kinetoscopes from Edison who would profit two hundred percent. When the kinetograph was ready they would allow Edison a similar profit on their purchases.

In total, the group stood ready to pay Edison sixteen thousand dollars once the deal was finalized, but even though he desperately needed the cash, Edison refused. Nothing but trouble had come from his selling off control of his phonograph, thus he felt this could be no different.

Tate and his associates did not give up. They waited for Edison to deliver the twenty-five kinetoscopes. When the kinetoscopes finally arrived, they came without "phonographic linkage," thus giving birth to silent movies. The group then approached Edison with a proposal to license the right to use Edison films and the coin-slot apparatus. This time, a deal was struck guaranteeing Edison a generous royalty and control of the kinetoscope itself. On April 14, 1894, Tate and his associates opened the first "Kinetoscope Parlor," with ten kinetoscopes in an old shoe store at

1155 Broadway in New York City. Ten were also sent to Chicago and five to Atlantic City. Billed as the "Wizard's Latest Invention," the kinetoscope was an instant success. On the first day in New York City, crowds were so large that Tate and his associates made one hundred twenty dollars, at twenty-five cents per person.

By November, Edison had leased the right to exhibit his kinetoscope in Europe to a second group of investors headed by Frank Z. Maguire and Joseph Baucus. Before long kinetoscope parlors were established in London, Liverpool, Copenhagen, and Paris, to name but a few locations. Edison now sold his kinetoscope to licensees for two hundred fifty dollars, a price they were more than willing to pay. When added to his royalties, Edison suddenly found himself reaping a fortune once again.

Advancements in motion-picture technology by others continued despite Edison's apparent monopoly on the market. Two brothers named Grey and Otway Latham, who operated a licensed kinetoscope parlor, approached Edison with a screen projector that showed promise and asked if he thought it would be a good idea to manufacture the instrument. Edison sternly responded:

> *No. If we make the screen machine that you are asking*
> *for, it will spoil everything. We are making these peep-*
> *show machines and selling a lot of them at a good profit.*
> *If we put out a screen machine there will be a use for*
> *maybe about ten of them in the whole United States.*
> *With that many screen machines you could show pictures*
> *to everybody in the country—and then it would be done.*
> *Let's not kill the goose that lays the golden egg.*

With this success came an end to Edison's day-to-day involvement with the enterprise. Surprisingly enough, Edison placed in charge of the business not Dickson, but William Gilmore, a one-time assistant of Samuel Insull at the Schenectady factory. Dickson was responsible for filming anything and everything Gilmore told him to (mostly boxing matches). Dissatisfied, Dickson formed a secret pact with the Latham brothers and another associate to form the LAMBDA Company and produce a marketable projector and manufacture a motion-picture camera based on Dickson's knowledge. When Gilmore became aware of Dickson's betrayal, on

April 2, 1895, he took his concerns to Edison, and Dickson was dismissed immediately. The LAMBDA Company successfully demonstrated their projector on April 21 to a group of journalists. In an interview with the *New York Sun*, Edison said that he would not be upset if the group made improvements and called it a kinetoscope, but if they called it anything else he would file charges against them.

The demonstration made Edison aware that he had to begin developing a projector or lose control of the market if projection systems captured consumers. Realizing this, or perhaps knowing that he could not develop a projector fast enough because of the numerous other projects going on at the same time at West Orange and Ogdensburg, the forty-nine-year-old Edison did something that the twenty-five-year-old Edison would never have done: He allowed his name to be used in association with someone else's invention. Thomas Armat, from Washington, D.C., had invented a projector he called a vitascope. Raff and Gammon, who purchased the rights to the device after Armat gave them a demonstration, brought it to Edison's attention. Edison was adamantly against lending his name to the projector, but changed his mind after seeing the invention in action. Armat was also against having Edison's name on his invention, but as Raff and Gammon pointed out to him, there were large profits to be made with Edison lending his name to the device; after all, industry representatives had been waiting a long time for an Edison projector system. The men assured Armat that Edison did not want to pose as the inventor but would lend his name to promote the product.

Armat struck a deal with Raff, Gammon, and Edison to manufacture the projector as Edison's Vitascope—Armat Design. The projector was introduced to the public on April 3, 1896, at Koster and Bial's Music Hall in New York City. Edison sat in a box seat while Armat ran the projector. Headlines praised "Edison's Latest Marvel, the Vitascope," and though the claim was not true, no one in either the Armat or Edison camp made a move to correct the misunderstanding.

Three months after the vitascope's debut, Edison made an improvement to the piece that controlled the movement of the film over the "eye" of the camera. By the end of July, he was filling orders for "Projecting Kinetoscopes" or "Edison Projectoscopes." Through the rest of the summer and early fall he worked on his own projector, which he introduced on November 15, again at Koster and Bial's Music Hall. He then stopped paying Armat for the use of his vitascope. Armat filed a lawsuit. The matter was settled out of court when rights to the vitascope were returned to Armat.

The projection of moving images across the big screen created as much of a stir as the kinetoscope had when it was introduced. After that the motion-picture industry grew at such an astonishing rate that by 1909 there were eight thousand movie theaters and nickelodeon parlors in the United States. In the years that followed, a number of individuals made improvements to projectors and motion picture cameras. Since Edison hadn't filed patents for his kinetograph and kinetoscope in Europe, people freely "borrowed" ideas from Edison's original inventions knowing that lawsuits would be hard to win. Undaunted, Edison filed a number of lawsuits in an effort to protect his original patents. Similar conditions existed for moviemakers, whose films were constantly reproduced without their permission and then shown to an audience for a fee.

These chaotic conditions persisted in the industry until Edison won a lawsuit in federal court in 1907 upholding his original patents of 1891. From this point forward, anyone using a motion-picture camera or projector that in anyway mechanically resembled Edison's originals would have to pay him a royalty.

As he had done in the past, Edison filled the gap left by the completion of his movie camera—at least at this point—by focusing his attention to an invention he had started years earlier and nursed along, a storage battery for use in automobiles. He had started conducting research and development on a storage battery in 1900. For more than a century, scientists had been trying to create an efficient and safe second cell or storage battery that would store the energy sent to it then send the charge back to the first cell. A series of complicated chemical reactions keep the current going back and forth. Ideally this process was to continue indefinitely until all the chemicals were used up. Today's car batteries are representative of this type of construction.

At the time that Edison began looking into creating a more effective storage battery in 1900, the only one available was the lead and acid battery, which was very heavy and extremely corrosive to its metal casing. Edison decided to use alkaline instead of acids, to prevent corrosion, and searched for the right chemicals to make a positive charge after settling on a type of iron for the negative chemical charge. He was excited to be experimenting with chemicals once again, his passion since boyhood. He employed upwards of ninety people, including leading physicists and chemists, in the search, which lasted for months, like the filament searches of the Menlo Park days.

After some success with nickel hydrate as a positive chemical source and iron oxide as the negative charge source, Edison began a campaign to market the new battery and started construction on a factory to meet a growing demand. In the summer of 1904, production got under way. Praise rang out across the country for the Wizard's latest invention, but problems appeared within the first year of production. The cells dropped thirty percent in power soon after being started and leaked when used in automobiles. Edison, against the advice of his financial advisors and the people selling the product, pulled his batteries off the market and even bought back all that had been sold at great expense. He told investors that he did not want an inferior product with his name on it, even if its performance surpassed anything else available. Never one to give up, Edison spent the next four years guiding the efforts of his assistants working on the problem of the battery.

As 1908 arrived, after dedicating himself to the project in the months after the court's ruling regarding his movie camera, Edison finally hit upon the solution to the battery problem. One of the chemicals used as an additive, lithium, boosted the capacity of the battery and gave it a longer life. Edison's trial-and-error method, not theory, stumbled upon this important chemical process. In fact, as late as the 1960s scientists still could not explain this chemical reaction.

While Edison had been conducting experiments on his storage battery, a number of officials from the larger movie companies approached him about forming a national trust to control the distribution and production of films. In return, producers would recognize Edison's patents and pay him royalties amounting to hundreds of thousands of dollars a year. Edison agreed, giving rise to the Motion Picture Patents Company. The agreement was signed in December 1908 in Edison's library at his West Orange laboratory, where guests were treated to dinner, drinks, and cigars. Edison ate quickly, then dismissed himself, saying, "You boys talk it over while I take a nap." He then walked over to a cot in a corner of the library, laid down, and fell soundly asleep. The men discussed the final terms and then woke Edison. Edison simply took a pen and asked, "All right, where do you want me to sign?"

Once his name was in all the appropriate places, Edison laid down his pen, and then turning to his distinguished guests he said, "Good-bye boys. I have to get back to work." He then walked out of the library, leaving his new business associates to fend for themselves.

With the agreement in place, the Patents Company collected a weekly fee from any movie theatre using their equipment. They also refused to sell films to distributors who used films from other independent producers. To make it even more difficult, the Patents Company cut a deal with George Eastman to sell raw stock film only to the Patents Company.

> *Of the nine film production companies making up the Motion Pictures Patents Company, only Vitagraph Films survived the break-up of the Trust, but only until 1925. Ironically, William Fox, the distributor who dared defy the Patents Company and make his own independent films, unknowingly founded one of the largest motion picture production companies in existence today, Twentieth-Century Fox. Another independent distributor turned producer, Carl Laemmle, founded the parent company of Universal Pictures in his own attempt to get away from the controlling arm of the Patents Company.*

The agreement lasted for over ten years. Edison's profits soon totaled over a million dollars a year. In April 1917, United States Supreme Court ordered the disbanding of the group when an independent distributor turned producer, William Fox, sued the

Motion Picture Patents Company under the country's anti-trust laws. During the ten years of the Patents Company's existence, the Edison film company made a hefty profit from royalties and distribution fees.

Because of the overwhelming growth of Edison business concerns connected to the phonograph and the motion picture from the turn of the century to the early 1910s, West Orange laboratory expanded dramatically. Buildings for record and film production appeared, as well as housing for the growing labor force. By 1911, managing the facility became such a large task that Edison undertook to reorganize his various enterprises under the name Thomas A. Edison, Incorporated. By now the assortment of companies founded by Edison to market and produce his inventions had grown to more than thirty. These companies ranged from the production of movie cameras to motion pictures and from residential phonographs to dictating machines for the office and averaged between twenty and twenty-seven million dollars in annual sales.

Edison's goal in restructuring these industries was not only to free up his time to focus on inventing, but also to keep up with the changing business environment. Gone were the days when the lone inventor could have his finger in every aspect of the business, or set up a self-sufficient company every time he felt an invention was ready for market. In the past, for example, different phonograph companies were founded to produce and market a model for a particular niche in the market, when the same management team could have overseen the marketing and labor force manufacturing all of them. Centralized management could have spotted when the same task was being replicated in different parts of the company.

Aside from the need for a centralized management structure to streamline the business practices of his various enterprises, Edison also realized that without sound centralized management, there would be no organization in place to guide his enterprises when he retired or passed away. This would leave the smallest of his companies to fend for themselves against the most powerful, which would lead to discord and possibly a breakup of the companies into their own entities, or an end to Edison's industries altogether. Edison was simply not going to let this happen, not if he could help it.

Edison tried to stay involved in every aspect of the business and had the final say in how business matters were handled. However, he was careful to respect the recommendations made by high-ranking executives, who often asked him to reconsider requests for money to support experiments. For example, when Edison wanted to conduct further research on his storage battery, he did not fight back when money he requested was denied, and even cancelled the request when he saw that it was only turning one group of executives against another. With this managerial organization in place, Edison guaranteed himself the time to focus on the business of inventing, and assured the survival of his company in the event that he should die.

After forming Thomas A. Edison, Incorporated, in 1911, Edison continued work on an improved model of his disc phonograph, a project that would take another three years to complete. He also worked on an electric safety lantern for use in the mining industry, receiving a patent on October 13, 1914. In the months prior, Germany had declared war on Russia, signaling the start of World War I, and by August 4, Britain declared war on Germany. For Edison, this meant that shipments of carbolic acid, an essential element in the production of phonograph records, could no longer be received from Britain and Germany, the two countries upon which he depended for them. An embargo was placed on shipments from Britain to America in the late summer of 1914, leaving Edison with enough material to continue until mid-October. A crisis looming, Edison undertook a study of the production of carbolic acid. He found that six methods could be used for its production. He selected the sulfonic acid process—but no one in America had ever attempted to produce the acid because it was believed that the quality of the coal mined in the States was substandard, although no one had ever challenged the findings.

Knowing that he needed to act quickly, Edison contacted a number of chemical producers asking them if they would be willing to construct a plant for making the acid. He was turned down at every turn. He then decided to gather leading chemists and engineers. He broke them into groups of three and posed the challenge. Work went on night and day in much the same way it had in Menlo Park. A week later, a design for the plant was agreed upon and work started immediately in Silver Lake, a few miles from West Orange. Eighteen days after work began, seven hundred tons of carbolic acid was sent to the phonograph factories. Before long, production grew to such an extent that excess acid was being sold to other industries in need of the material to manufacture dyes and even explosives. Similar plants were also constructed to produce benzol and paraphenylenediamine.

By December 1914, the sixty-seven-year-old Edison had once again managed to overcome a major challenge that could have had dire consequences on a revenue source Edison Incorporated depended upon. However, before the end of the year, there was one last challenge to overcome. A fire on the evening of December 9 burned to the ground Edison's West Orange laboratory and thirteen other buildings covering four blocks. As crews struggled to put the blaze out, Edison was seen with a pad and pencil in hand, hard at work designing a new and improved laboratory. The next day, he led fifteen hundred laborers in cleaning up the site and hauling away debris. Edison Incorporated records estimated the loss at $919,788. "I am sixty-seven," Edison declared, "but I'm not too old to make a fresh start."

Days later, salvaged machinery was installed in leased buildings nearby. The men were back to work before the week was out. From Henry Ford, by now a close friend, Edison received seven hundred fifty thousand dollars, an amount he would pay back in coming years, but for which Ford refused interest. Edison also managed to secure bank loans using money owed Edison Incorporated as collateral. Three weeks after the fire, the laboratory and most of the surrounding buildings had essentially been rebuilt. By January 1915, employees would be manufacturing the disc phonograph that Edison had started making improvements upon years earlier.

Now that Edison had rescued his phonograph works and his laboratory, he could get back to working on inventions of his own choosing and not mothered by necessity. The coming years would also find him sharing camping trips with Henry Ford and their companions. He would continue to conduct annual birthday interviews with reporters eager to share his views with Americans.

However, the United States military would come calling with a request for Edison to aid America as it prepared to enter World War I.

Chapter 13

Twilight Comes

Mr. Edison himself did not grow old. He was like a young driver in a worn-out car. He has just gone, I believe, to get new facilities to continue his work. But the sense of personal loss is very heavy. There was only one Edison.

—Henry Ford, October 19, 1931, the day after Edison's death

With tensions rising in the United States over the war in Europe, the question of military preparedness divided the nation. On one side of the issue stood men like Henry Ford, who urged a diplomatic end to the war, while on the other were men like Edison who supported diplomatic negotiations but believed in the build-up of a strong military in case the United States was left with no choice but to enter the war. The fight to sway public opinion was often fought in the newspapers. Ford called military preparedness a waste of resources, while Edison argued that "even a man has insurance on his home just in case anything happened to it."

Edison's strong support of military preparedness caught the eye of the secretary of the Navy, Josephus Daniels, who was trying to gain support in Washington for the build-up of armaments.

Knowing that a man like Edison could sway public opinion and the Congress, Daniels approached him with the offer to lead the Naval Consulting Board. The group would consist of advisors charged with examining shortcomings in naval technology and then recommend how to improve the equipment. The board would also review ideas for weapons submitted by the public and professionals and select those worthy of further consideration. Edison would be in charge of organizing and selecting who would serve on the board.

On July 7, 1915, Edison accepted. It was not the first time he had played a part in supporting the nation's military. In the 1880s, he had designed a torpedo for the Navy, considered the first remote-controlled weapon in the world, and in 1898, he had made a number of suggestions for weapons for use in the Spanish-American War. In February 1915, he had signed an agreement with the Navy to supply them with his storage battery for use aboard Navy submarines. At the signing of this contract, worth an estimated ten million dollars, that Daniels had approached him.

The board met for the first time on October 7, 1915. Edison was soon elected president. In order for Edison to understand what was being said, an assistant tapped the words out in Morse code on Edison's knee. Edison's most significant contribution was his proposal to establish a Naval research laboratory. It didn't pass through Congress until after the end of the war because of bickering among Naval military leaders over where it would be located and who would be in charge of the operation. Edison would serve on the board until December 1920, the year construction started on the laboratory.

During the summer of 1916, Edison took the first of a number of camping trips with Henry Ford, Harvey Firestone, and John Burroughs. The trip was suggested by Ford, who had met Edison for the first time at the Association of Edison Illuminating Companies Conference at Manhattan Beach, New York, in 1897. In attendance in his capacity as chief engineer at the Detroit Edison Company's powerhouse, Ford was asked to sit next to Edison and explain his idea for an automobile powered by gasoline. Reluctant at first, Ford soon sat next to the man he had admired for years and explained his concepts while Edison, his hand cupped over his ear, listened intently. Edison had long been a supporter of the "electric" automobile; no one knew how he would react to what was being said to him.

Once Ford finished talking, Edison asked him a series of questions, which Ford quickly answered, then, in a move that took everyone by surprise, Edison brought his fist down on the table saying, "Young man, that's the thing! You have it! The self-contained unit carrying its own fuel with it. Keep at it!"

Ford, who had been close to giving up on the project, returned to Detroit with renewed vigor. He went back to work on the horseless carriage he called the "quadricycle." Two years later, Ford would leave the Detroit Edison Company and, with the aid of investors, launch his first automotive manufacturing plant.

Of his encounter with Edison in 1887, Ford would later say, "It meant the world to me." The two men became great friends and often spent time at each other's homes. In 1916, Ford planned the camping trip, but was unable to attend due to a business matter. Prior to backing out he had arranged for a Ford touring automobile for Edison and Firestone to ride in, and a Ford truck to carry their supplies. Edison and Firestone started their journey from West Orange. They drove through the Catskill Mountains to the home of John Burroughs in Roxbury, New York, then drove across the Adirondacks to upper Vermont. In all, they spent ten days "roughing it"—as servants and drivers took care of their every need.

Ford made it a point to be there for the next "vagabond" outing in 1918. This time the group traveled through the Great Smoky Mountains. Having released the itinerary to reporters prior to the trip, Ford, Edison, Firestone, and Burroughs were hounded at every turn. However, as the caravan drove deep into the mountain forests, newspapermen soon called off the chase. Burroughs later recalled that Edison liked to read, or sleep for hours anywhere he could lay down. Ford made sure that the firewood never ran out by swinging his ax throughout the day. Burroughs also reminisced later that the "backwoods" people called Edison, "Mr.

Phonograph," and didn't know what an automobile was, much less recognize Ford.

By the next year, the caravan of cars numbered fifty. Ford trucks bore signs reading, "Buy Firestone Tires." As they drove through West Virginia, the caravan stopped long enough for the celebrated "vagabonds" to make a promotional stop at a Ford dealership. President Warren Harding dropped by the campsite to have his picture taken by the army of photographers that now followed the foursome no matter where they went. So overcrowded was the experience becoming that Edison no longer took part after 1921, the same year John Burroughs passed away.

> Edison toured the massive General Electric plant and laboratory at Schenectady, New York, in the fall of 1922. This facility sprang out of the old Edison Machine Works. It was now a huge complex, miles long, housing eighteen thousand employees. All workers came together to greet and praise Edison. A bronze plaque was placed by the door of the laboratory to honor the founding father of this facility. The research demonstrations for the elderly inventor delighted him, but he later admitted that it was not the same anymore even though he expressed a nostalgic attachment to the place.

Now in his mid-seventies, Edison no longer spent the bulk of his time at the West Orange laboratory. Instead, he worked at a laboratory in a room of his home. To escape Eastern winters, he retreated to his Fort Myers estate, where he continued his experiments in a laboratory there. His focus was on further perfecting the various models of his phonograph, business machines, and batteries, both primary and secondary.

Edison's last extensive research and development efforts started in 1927 and would continue until his death in 1931, trying to find a plant from which rubber or a rubber substitute might be derived. The request and funding for research came from Henry Ford and Harvey Firestone, who contributed nintey thousand dollars apiece. Characteristically, after taking up the cause Edison was so immersed in it that Mina would say, "Everything has turned to rubber in our family. We talk rubber, think rubber, dream rubber. Mr. Edison refuses to let us do anything else."

Over the next two years over seventeen thousand plants were gathered. Experiments showed that an estimated two hundred of them contained rubber latex. After further testing, Edison concluded that goldenrod held the answer. Intensive crossbreeding produced a twelve-foot goldenrod variety containing a large amount of latex. Four tires were manufactured by Firestone and placed on a Ford automobile belonging to Edison. The process of extracting and preparing the material for production was not cost-effective, but Edison felt it could be refined to compete with imported rubber.

A year after Edison undertook the challenge of discovering a rubber substitute, Henry Ford decided to join others in celebrating the fiftieth anniversary of Edison's incandescent lamp by dedicating a museum and turn-of-the-century village he was going to build in Dearborn, Michigan, to his trusted friend and mentor, Thomas Alva Edison. In September 27, 1928, Edison was present in Dearborn, when the cornerstone of what would become the Edison Institute, today known as the Henry Ford Museum and Greenfield Village, was laid. Edison signed his name, the date, and put his footprints in a square of concrete at the entrance of the museum, and implanted a spade that once belonged to Luther Burbank, the famed botanist and camping companion of Edison and Ford. The spade represented the America of days gone by, and Edison's signature represented the America that had risen from his efforts.

Following the event, newspapers and newsreels reported that the eighty-one-year-old Edison was returning to his work, a search for a domestic source of natural rubber. Meanwhile, Ford was busy collecting items for his museum and village. He was gathering structures from all over Michigan and as far away as New Haven, Connecticut. Among these was the Eagle Tavern from Clinton, Michigan; the Loranger Grist Mill from Stoney Creek, near Monroe, Michigan; the Logan County Courthouse, where Abraham Lincoln traveled the circuit during his early days as an attorney; Noah Webster's New Haven, Connecticut, home; the home and bicycle shop of Wilbur and Orville Wright from Dayton, Ohio; and the Smith's Creek Grand Trunk Railroad Depot, where young Edison, his laboratory, and his printing press were tossed from the train.

Edison in 1892.

Work was also progressing on the Ford museum, a reproduction of Independence Hall in Philadelphia. The crowning achievement of the entire project, however, was in the village, where a Edison's

Menlo Park laboratory and complex were being painstakingly restored, as well as Sarah Jordan's boarding house and Edison's original Fort Myers laboratory, which Ford secured from Edison by building him another. Ford pushed his supervisors to the limit to have everything completed on time. As the summer drew to a close, there was no doubt that the museum and village would be ready by October. Even so, a dark cloud developed in August, with news that Edison was ill and in bed at home. Ford rushed to his side. Edison assured him that he would be in Dearborn come October.

True to his word, and despite the fact that he was still suffering the after-affects of his three-week battle with pneumonia, Edison and his wife arrived in Dearborn aboard Ford's personal railroad car a few days before the official dedication of the museum and village on October 21, 1929. Ford led Edison and Mina to the building where Edison had achieved his greatest success. Walking through the gate surrounding the compound, the first thing Edison did was to reach down and take a handful of the soil that Ford had bought by the trainloads from the original site in New Jersey. He held it in his hands for a moment and then said, "H'm, the same damn old New Jersey clay."

Inside his legendary laboratory, Edison was escorted to the second floor. Astounded by what he found, Edison walked to a chair and sat down. The next day, a reporter for the *Detroit Free Press* wrote ...

> [H]is companions in the party remained where they stood,
> apart from him a dozen feet. No word was spoken; it was
> if by common consent the spectators instinctively felt awed
> here, in the presence of an old man upon whom memories
> of eighty-two years were flooding back. He sat there,
> silent, his arms folded, an indescribably lonely figure,
> lonely in the loneliness of genius, of one who, somehow,
> has passed the others, who no longer has equals to share
> his world, his thoughts, his feelings.

For five, perhaps ten minutes, the scene was uninterrupted. Now and then Edison looked about him and his eyes glazed over. Suddenly he cleared his throat and the spell was broken.

Ford stepped forward and handed Edison the old mortar and pestle he had once used at Menlo Park. Found in pieces on the original site, Ford had glued them together personally. Edison took the mortar bowl and lifted the pestle. After a minute, Ford asked him what he thought of his restoration, Edison stared around the room and then said, "Well, you've got this just about ninety-nine and one half per cent perfect."

"What is the matter with the other one half per cent?" Ford asked.

"Well," Edison answered, "we never kept it as clean as this!"

The day of the dedication, October 21, 1929, was cold and rainy. Skies were to remain cloudy well into the night. Distinguished guests invited by Ford arrived in Dearborn from all over the world throughout the day. President Hoover and his wife arrived on a special train from Washington, D.C. In Detroit, the Hoovers joined the Edisons, the Fords (including Edsel, Ford's son, and his wife), and Firestones, as well as a few other guests. The group rode to Dearborn aboard an 1860s train decorated to resemble a locomotive on which Edison had served as a candy butcher, complete with a laboratory in the luggage car. Somewhere along the route, Edison took a box filled with an assortment of items and walked the isle calling, "Candy and fruits for sale!"

President Hoover took Edison up on his proposition, exclaiming, "I'll take a peach," and handing over a coin.

The train pulled into the restored Smiths Creek Depot at Greenfield Village around ten o'clock. As Edison stepped down from the passenger car, guests clapped and cheered. Scattered among them was found Madam Curie, Lee DeForest, George Eastman, Orville Wright, Will Rogers, John D. Rockefeller, Walter P. Chrysler, Cyrus Eaton, Charles Schwab, Fielding H. Yost, and Dr. Charles Mayo. An informal gathering was held inside Clinton Inn on the Village grounds, then guests rode in horse-drawn carriages on a tour of the Village's twenty-eight buildings and were given an opportunity to visit the museum.

Later in the day, guests were driven in Ford automobiles to their hotel rooms where they freshened up before the formal banquet and dedication ceremony. As guests returned for the evening festivities, Edison, Ford, President Hoover, Jehl, and few others were found at the Menlo Park laboratory. Edison sat at a table on the second floor repeating the same final preparations taken fifty years earlier in making the first incandescent lamp. Millions of people around the world listened in darkened homes to the reenactment on their radios. His work completed, Edison handed the lamp to Jehl, who then placed it on a Sprengel pump in order to form the vacuum that was found so many years before to be one of the secrets to inventing a functional incandescent lamp. Finished, Jehl called to Edison that the time had come to give the lamp a try. In their homes, people listened as radio announcer Graham McNamee proclaimed …

> The lamp is now ready, as it was a half century ago! Will
> it light? Will it burn? Edison touches the wire.
> Ladies and gentlemen—it lights! Light's Golden Jubilee
> has come to a triumphant climax!

As the filament came to life and grew stronger, Edison loudly proclaimed, "*Let there be light!*"

In homes throughout the world, people added to the celebration by turning on their lights in a show of gratitude for the old Wizard. In the packed banquet hall, lights were turned up in intensity, and an airplane flew across the overcast Dearborn sky pulling an electrified banner reading: "Edison, 1879–1929." As Edison and those present exited the laboratory and made their way to the celebration dinner, Ford turned to a workman and ordered him to nail the chair in which Edison had been seated to the floor. The workman did as he was told. The chair was fixed in place, where it has remained to this day, undisturbed.

Though the night was still young, Edison's stamina was wearing thin. On his arrival at the banquet hall, he nearly collapsed. He was given warm milk, and he cried as Mina comforted him and convinced him to go on with the evening's events. Once he was seated in his place of honor, a number of tributes sent from every corner of the world were read. Through the magic of radio, Albert Einstein was able to offer a word of praise from his home: "The great creators of technics, among whom you are one of the most successful, have put mankind into a perfectly new situation, to which it has not at all adapted itself."

Owen D. Young, the chairman of the board of General Electric, declared to Edison that "the same unconquerable will and unquenchable fire which took you out of [the Smith Creek] depot, and set you on your career, brings you back today." He then read additional tributes to Edison from the Prince of Wales and German president Paul von Hindenburg.

President Hoover then gave a speech commending Edison's lifelong achievements, and he praised him for "repelling darkness." When Edison's turn came to speak, he could hardly stand. However, with Mina's encouragement, he took the podium. With an unsteady voice, he read his prepared speech into the microphone:

> I would be embarrassed at the honors that are being
> heaped on me on this unforgettable night were it not for
> the fact that in honoring me you are also honoring that
> vast army of thinkers and workers of the past without
> whom my work would have gone for nothing.

Edison could hardly be heard as he thanked Henry Ford, saying, "Words are inadequate to express my feelings. I can only say to you, that—in the fullest and richest meaning of the term—he is my friend. Good night."

Once finished, Edison was quickly ushered from the stage. Mina and President Hoover's physician helped him to a back room, where they laid him on a sofa. He was then taken to his quarters at Ford's Fair Lane estate and was placed in bed, where he was later heard to say, "I am tired of all the glory, I want to get back to work."[1] The next day, the story of his collapse took precedence over the celebration. People found it hard to believe that the once-robust Edison was now in failing health.

In a related story, newspapers also announced that the domestic recording branch of Edison's phonographic company was closing. Six days later, recording operations were halted completely. Sixty-two men found themselves without a job. The next day, October 29, the stock market crashed; the Great Depression had arrived.

Edison transcribing notes from a piece of paper into a laboratory notebook, circa 1928.

Edison now spent less time at his laboratory and more time at Glenmont and his residence in Florida. He continued to conduct experiments in his search for a rubber substitute. For a generation that had grown up and had grown old with Edison, news that he was still hard at work despite questionable health was no surprise.

His work ethic was one of his most admired and respected qualities. Adoration for Edison had grown to the point that, in survey after survey, when people were asked to name the greatest American in history, Edison's name was often at the top of the list, or second only to that of George Washington, or Abraham Lincoln. When informed of these results, Edison would only say that he was humbled by the honor, and he meant it.

German-born biographer Emil Ludwig, who won fame and criticism for his biographies, *Kaiser Wilhelm II* and *Jesus, The Son of Man*, witnessed the public's admiration for Edison while traveling with him and Henry Ford in Florida. Ludwig wrote of the experience and included the piece in a collection of reminiscences, *Gifts of Life*.

> On the expedition to the south of Florida with Edison and Ford, we arrived late in one of those small new towns. Lunch was over, so we went into the café and ordered something. So as not to attract attention, Ford had a table laid quite at the back in semi-obscurity. Edison, who never takes lunch, stayed in the car, sitting in his usual place in front, for he sees better from there. He sent his chauffeur in to lunch with us. The car stood in the shade on the other side of the broad empty street, about ten yards from our café.
>
> Somebody had meanwhile spied the old man in his solitary car and probably called out his name, so he was done for! When after a short time, I went to the window, the street was literally dark with people, and I vainly tried to fight my way through to the car.
>
> There he sat, and every one was holding out a slip of paper, either to ask some stupid question or merely get his autograph; and he was writing on his little slips, nodding, laughing, waving, to the people. When we, stranded as we were, asked him by gestures across the sea of human beings whether he wanted a lifeboat, and the crowd drew his attention to us, he looked over, nodded, laughed, and shouted:
>
> "Don't worry! It's all right!"

*Then he turned back to the throng with a friendly
nod, and I thought to myself: "There sits the uncrowned
King of America."*

Aside from the profiles and photographs published over the
years, people around the world had come to know Edison from the
yearly birthday interview he granted reporters. The Wizard's personality showed through in the frank and often humorous answers
he gave to reporters' questions, and while his hair had grayed and
his face had wrinkled, his mind and the ideas germinated there
were as fresh as ever. It seemed Edison would live forever. In 1931,
the event took place at Edison's laboratory office on his estate in
Fort Myers, Florida, where Edison and Fred Ott, one of his trusted
assistants dating back to his Newark factory, were "on the job," as
Edison put it, uncovering a natural source of rubber. Edison
appeared dressed in a blue three-piece suit with loose fitting
bowtie. His outfit was accented by a brilliant sunflower in the lapel
of his coat, a symbol of his latest interest. The newspapermen fired
a battery of thirty questions; some were quickly dismissed with a
yes or a no, while others, like, "Whom do you regard as the five
outstanding men in the world?" received no answer at all.

Asked about the depression gripping the country, Edison said
that business had started a three-year trend toward the level of
activity that prevailed prior to the depression and that the "cycle
of business depression" was one that "we will always have" because
it lay "in the very nature of man." He declared Prohibition and
Hoover's administration successes. Unemployment was "a question
several sizes too large" for him to answer, and "ambition and the
will to work" were the chief aids to success. Of turning eighty-four,
Edison simply said, "It feels fine to be eighty-four years old." He
then abruptly changed the subject by pointing at the sunflower on
his lapel saying, "There's a lot of rubber in that."

The tire magnate, Harvey S. Firestone, asked Edison, "Are you
going to send me enough rubber this year to make a set of tires for
you?"

"I think," the inventor replied, smiling broadly, "I will have
enough rubber on hand within two years to send it to the Firestone
works and have them make me a set of home grown tires."

As for life in general, Edison felt the current pace was not too fast and that "the present trend of life is improving as pertains to morals."

The interview was to be the first in a string of events celebrating his birthday, including a gala parade to a new seven hundred fifty thousand dollars bridge spanning the Callosahatchee River named in Edison's honor. Later in the day, he would also speak to the annual convention of Edison Pioneers, a group that at the time consisted of men who had been employed at Menlo Park during the 1870s and early 1880s.

The question most often asked Edison was which invention he considered his favorite, or most satisfying? Edison never tired of the question, and always answered that he was most proud of his phonograph. Edison's affection for the invention was not because it brought him worldwide fame and eventually untold riches, but because he considered the device as something that was entirely his and his alone. No one could claim that he had borrowed any facet of the invention from work in which they were involved, or had completed. Beyond the fact that the phonograph was Edison's most treasured invention, it should also be remembered as a benchmark in his career. His life experiences up to that point not only made the invention of the device possible, but it was a point in Edison's history by which he was clearly prepared to take advantage of the opportunity for publicity and acclaim.

The next day, Edison returned to his work. Over the next few months, his health went through a series of highs and lows; he would be well for a couple of weeks and then suddenly bed-ridden for a few days. On June 11, he sent words of encouragement to the National Light Association convention in Atlantic City, which read:

> *My message to you is to be courageous. I have lived a long time. I have seen history repeat itself again and again. I have seen many depressions in business. Always America has come out strong and more prosperous. Be as brave as your fathers were before you. Have faith—go forward.*

Edison's words of encouragement seemed to be directed more toward himself than to the economic hardship the industry was facing, and as June came to an end Edison was battling a combination of illnesses which doctors had diagnosed as Bright's disease, uremic poisoning, and diabetes. On August 1, 1931, he collapsed; the end, it was feared, was once again near.

Tributes praising Edison's contributions to humanity were published in the world's newspapers. None captured the significance Edison had played in redefining the world more than *The New York Times* on June 24, 1923, which reported that Edison's genius was responsible for the employment of over 1,500,000 men and that the value of his inventions to society was $15,000,000,000, a sum that was "within 20 per cent of equaling the value of all the gold dug from the mines of the earth since America was discovered."

Edison, however, was not yet ready to give up the fight. By September he was up and around once again. He questioned his doctors regarding his treatment, received a visit from Henry Ford, and sent directives and questions to his employees at West Orange on the work taking place in his absence. He resumed drives in the countryside with Mina. However, by mid-September he grew worse. He was confined to his bed. *The New York Times* later wrote ...

> *With the interest and sympathy which it reveals only for*
> *its great, the entire world followed the illness and passing*
> *of Thomas Alva Edison. Throughout the long weeks of*
> *his illness, the old-fashioned Victorian home ... where the*
> *enfeebled white-haired inventor awaited death, was the*
> *focal point of universal solicitude.*

On October 13, after presenting Harvey Firestone with four vulcanized specimens of goldenrod rubber, Edison slipped into a coma. Outside, newspapermen waited in the makeshift newsroom at the ten-car Glenmont garage, while inside Edison's family and laboratory assistants awaited the inevitable. The scene was reminiscent of the day some fifty-two years earlier when Edison and his workers sat up all night watching to see when his carbon filament would burn out. Periodically, his son, Charles, would step out of Edison's room to say, "The light still burns."

The vigil lasted until the early morning hours of October 18, when the lights went on in Edison's bedroom at 3:24, an indication to those outside that Thomas Alva Edison had passed away.

Reaction to the news of Edison's death was swift and all-consuming. In gratitude, the flags on all Edison Company buildings flew at half-staff and the factories surrounding Glenmont were closed until after the funeral. In New York City, officials of the Edison Company placed a wreath at the Pearl Street building that had been the first electric power house in the world; the National Broadcasting Company paid homage with a special musical tribute, and in Fort Myers, the City Council passed a resolution of sympathy and immediately dispatched it to Mrs. Edison. The *London Times* wrote that Edison ...

> *seemed to belong to a past which was already becoming*
> *remote, a past without the incandescent electric light, and*
> *without the phonograph, and without other gifts with*
> *which his ingenuity and persistence endowed the world.*

Tributes arrived at Glenmont from world leaders and dignitaries around the world. Aboard the battleship *Arkansas*, President Hoover announced that he planned to attend the funeral and sent a note to Mina that read, "Mr. Edison was as great in his fight for life as he was in the achievement which has made the whole world his debtor. I mourn his passing, not only as one of the greatest men our nation has produced, but as a personal friend ...." From France, Premier Laval sent his condolences, and Pope Pius XI expressed deep sorrow from his office at the Vatican. Voicing their feelings on Edison's passing were New York governor Franklin D. Roosevelt, George Eastman, Harvey S. Firestone, Adolph S. Ochs, publisher of *The New York Times*, Albert Einstein, and William Randolph Hearst.

In a mixed reaction to Edison's passing, Nikola Tesla, himself a recognized leader throughout the world in the area of electricity, criticized Edison's methods:

> *[He] was inefficient in the extreme, for an immense*
> *ground had to be covered to get anything at all unless*
> *blind chance intervened and, at first, I was almost a sorry*
> *witness of his doings, knowing that just a little theory and*
> *calculation would have saved him 90 percent of the labor.*

He concluded, however, by saying, "The recurrence of a phenomenon like Edison is not very likely .... He will occupy a unique and exalted position in the history of his native land, which might well be proud of his great genius and undying achievements in the interest of humanity."

Edison's body lay in state for two days in the library of his West Orange laboratory. Thousands of people lined up to pay their final respects, including Mr. and Mrs. Henry Ford, Mr. and Mrs. Calvin Coolidge, Andrew Carnegie, Dr. Karl Compton, Hamilton McK. Twombly Jr., Charles Batchelor's widow, Francis Upton's two daughters, Lillian Gilliland, Francis Jehl, and Samuel Insull. Mrs. Herbert Hoover was there alone; the president was unable to attend due to a meeting with the premier of France. Fred Ott also arrived alone; his brother John, who had been ill, had passed away shortly after hearing of Edison's death. John's crutches were placed symbolically next to Edison's coffin.

Edison's lieutenants from his days at Newark and Menlo Park all enjoyed prosperous lives. John Kruesi, the manufacturer of Edison's original phonograph, managed the Edison Machine Works. In 1883, he was awarded a patent for an underground electric tube system. He founded the Electric Tube Company to manufacture and sell the system. A short time later the company merged with Edison Machine Works, where Kruesi served under Batchelor as assistant general manager until 1885, at which point he took over the position. When the company was merged with Edison General Electric, and moved to Schenectady, New York the following year, Kruesi became the assistant general manager under Samuel Insull. During six years in this position, Kruesi expanded the shops as the number of employees rose from two hundred to four thousand. He became the general manager of the General Electric Company in 1892, after the reorganization of the Edison General Electric Company, and chief mechanical engineer in 1896. He passed away on February 22, 1899.

Charles Batchelor led the construction of Edison's West Orange laboratory and was the general manager of Edison Machine Works. He later became the treasurer and general manager of the General Electric Company in 1892. He retired from the company and soon thereafter assisted Edison at the Ogdensburg milling project.

When he passed away on January 1, 1910, he was president of the Taylor Foundry Company.

Francis Upton gave up his position with the Edison Lamp Works in 1894. Four years later he returned to work for Edison becoming the efficiency engineer at the New Jersey and Pennsylvania Concentrating Works. In this role, Upton was able to excel in selling sand, the by-product of Edison's Ogdensburg mill, to cement companies. He was so successful that it became one of the deciding factors in convincing Edison to start his Portland cement company. With the close of the Ogdensburg mill, Upton went to work for the Edison Portland Cement Company, where he was to become the company representative for northern New Jersey. He left the company in 1911, selling cement products on his own. He was married twice and, like Edison, had three children with each wife. He assumed the post of president in the Edison Pioneers, a group of men who had worked for Edison over the years, in 1918. In retirement, Upton moved to California, but died in Orange, New Jersey, on March 10, 1921. With the passing of these men, Edison had lost trusted employees and lifelong friends.

As the crowds disappeared, on Wednesday, October 21, Edison's body was returned to Glenmont at three o'clock that afternoon. Mina spent an hour alone with the body before the private funeral service. The two-hour service began with the playing of two of Edison's favorite tunes, "I'll Take You Home Again, Kathleen," and "Little Grey Home in the West." These songs were then followed by a classical medley consisting in part of Beethoven's "Moonlight Sonata," and Wagner's "Evening Star." Dr. Stephen J. Herben, former pastor of the Orange Methodist Episcopal Church, where Mina was a member, read the twenty-third Psalm and closed by saying, "His fertile brain has ceased to do its accustomed work. His gleaming eye is dimmed. His quick hand is folded in rest."

A eulogy written by Arthur J. Palmer, an Edison Industries employee, was then read by Dr. Lewis Perry, a family friend, which concluded, "Of this man, this super-being who defies classification, what more can be said, what greater tribute can be paid than this: He is humanity's friend."

Asthe invited guests departed, the song "Now the Day is Over" marked the close of the proceedings. Mina, the rest of the Edison family, Mr. and Mrs. Ford, Mr. and Mrs. Firestone, and Mrs. Hoover accompanied the coffin to the Rosedale Cemetery, where final words of praise were offered. The coffin was lowered into the ground as Dr. Herben delivered the grief poem:

Earth to earth, and dust to dust,
Calmly now the words we say,
Left behind, we wait in trust
For the Resurrection day.
Father, in Thy gracious keeping
Leave we now Thy servant sleeping.

Those present took their turn at dropping a solitary white rosebud into the grave. Mina was to rest next to Edison after she passed away on August 24, 1947, where they would remain until sixteen years later when they were reinterred on the grounds of Glenmont.

In tribute to Edison, on the evening of October 21 at 6:59 Pacific time, 7:59 Mountain time, 8:59 Central time, and 9:59 Eastern time, across America all but essential lights were turned off. Even the bright lights of Broadway and the torch held high by the Statue of Liberty, which had greeted the down-and-out inventor on his arrival in New York City were extinguished. One minute later, from the Pacific to the Atlantic, with a simple flip of a switch, Americans turned off the darkness, forever.

The uncrowned king of America now belonged to the ages.

Testimonials from dignitaries were published in newspapers throughout the world. They referred to Edison as an example of Americans at their finest, and a model of what was possible when genius was combined with indomitable courage and purpose. He was lauded for his humorous, enthusiastic, humble, inquisitive, and persevering personality. He was described as a man of the people, the best scientist since Farraday, the last of the great electrical pioneers, a person who was not afraid to take risks. He was complimented for discovering practical and marketable inventions, for his broad-based knowledge of a variety of subjects. He was eulogized for contributions from his idea of a research and development laboratory, to his invention of the phonograph, the motion-picture camera, his incandescent lamp, and his electrical distribution system. It was recalled how Edison invested his money in furthering his career, how he placed into use the knowledge gained from one area into another, and the passion he held for his profession, not for monetary gain, but because of his true love for inventing. Overall, it was agreed that humanity would never have a greater benefactor than Thomas Alva Edison.

Today, for the average American and others around the world, Edison's name no longer holds much significance outside of the fact that he invented the light bulb, or that they pay their electrical light bill to a company that still bears his name. His story and his other contributions have been all but forgotten. This would have suited the humble side of Edison's personality, but the side of Edison's personality that demanded the spotlight would never have been satisfied.

For this reason, there can be no doubt that wherever Thomas Alva Edison is today, he is surely smiling when rolling blackouts in California are somehow attributed to his name, or when he once again makes headlines, as when he was named number one in *Life* magazine's list of people who made the Millennium; an honor that placed him ahead of Christopher Columbus, Martin Luther, Galileo Galilei, Leonardo da Vinci, Issac Newton, Ferdinand Magellan, Louis Pasteur, Charles Darwin, and Thomas Jefferson.

Then again, this acclaim might have been too much for Edison, who would have preferred to be remembered as nothing more than a man who made something of his life through hard work, determination, and perseverance.

At the turn of the century, electricity had changed life dramatically. The electric elevator allowed for towering skyscrapers. Electric motors streamlined and sped up factories that had depended on monstrous steam engines. Yet no matter how many inventors contributed to this modern age of electricity, people around the world attributed the transformation to Edison. Edison became a folk hero in his old age, especially for Americans, and he fit the role perfectly. He looked the part, being a bit disheveled and paternal. His wit and ability to coin catchy phrases added to his charm.

Today, for the average American and others around the world, Edison's name no longer evokes the hero worship of the early twentieth century. However, Edison's legacy lives on in our everyday lives through his many inventions and the spirit of perseverance that inspires modern inventors. Perhaps the most prominent yet least recognized of Edison contributions to the modern age is the industrial research facility. Edison's Menlo Park was the precursor of all the major industrial research facilities. Most major companies involved in technological and industrial research world never dream of operating without such a facility, yet few are aware of their direct connection to Thomas Alva Edison's idea. Edison's phonograph and motion-picture camera were the beginnings of the vast entertainment industry we have today. The electrical wiring in our houses and the switches and plugs on all of our appliances are direct descendants of Edison's innovations. Even excluding the light bulb, a person does not have to look far to find an Edison idea.

Beyond all the material items that Edison helped to create, perhaps his inspiring character is his most important legacy. Thomas Alva Edison's accomplishments at such an early age and the sheer volume of output in his lifetime leave one astounded by his energies, asking how it was all possible. He was a man who never gave up. He kept a positive attitude even when working long hours for weeks—and, in addition to his gifts, he worked hard to accomplish what he achieved. His famous quote that "genius is one percent inspiration and ninety-nine percent perspiration" represented his work ethic and lifestyle. Even vacations included work, and he never stopped thinking and putting ideas and experience together to create newer and better products. This legacy of perseverance is perhaps Edison's most important legacy, one that can inspire and motivate people towards an even brighter future.

Appendix A

Chronology

1828: Nancy Elliott and Samuel Edison married in Vienna, Ontario.

1847, February 11: Thomas Alva Edison was born in Milan, Ohio. He was the seventh child of Samuel and Nancy Elliot Edison.

1854: Edison family moves to Port Huron, Michigan.

1859: Young Edison secures job as a "candy butcher" on the Grand Trunk Railroad running between Port Huron and Detroit.

1862, August: Printed and published a newspaper, *The Weekly Herald*, on the Grand Trunk Railroad. This was the first newspaper ever printed on a moving train.

1862: Edison snatched the son of Mt. Clemens, Michigan, station agent, J. U. Mackenzie, from the path of a moving freight car. In gratitude, Mackenzie gives Edison's formal lessons in the art and technology of telegraphy. Years later, Mackenzie would spend a great deal of time at Menlo Park.

1863, May: Secures position as a regular telegraph operator on Grand Trunk Railway at Stratford Junction, Ontario, Canada.

1863: Began five-year period as an itinerant telegrapher in various cities of the Midwest. This period in his life can be considered his "collegiate" years.

1868: Arrives in Boston, where he became a telegraph operator in the offices of the Western Union Company. Began work with duplex system of telegraphy. Receives first patent for the telegraphic vote recorder.

1869: Arrives in New York City, a washed-up inventor. Shortly afterwards, he secures a position with the Gold Indicator Company after repairing its central transmitting apparatus when no one else could.

1869, October: Establishes a partnership with Franklin L. Pope and James Ashley as electrical engineers. Believed to be the first firm of this type established in the United States. Partnership lasts until summer of 1870.

1870: Received forty thousand dollars from the Gold and Stock Telegraph Company, a Western Union subsidiary, for improvements made to several devices owned by the company and for his stock ticker. With this money, Edison opens a manufacturing shop in Newark, New Jersey, where he made stock tickers and telegraph instruments.

1871, December 25: Married Mary Stilwell, daughter of Nicholas Stilwell of Newark.

1872: Began a four-year period during which he manufactured telegraph instruments for Western Union Telegraph Company and Automatic Telegraph Company. He had several shops during this time in Newark, New Jersey. He worked on and completed many inventions, including the motograph, automatic telegraph system, duplex, quadruplex, and multiplex systems; also paraffin paper and the carbon rheostat.

1874: Invented the electric pen and manual duplicating press for making copies of letters. Patent granted 1876. Improved and manufactured at Menlo Park in 1877.

1875: Devised an automatic copying machine. He later sold the machine to the A. B. Dick Company of Chicago.

1875, November 22: Discovered a previously unknown and unique electrical phenomenon he referred to as etheric force. Twelve years later, this phenomenon was recognized as being due to electric waves in free space. This discovery is the foundation of wireless telegraphy.

1876, April: Moved from Newark to the newly constructed laboratory at Menlo Park, New Jersey. This was the first laboratory for organized industrial research. He was twenty-nine at the time.

1877, April 27: Applied for patent on the carbon telephone transmitter, which made Alexander Graham Bell's telephone commercially practicable. This invention included the microphone, which is used in radio broadcasting.

1877, December 6: Recorded "Mary Had a Little Lamb" on the tin-foil phonograph. This was the first time a machine recorded and reproduced sound.

1877, December 24: Applied for patent on the phonograph.

1878, April 18: Took the tin-foil phonograph to Washington, D.C., to demonstrate it before the National Academy of Sciences and to President Rutherford B. Hayes, his wife, and White House guests.

1878, July 29: Using the heat of the sun's corona during an eclipse at Rawlins, Wyoming, he tested the microtasimeter, a device indicating minute heat variations by electrical means.

1878, October 15: Incorporation meeting of the Edison Electrical Lighting Company.

1879, July: First Edison experimental marine electrical plant installed aboard SS *Jeanette* for the George Washington De Long expedition to the Arctic.

1879: Invented the first practical incandescent electric lamp on October 21. The lamp maintained its incandescent for more than forty hours.

1879: Conceived and implemented radical improvements in construction of dynamos making them suitable as generators for his system of distributing current for light, heat, and power. Invented system of distribution, regulation, and measurement of electric current, including sockets, switches, fuses, and so on.

1879, December 31: Gave a public demonstration of his electric lighting system in streets and buildings at Menlo Park, New Jersey.

1880: Discovered a previously unknown phenomenon. He found that an independent wire or plate placed between the legs of the filament of an incandescent lamp acted as a valve to control the flow of current. This became known as the Edison Effect. This discovery covers the fundamental principal on which rests the science of electronics.

1880, April 3: Invented the magnetic ore separator.

1880, May 1: First commercial installation of the Edison lighting system on land or water aboard the SS *Columbia*.

1880, May 13: Started operation of the first passenger electric railway in this country at Menlo Park, New Jersey.

1880: Ushered in seven strenuous years of invitation and endeavor in extending and improving the electric light, heat, and power systems. During these years he took out more than three hundred patents. Of 1,093 patents issued to Thomas A. Edison, 365 deal with electric lightning and power distribution.

1880, October 1: First commercial manufacturer of incandescent lamps began at Edison Lamp Works, Menlo Park, New Jersey.

1881, January 31: Opened offices of the Edison Electric Light Company at 65 Fifth Avenue, New York City.

1881, March 2: Edison arranged to open the Edison Machine Works at 104 Goerck Street, New York City.

1882, January 12: Opened the first commercial incandescent lighting and power station at Holborn Viaduct, London, England.

1882, May 1: Moved the first commercial incandescent lamp factory from Menlo Park to Harrison, New Jersey. Organized and established shops for the manufacture of dynamos, underground conductors, sockets, switches, fixtures, meters, and so on.

1882, September 4: Commenced the operation of the first commercial center station for incandescent lighting in this country at 257 Pearl Street, New York City.

1883, July 4: First three-wire system central station for electric lighting started operation at Sunbury, Pennsylvania.

1883, November 15: Filed patent on an electrical indicator using the Edison Effect. This was the first patent in the science now known as electronics.

1884, August 9: His wife, Mary Stilwell Edison, died at Menlo Park, New Jersey.

1885, March 27: Patent granted on a system for communicating by means of wireless induction telegraphy between moving trains and railway stations.

1885, May 14: Patent executed on a ship-to-shore wireless telegraphy system by induction.

1886, January: Bought Glenmont, a residence in Llewellyn Park, West Orange, New Jersey.

1886, February 24: Married Mina Miller, daughter of Lewis Miller of Akron, Ohio.

1886, December: Moved plant of Edison Machine Works from 104 Goerck Street, New York City, to Schenectady, New York.

1887: Work begins on West Orange laboratory. Laboratory equipment and machinery moved into space before construction completed.

1888: West Orange, New Jersey laboratory completed. During the first four years, Edison took out over forty patents concerning improvements on the cylinder phonograph.

1889, January: Formation of Edison General Electric.

1889, October 6: First projection of an experimental motion picture. This was a "talkie" shown at the West Orange laboratory; the picture was accompanied by synchronized sound from a phonograph record.

1891, August 24: Applied for patent on the motion picture camera. With the invention of this mechanism, which used a continuous tape like film, it became possible to take and reproduce motion pictures as we do today.

1891: This year marked the culmination of his preliminary surveys and experimental work on iron-ore concentration that he had started while in Menlo Park in 1880. Edison did some of his most brilliant engineering work in connection with this project.

1893, February: "Black Maria," the world's first motion-picture studio constructed in West Orange Laboratory complex.

1893: Edison-Lalande primary cells supplied power for the first electric semaphore signal installed on railroad near Phillipsburg, New Jersey.

1894, April 14: First commercial showing of motion pictures took place with the opening of a kinetoscope parlor at 1155 Broadway, New York City.

1896: Experimented with the x-ray discovered by Roentgen the year before. Developed the fluoroscope but did not patent, choosing to leave it to the public domain because of its universal need in medicine and surgery.

1896, February 26: His father, Samuel Edison, died in Norwalk, Ohio.

1896, April 23: First commercial projection of motion pictures at Koster and Bial's Music Hall, New York City, by Edison Vitascope.

1896, May 16: Applied for a patent on the first fluorescent electric lamp. This invention sprang directly from his work on the fluoroscope.

1900: Beginning of a ten-year period of work that resulted in the invention and commercial introduction of the Edison nickel-iron-alkaline storage battery. The alkaline battery is widely employed as a power source in mine haulage, inter- and intra-plant transportation, for railway train cat lighting and air-conditioning, signaling services, and many other industrial applications.

1901: Commenced construction on the Edison cement plant at New Village, New Jersey, and started quarrying operations at nearby Oxford. In his cement industry, Edison proceeded to apply the fruits of experience gained in the iron-ore concentrating venture.

1902: Worked on improving the Edison copper oxide primary battery.

1903, July 20: Applied for patent on long rotary kilns for cement production.

1904: *The Great Train Robbery*, the first motion-picture story on film is produced and filmed by Edison film company. Edison Studios goes on to produce over seventeen hundred films.

1907: Developed the universal electric motor for operating dictating machines on either alternating or direct current.

1909: After close to ten years of research, the improved Edison nickel-iron alkaline battery appeared. It was a success in industrial and naval applications.

1910: This year initiated a four-year period of work on an improved type of disc phonograph. His work resulted in production of the diamond disk instrument and records, which reproduced vocal and instrumental music with improved fidelity.

1912: Introduced the kinetophone for talking motion pictures.

1914, October 13: Patent executed on electric safety lanterns, which are used by miners for working lights. These miners' lamps have contributed in an important degree to the reduction of mine fatalities.

1914: Developed a process for the manufacture of synthetic carbolic acid. Designed a plant, and within a month was producing a ton a day to help overcome the acute shortage due to World War I.

1914, December 9: Edison's great plant at West Orange, New Jersey, was destroyed by fire. Rebuilding was planned immediately, and new buildings began to arise almost before the ruins of the old ones were cold.

1915: Established plants for the manufacture of fundamental coal-tar derivatives vital to many industries previously dependent on foreign sources. These coal-tar products were needed later for the production of wartime explosives. Edison's work is recognized as having paved the way for the important development of the coal-tar chemical industry in the United States today.

1915, October 7: Became president of the Naval Consulting Board, at the request of Josephus Daniels, then secretary of navy. During the war years (1915–18), he did a large amount of work connected with national defense, particularly with reference to special experiments on over forty major war problems for the United States government.

1923: Made a study of economic conditions, publishing results in a pamphlet in 1924, when Edison presented to the secretary of the treasury a proposed amendment to the Federal Reserve Banking System.

1927: A four-year period began during which Edison searched for a domestic source natural rubber. This project was completed with the vulcanization of goldenrod rubber shortly before his death.

1928, May 21: Received a special Congressional Medal of Honor, which was presented by Andrew W. Mellon, Secretary of the Treasury.

1929, October 21: Commemorating the fiftieth anniversary of the incandescent lamp and in the presence of President Herbert Hoover, Henry Ford, and other world leaders, Edison re-enacted the lighting of the first practical incandescent lamp.

1931, October 18: Died at Llewellyn Park, West Orange, New Jersey, at age eighty-four. He was survived by his wife, Mina Miller Edison; his four sons, Thomas Alva Jr., William Leslie, Charles, and Theodore; and his daughters Marion Edison Oser and Madeleine Edison Sloane.

Appendix B

Honors

1878: Doctor of Philosophy, Union College Chevalier of the French Legion of Honor Medal of Superiority, The American Institute.

1879: Medals of Excellence, the American Institute.

1881: Diploma of Honor, General Congress, Paris.

1889: Insignia of Grand Officer of the Crown of Italy.

1892: The Alvert Medal, British Society of Arts.

1904: Honorary Chief Consulting Engineer, American Institute of Electrical Engineers.

1908: The John Fritz Gold Medal.

1913: Rathenau Gold Medal, American Museum of safety.

1915: The Civic Forum Gold Medal of the Franklin Institute Doctor of Science, Princeton University.

1916: Honorary Member of the Illuminating Engineering Society Doctor of Laws, University of the State of New York.

1920: Distinguished Service Medal, U.S. Department of the Navy.

1923: Honorary Life Member of the Royal Order of Loyal Knights of the Round Table.

1925: Medal of Public Instruction, Venezuelan Government.

1928: Gold Medal for Sciences, the Society of Arts and Science.

1928: May 21: Awarded Special Congressional Medal of Honor.

1992: Bachelor of Science degree in Applied Science and Technology Thomas Edison State College, Trenton, New Jersey.

2000: Named number one in *Life* magazine's list of People Who Made the Millennium.

Appendix C

Further Reading

Books

Alvarado, Rudolph, and Sonya Alvarado. *Drawing Conclusions on Henry Ford*. Ann Arbor, MI: University of Michigan Press, 2001.

Baldwin, Neil. *Edison: Inventing the Century*. New York: Hyperion, 1995.

Brown, J. J. *Ideas in Exile: A History of Canadian Invention*. Toronto: McClelland and Steward Ltd., 1967.

Bryan, George S. *Edison: The Man and His Work*. New York: Knopf, 1926.

Cheney, Margaret. *Tesla: Man Out of Time*. New Jersey: Prentice-Hall, Inc., 1981.

Clark, Ronald W. *Edison: The Man Who Made the Future*. New York: G. P. Putnam's Sons, 1977.

Conot, Robert. *A Streak of Luck*. New York: Seaview Books, 1979.

Cousins, Margaret. *The Story of Thomas Alva Edison*. New York: Random House, 1965.

Dickson, W.K.L., and Antonia Dickson. *Life and Inventions of Edison*. New York: Thomas Y. Crowell Publishing, 1894.

Dyer, Frank L., and Thomas C. Martin. *Edison: His Life and Inventions*. Vol. I & II. New York: Harper and Brothers, 1910.

Egan, Louise. *Thomas Edison: The Great American Inventor*. Barron's Educational Series, Incorporated, 1987.

Ford, Henry, with Samuel Crowther. *Edison as I Know Him*. New York: Cosmopolitan Book Corporation, 1930.

Friedel, Robert, and Paul Israel. *Edison's Electric Light: Biography of an Invention*. New Brunswick, NJ: Rutgers University Press, 1986.

Gabler, Edwin. *The American Telegrapher: A Social History, 1860–1900*. New York: Rutgers University Press, 1988.

Gelatt, Roland. *The Fabulous Phonograph: The Story of the Gramophone from Tin Foil to High Fidelity*. New York: Appleton-Century, 1966.

Greusel, John Hubert. *Thomas A. Edison: The Man, His Work and His Mind*. John Hubert Greusel, 1913.

Hammond, John Winthrop. *Men and Volts: The Story of General Electric*. Lippincott, 1941.

Harlow, Alvin F. *Old Wires and New Waves: The History of the Telegraph, Telephone and Wireless*. Appleton-Century, 1936.

Hatfield, H. Stafford. *The Inventor and His World*. London: Kegan Paul, Trench, Trubner & Co. Ltd., 1933.

Insull, Samuel. *Central Station Electric Service*. Chicago: Samuel Insull, 1915.

Israel, Paul B. *Edison: A Life of Invention*. New York: John Wiley & Sons, Incorporated, 1998.

Jehl, Francis. *Reminiscences of Menlo Park*. Vol. I, II, III. Dearborn, MI: Edison Institute, 1937-39.

Jewkes, John, et al. *The Sources of Invention*. New York: Macmillan, 1958.

Jones, Francis Arthur. *Thomas Alva Edison: An Intimate Record.* New York: Thomas Y. Crowell & Co., 1907.

Josephson, Matthew. *Edison: A Biography.* New York: McGraw-Hill Book Company, Incorporated, 1959.

Martin, Thomas C. *Forty Years of Edison Service: 1882–1922.* The New York Edison Company, 1922.

Mast, Gerald. *A Short History of the Movies.* Indianapolis: The Bobbs-Merrill Company, Incorporated, 1976.

Melosi, Martin V. *Thomas A. Edison and the Modernization of America.* New York: HarperCollins Publishers, 1990.

Millard, Andre. *Edison and the Business of Innovation.* Johns Hopkins University Press, 1990.

Miller, F. T. *Thomas Alva Edison: Benefactor of Mankind: The Romantic Life Story of the World's Greatest Inventor.* John C. Winston, 1931.

Nerney, Mary C. *Thomas A. Edison: A Modern Olympian.* New York: Harrison Smith & Robert Haas, 1934.

O'Neil, John. *Prodigal Genius: The Life of Nikolas Tesla.* New York: Ives, Washburn, Inc., 1944.

Read, Oliver, and Walter L. Welch. *From Tin Foil to Stereo.* New York: Howard W. Sams & Company, Incorporated, 1976.

Rosenburg, Robert, and Paul Israel, et al. *The Papers of Thomas A. Edison.* Baltimore: John Hopkins University Press, 1989 [on-going].

Rossman, Joseph. *The Psychology of the Inventor: A Study of Patentee.* Washington, D.C.: The Inventors Publishing Company, 1931.

Runes, Dagobert D. *The Diary and Sundry Observations of Thomas Alva Edison.* New York: Philosophical Library, 1948.

Silverberg, Robert. *Light for the World: Edison and the Power Industry*. New Jersey: D. Van Nostrand Company, Incorporated, 1967.

Simonds, William Adams. *Edison: His Life, His Work, His Genius*. Allen & Unwin, 1935.

————. *The Great Robber Barons: The Great American Capitalists, 1861–1911*. Harcourt Brace Jovanovitch, 1962.

————. *Thomas Alva Edison: Sixty Years of an Inventors Life*. London: Hodder and Stoughton, 1907.

Vanderbilt, Byron M. *Thomas Edison, Chemist*. American Chemical Society, 1971.

Wachhorst, Wyn. *Thomas Alva Edison: An American Myth*. The MIT Press, 1981.

Welch, Walter L. *Charles Batchelor: Edison's Chief Partner*. Syracuse University Press, 1972.

Articles, Magazines, Periodicals

"A Call Upon the Phonograph." *Newark Daily Advisor*. 3 May 1878.

"A Great Triumph." *New York Sun*. 10 September 1878.

"A Marvelous Discovery." *New York Sun*. 22 February 1878.

"A Night with Edison." *New York Herald*. 31 December 1879.

"A Talk with Edison." *Scientific American*. 2 April 1892.

"A Wonderful Invention." *Scientific American*. 17 November 1877.

"A Wonderful Workshop." *New York Post*. 25 October 1887.

"Abnormality Like His a Blessing." *New York Times*. 12 December 1914.

Adams, Milt F. "Automatic Telegraphing." *Journal of the Telegraph*. 25 May 1868.

"An Evening with Edison." *New York Times*. 4 June 1878.

"An Inventor's Workshop." *New York Times*. 9 August 1880.

Baldwin, Neil. "The Laboratory Notebooks of Thomas Edison." *Scientific American*. October 1995.

Ballentine, Caroline Farrand. "The True Story of Edison's Childhood and Boyhood." *Michigan Historical Collection*. Vol. IV. February 1920.

Bancroft, William L. History of Military Reservation at Fort Gratiot." *Michigan Pioneer & Historical Society*. Vol. XI. 1888.

Beach, Alfred. "The Talking Phonograph." *Scientific American*. 22 December 1877.

Benson, A. L. "The Wonderful World Ahead of Us." *Cosmopolitan Magazine*. Vol. 50. February 1911.

"Chirography." *Telegrapher*. 1 August 1868.

"Controlling the Phonograph and Graphophone. *Scientific American*. 1 March 1890.

"Echoes from Dead Voices." *New York Sun*. 6 November 1877.

"Edison and His Electric Light." *Scientific American*. 3 January 1880.

"Edison and the Electric Light." *Nature*. 12 February 1880.

"Edison at Home: A Ninety Minute Interview by Telephone." *Philadelphia Record*. 5 June 1878.

Edison Electric Light Company Bulletin, 2:1. Thomas Alva Edison Microfilm, 96: 672.

"Edison Is Mourned as Leader of Age." *New York Times*. 19 October 1931.

"Edison Sees Business Normal Within 3 Years." *Detroit Free Press.* 12 February 1931.

Edison, Thomas Alva. "Premiums." *Weekly Herald.* Undated.

Edison, Thomas Alva. "The Phonograph and its Future." *The North America Review.* June 1878.

Edison, Thomas Alva. "The Wonderful New World Ahead of Us." *Cosmopolitan Magazine.* Vol. L. February 1911.

"Edisoniana." *The Daily Graphic.* 9 May 1878.

"Edison's Double Transmitter." *Telegrapher.* 12 December 1868.

"Edison's Electric Light." *New York Herald.* 27 March 1879.

"Edison's Electric Light." *New York Sun.* 12 April 1879.

"Edison's Electric Light." *New York Sun.* 20 October 1878.

"Edison's Electric Light." *New York Times.* 5 September 1882.

"Edison's Home Life." *Scientific American.* 27 July 1889.

"Edison's Improved Phonograph." *Scientific American.* 19 November 1887.

"Edison's Incandescent Light." *New York World.* 5 September 1882.

"Edison's Inventions." *New York World.* 12 January 1878.

"Edison's Kinetograph." *Harper's Weekly.* 13 June 1891.

"Edison's Latest Electric Light." *Scientific American.* 10 January 1880.

"Edison's Lieutenants." *New York Evening Sun.* 22 December 1884.

"Edison's New Laboratory." *Scientific American.* 17 September 1887.

"Edison's New Phonograph." *Scientific American.* 29 October 1887.

"Edison's Newest Marvel. Sending Cheap Light, Heat, and Power by Electricity." *New York Sun.* 16 September 1878.

"Edison's Perfected Electric Light." *Frank Leslie's Illustrated Newspaper.* 10 January 1880.

"Edison's Phonograph in England." *Scientific American.* 15 September 1888.

"Edison's Phonographic Doll." *Scientific American.* 26 April 1890.

"Edison's Revolution in Iron Mining." *McClure's Magazine.* November 1897.

"Electric Light." *New York Herald.* 17 January 1879.

"Electrical Lighting in America." *The Electrician.* 17 April 1880.

"Far Worse Than Hanging." *New York Times.* 7 August 1890.

"Four Hours with Edison." *New York Sun.* 29 August 1878.

"Honors Conferred on Thos. A. Edison." *Scientific American.* 7 September 1889.

Houston, Edwin J. "The Gramophone." *Journal of the Franklin Institute.* 2 March 1888.

Lathrop, George Parsons. "Edison's Kinetograph." *Harper's Weekly.* 13 June 1891.

Lathrop, George Parsons. "Talks With Edison." *Harper's Monthly Magazine.* February 1890.

"Lighting A Great City." *New York Times.* 7 February 1880.

"Ludwig Saw in Edison Our 'Uncrowned King'; Tells of His Pleasure of Crowd's Homage." *New York Times.* 19 October 1931.

MacInnes, Margo, ed. *Thomas A. Edison's Menlo Park Laboratory including Sarah Jordan Boarding House.* Michigan: Henry Ford Museum & Greenfield Village, 1990.

MacLaurin, Richard C. "Mr. Edison's Service for Science." *Science*. 4 June 1915.

May, George S., and Victor F. Lemmer. "Thomas Edison's Experimental Work with Michigan Iron Ore." *Michigan History*. Vol. 52–53. 1968–1969.

"Menlo Park Laboratory." *New York Times*. 16 January 1880.

"Muybridge's Zoogyroscope." *Scientific American*. 5 June 1880.

"Newsboy Enterprise." *Detroit Free Press*. 11 April 1862.

Palmer, Arthur J. *Edison: Inspiration to Youth*. Ohio: Edison Birthplace Association, 1928.

Passer, Harold C. *The Electrical Manufacturers, 1875–1900*. Massachusetts: Harvard University Press, 1953.

Ponce de Leon, Charles. "Idols and Icons: Representations of Celebrity in American Culture, 1850–1940." Ph.D. dissertation, Rutgers University, 1992.

"Possibilities of the Phonograph." *Scientific American*. 16 November 1889.

"Salute to The Incredible Talking Machine: 1877–1977." *High Fidelity*. January 1977.

Shaw, G. M. "Sketch of Edison." *Popular Science Monthly*. August 1878.

"Song Edison Liked Given in Tribute." *New York Times*. 19 October 1931.

Swan, Joseph W. "Edison's New Lamp." *Nature*. 1 January 1880.

"Telegraph Statistics." *Scientific American*. 7 February 1852.

"Tesla Says Edison was an Empiricist." *New York Times*. 19 October 1931.

"The Dangers of Electric Lighting." *North American Review*. November 1889.

"The Edison Exhibit at the Paris Exhibition." *Scientific American.* 15 June 1889.

"The Edison Light." *Science.* July 1880.

"The Edison Phonograph." *The Popular Science Monthly.* Vol. XII. November 1877 to April 1878.

"The Inventor of the Age." *New York Sun.* 29 April 1878.

"The Latest by Telegraph." *Detroit Free Press.* 9 April 1862.

"The Man Who Moves the World." *The Daily Graphic.* 26 October 1878.

"The Manufacture of Edison's Talking Doll." *Scientific American.* 26 April 1890.

"The Papa of the Phonograph: Afternoon with Edison." *New York Graphic.* 2 April 1878.

"The Perfected Phonograph." *North American Review.* June 1888.

"The Phonograph." *Scientific American.* 30 March 1878.

"The Scientific Use of the Phonograph." *Scientific American.* 19 April 1890.

"The Success of the Electric Light." *North American Review.* October 1880.

"The Two Railroad Projects Compared"; "New Streak of Lighting"; "Discovery of Steam Power"; "Electrical Drummond Light." *Scientific American.* 13 February 1847.

"The Wizard of Menlo Park." *The Daily Graphic.* 10 April 1878.

"Thomas A. Edison." *Chicago Tribune.* 8 April 1878.

"Thomas A. Edison." *The Phrenological Journal.* Vol. 66. February 1878.

"Thomas Alva Edison." *New York Times.* 19 October 1931.

"Thomas Alva Edison." *Scientific American.* December 1931.

"Thomas Alva Edison." *Scientific American*. 12 October 1889.

"Thomas Edison." *London Times*. 19 October 1931.

"To Catch a Speaker's Gestures." *New York Herald*. 2 February 1890.

Uzzell, Thomas H. "An Interview with Thomas A. Edison." *Colliers Weekly*. 2 December 1916.

"Value of Edison's Genius Is Put at Fifteen Billions." *New York Times*. 24 June 1923. Special Features.

Westinghouse, George. "A Reply to Mr. Edison." *North American Review*. December 1889.

"Westinghouse Is Satisfied." *New York Times*. 7 August 1890.

"When Edison Was Young." *Scientific American*. 8 April 1893.

"Who's Who in the Film Game." *The Nickelodeon*. 1 August 1910.

"With Mr. Edison on the Eiffel Tower." *Scientific American*. 14 September 1889.

"Wizard Edison at Home." *New York World*. 17 November 1889.

"World Followed News of His Illness." *New York Times*. 19 October 1931.

Correspondence

Adams, Milt F., to Thomas Alva Edison. 13 May 1878. Thomas Alva Edison Microfilm, 15:649.

Cook, Joel, to Thomas Alva Edison. 31 December 1879. Thomas A. Edison Microfilm, 49:757.

Croffut, William, to Thomas Alva Edison. 3 February 1879. Thomas Alva Edison Microfilm, 50:242–243.

Edison, Thomas Alva, to Ezra Gilliland. 11 September 1888. Thomas Alva Edison Microfilm, 124:410.

Edison, Thomas Alva, to George Edward Gouraud. 21 July 1887. Thomas Alva Edison Microfilm, 120:277.

Edison, Thomas Alva, to Samuel Insull. 27 June 1885. Thomas Alva Edison Microfilm, 77:117.

Fox, Edwin Marshall, to Thomas Alva Edison. 26 January 1879. Thomas Alva Edison Microfilm, 50:241.

Gilliland, Ezra, to Thomas Alva Edison. 13 September 1888. Thomas Alva Edison Microfilm, 124:410.

Goddard, Calvin, to Thomas Alva Edison. 22 January 1879. Thomas Alva Edison Microfilm, 50:227.

Gouraud, George Edward, to Thomas Alva Edison. 21 December 1880. Thomas Alva Edison Microfilm, 54:359.

Gouraud, George Edward, to Thomas Alva Edison. 2 July 1887. Thomas Alva Edison Microfilm, 120:274.

Insull, Samuel, to Alfred O. Tate. 1 September 1887. Thomas Alva Edison Microfilm, 119:698.

Insull, Samuel, to Alfred O. Tate. 30 July 1889. Thomas Alva Edison Microfilm, 139:594.

Johnson, Edward, to Thomas Alva Edison. 9 December 1887. Thomas Alva Edison Microfilm, 120:250.

Moses, Otto, to Thomas Alva Edison. 1 June 1879. Thomas Alva Edison Microfilm, 49:914.

Raff, Norman, and Frank Gammon to G. Armat, 5 March 1896. Quoted in *Edison vs. American Mutascope Co. & Keith.* Thomas Alva Edison Microfilm, 116:75.

Reiff, Josiah, to Thomas Alva Edison. November 18, 1877. Thomas Alva Edison Microfilm, 3:1117.

Appendix D

Sights and Sites

Henry Ford Museum and Greenfield Village, Dearborn, Michigan

Founded in 1929 by Henry Ford in honor of Thomas Alva Edison. Located in Dearborn, Michigan, the huge museum contains a collection of Americana dating from the founding of America to the present. Greenfield Village consists of a collection of historical and landmark buildings. Included among these buildings are Edison's Menlo Park laboratory and complex buildings, Sarah Jordan's Boarding House, and Edison's Fort Myers Laboratory. The museum and the village are a must-see for Edison aficionados. For information call 313-271-1620, or visit www.hfmgv.org on the Web.

Edison National Historic Site, West Orange, New Jersey

Supported by the National Parks Service, visitors to the site can tour Edison's West Orange laboratory and home. Provides a unique opportunity to interpret and experience important aspects of America's industrial, social, and economic past, and to learn from the legacy of the world's best-known inventor. For directions and information visit www.nps.gov/edis/.

Edison Memorial Tower and Museum, Edison, New Jersey

Located on the site of Edison's laboratory, the Edison Memorial Tower pays homage to the inventor of the incandescent bulb. The museum contains several pieces of Edison memorabilia and some of his early inventions. For information call 732-549-3299 or visit www.ohwy.com/nj/t/thedmetm.htm.

The Winter Estates of Thomas Alva Edison and Henry Ford, Fort Myers, Florida

Longtime friends, Edison and Ford built these winter estates to get away from cold Michigan winters. Visitors to the estates can catch a glimpse of the good life enjoyed by two of America's pre-eminent citizens. For information call 941-334-7419, or visit www.edison-ford-estate.com/index2php3.

Thomas Edison Birthplace Museum, Milan, Ohio

This intimate museum offers visitors the experience of walking through the birthplace of Thomas Alva Edison and features a collection of rare Edisonia, including examples of many early Edison inventions, documents, and family mementos. The museum is located at 9 Edison Drive, near Exit 7 of the Ohio Turnpike. For further information call 419-499-2135, or visit www.tomedison. org.

Thomas Edison Depot Museum, Port Huron, Michigan

Opened in 2001, the Thomas Edison Depot Museum is housed inside the historic Fort Gratiot depot. The museum offers an appreciation for Edison's life and accomplishments. Exhibits support Edison's multi-faceted story of creativity, family support, adversity, perseverance, and ultimate triumph as the greatest inventor of our times. Located under the Blue Water Bridges on Edison Parkway. For further information call 810-982-0891, or visit www.phmuseum.org.

Appendix E

The Edison Family

Thomas Alva Edison's marriages to Mary Stilwell and to Mina Miller resulted in the birth of six children, three from each marriage. In both cases a daughter came first followed by two boys.

Children of Thomas Alva and Mary Stilwell Edison

Marion Estelle Edison

Marion was born to Thomas and Mary on February 18, 1872. Growing up, she was nicknamed "Dash" by her father, because of his passion for telegraphy. As a child, she spent a good deal of her time at the Menlo Park laboratory, where she was responsible for keeping her father's cigar box stocked. After her mother's death on August 9, 1884, she became even closer to her father, traveling with him on several occasions to Europe and cities throughout the United States.

She was educated at Somerville Seminary in Somerville, New Jersey, and Bradford Academy in Bradford, Massachusetts. In 1892 she married Karl Oscar Oeser, a German army lieutenant. They lived in Germany, and when Word War I began Marion remained with her husband. However, they were divorced in 1921, at which point she returned to the United States, where she died on April 16, 1965.

Thomas Alva Edison Jr.

Thomas Alva Edison Jr. was born on January 10, 1876. He was nicknamed "Dot" by his father to go with the nickname "Dash," he bestowed on his daughter. As a boy, he often took his father's lunch to the laboratory at Menlo Park. In adolescence, he boarded at St. Paul's School in Concord, New Hampshire, and the J. M. Hawkins School in Staten Island, New York. In 1899, he secretly married stage actress Marie Louise Toohey. They were divorced before the end of the year. He then married Beatrice Heyzer. They remained married for the rest of their lives.

Thomas Jr. did not care for school, or work. Taking note of his son's attitude, Edison often spoke badly of his son to his associates. To support himself as a young man, Thomas Jr. sold the rights to use his name to publicize medicines and inventions that were not reliable. Upon learning of his son's escapade, Edison offered him a fifty dollar weekly allowance and the funds to start up a mushroom farm if he dropped the commercial use of the Edison name. Thomas Jr. agreed, changing his name to Thomas Willard. The endeavor failed. In the years that followed, Thomas Jr. reconciled with his father thanks in part to Mina's intersession on his behalf. He was given a job at the Research Engineering Division of Thomas Alva Edison, Incorporated, as a marketing specialist. He died on August 25, 1935, in a Springfield, Massachusetts, hotel room, where he had signed in under the name J. J. Byrne. The Hampden medical examiner attributed his death to heart disease; however, speculation that he committed suicide soon appeared in newspapers.

William Leslie Edison

William was born on October 26, 1878. He also boarded at St. Paul's School in Concord, New Hampshire, and the J. M. Hawkins School on Staten Island. Unlike his older brother, William excelled academically, attending the Sheffield Scientific School at Yale following his graduation from the Hawkins School. However, like his brother, he was berated and even disowned by his father for allowing his name to be used in a number of business ventures. He married Blanche Travers. In an effort to find work, the couple moved from town to town. Over seven years they lived in Staten Island, Washington, D.C., Yonkers, Philadelphia, and Pittsburgh, where William was employed as a factory worker, or a mechanic.

They also received public assistance when times were bad. With the assistance of his father, William eventually established a poultry farm in Waterview, Virginia, breeding chickens, turkeys, pheasant, homing pigeons, quail, ducks, and leghorns. In 1898, he served in the military during the Spanish-American War and he also took part in World War I. He died on August 10, 1937, after battling cancer for the last two years of his life.

Children of Thomas Alva and Mina Miller Edison

Madeleine Edison Sloane

Madeleine was the first child born to Thomas and Mina on May 31, 1888, at the home in West Orange, New Jersey. She was nicknamed "Toots" by her relatives. Known for her intellect and sharp wit, she would have fit in well at the West Orange laboratory if she hadn't been a girl. She attended Bryan Mawr College in Pennsylvania starting in the fall of 1906. However, after two years, she left the college. She married John Eyre Sloane in the drawing room at Glenmont on June 17, 1914. Her parents approved of the marriage, but with some trepidation. Mina was concerned because John was Catholic. Edison was skeptical because John's father was a noted aviator and not an inventor or industrialist. The Sloanes had four sons, the only Edison grandchildren.

Involved in politics and public service, Madeleine was a candidate for Congress in 1938, running as a Republican, the party to which her father was a lifelong member. With the start of World War II, she volunteered her time to blood drives for the New Jersey Red Cross. After Mina's death on August 24, 1947, she became involved with preserving the home in which her father was born in Milan, Ohio. She was also named to the Board of Directors for Western Union in the 1950s. She died on February 14, 1979, leaving an endowment to the Edison Birthplace.

Charles Edison

Charles Edison was born at the Edison home in West Orange, New Jersey, on August 3, 1890. He graduated from the Hotchkiss School in Lakeville, Connecticut in 1909. He married Carolyn Hawkins, a girl he met at college, in a ceremony at the Edisons' winter home in Fort Myers, Florida, on March 27, 1918. Charles joined Thomas Alva Edison, Incorporated, in 1914 as an executive in training overseeing a number of departments. He became president of his father's company in 1927 and held the position until the company was sold in 1959.

Like his sister, Madeleine, Charles was also involved in politics and public service. In the mid-1930s he served as assistant secretary of the Navy in President Franklin Roosevelt's Cabinet, and eventually became the acting secretary. In 1940, he was elected to one term as the governor of New Jersey. However, he ran as a Democrat, a break from the Republican Party to which his father had been a member. In his most noted legislation, Charles proposed a revision of the state's outdated constitution, but voters rejected it in a statewide referendum. However, after his term, the state soon adopted a modern constitution. Prior to his death, Edison established a charitable foundation that today is known as the Charles Edison Fund. He died of a heart attack on July 31, 1969.

Theodore Miller Edison

Theodore was born at Glenmont on July 10, 1898, and was named in honor of Mina's brother who had just died in the Spanish-American War. From an early age, he was known in the family as "the little laboratory assistant," because of his attraction to science and experimenting. His father, however, was concerned with his son's inclination to mathematics; so much so, that on one occasion, Edison stated, "Theodore is a good boy, but his forte is mathematics. I am a little afraid … he may go flying off into the clouds with that fellow Einstein. And if he does … I'm afraid he won't work with me." Theodore attended the Haverford School in Haverford, Pennsylvania, and then Montclair Academy in Montclair, New Jersey. He went on to attend the Massachusetts Institute of Technology, where he earned a degree in physics in 1923. In being awarded his diploma, he became the only member of the Edison family to graduate from college.

After graduation, he joined Thomas Alva Edison, Incorporated, as a lab assistant, eventually becoming the technical director of research and engineering. In 1925 he married Anna Maria Osterhout, a classmate from MIT. In 1931, he started Calibron Products, Inc., a company that conducted research and experimental work, as well as engineering advice on a consultation basis. He also established a laboratory in West Orange. Over his career, he was awarded eighty patents. In his old age, Theodore fought for the protection of the environment, was an outspoken critic of the Vietnam War, and supported the idea of zero population growth. He was to reside in West Orange with his wife until his death on November 24, 1992.

Index

arc lighting, invention of, 91
articles
  "Edison's Combination Repeater," 34-35
  "Edison's Double Transmitter," 33-34
assistants
  hiring process, 109-110
  Wizard's laboratory, 109-110
Automatic Telegraph Company
  business ventures, 51-54
  Jay Gould, 54

B

Bachelor of Science degree, 234
bamboo, electric lighting, discoveries, 110
Batchelor, Charles, 49
batteries, alkaline, Edison, 196-197
Battle of Shiloh, 11
Baucus, Joseph, 193
Bechtelsville, Pennsylvania, iron-ore plant, 165-166
Bell, Alexander Graham
  graphophone, 145-146
  telephone, invention of, 66-67

Bell, Chichester, graphophone, 145-148
Bergmann, Sigmund, 49-50
Berliner, Emile, gramophone, 159
Bernhardt, Sarah, 113-114
birthday, Edison, 4-6
  celebration, 216
Black Friday, 44
Black Maria, 191
books
  Decline and Fall of the Roman Empire, 7-8
  Dictionary of Science, 7-9
  Edison as I Knew Him (Henry Ford), 173
  Electric Telegraph Manipulation (Charles Walker), 28
  Experimental Researches in Electricity, 32-33
  Gifts of Life (Emil Ludwig), 214-215
  Handbook of Practical Telegraphy (Richard Culley), 28
  History of England, 7-8
  History of the World, 7-8
  Horse in Motion, The, 182
  Jesus (Emil Ludwig), 214
  Kaiser Wilhelm II (Emil Ludwig), 214